"GIE I BURTLE": *A Village Apart*

Cover: Geoff Moxey and Bill Reece enjoying a joke at the Lunch Club.

Overleaf: George Pringle's 1870 map of area.

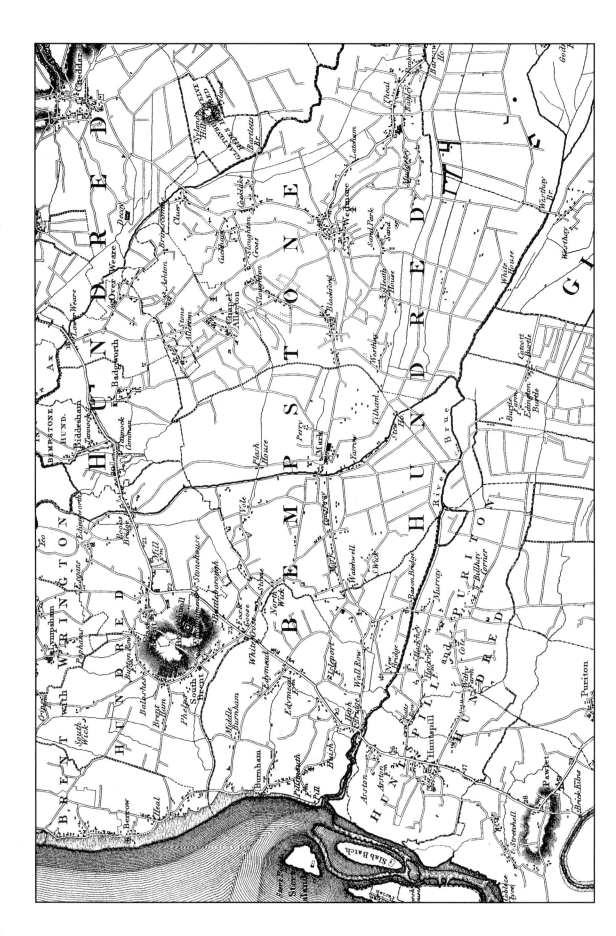

"*Gie I Burtle*"

– A VILLAGE APART –

C.S. John Sparkes

Foreword by the Right Hon. The Lord Biffen

Many years ago a young man from Burtle
visited London, an unusual event in those days.
When he arrived back the villagers were keen to
learn about his impressions of the big city.

"Oh, Lunnon be alright", he said, **"But gie I
Burtle".**

ELSP

Published in 2001 by
ELSP
1 The Shambles
Bradford on Avon
Wiltshire   BA15 1JS

Design and typesetting by Ex Libris Press

Printed in Britain by
Cromwell Press, Trowbridge, Wiltshire

ISBN 0 903341 62 0

Acknowledgement: The author is grateful to all
his Burtle friends who loaned him
photographs for publication in this book

CONTENTS

FOREWORD

by the Right Hon. The Lord Biffen

Alas, I was not born in Burtle or spent my childhood in the Somerset Levels but I have the privilege of close family connections. My father was born in Catcott Burtle in 1896 and my mother spent her youth on the family farm in nearby Huntspill and would row cheese in a flat boat down the river Brue to Highbridge market. I can only claim to have used the Somerset and Dorset Railway to travel from Bridgwater to Glastonbury in order to offer full-hearted but vain support to Somerset County Cricket.

Such memories and recollections as I possess have been quickened by John Sparkes' delightful book on Burtle and its surrounds. He writes with a discerning eye, showing reverence for history and occasional indignation in the spirit of William Cobbet who chronicled the British countryside two centuries ago in his *Rural Rides*.

The levels, the moors and the Polden Hills were distinctive locations but Burtle 'almost an island community' was a village set apart, largely because it had a low lying topography and a wealth of peat. The village had no substantial landowners but rather a host of small dairy farmers, as many as forty between the wars. They were independent minded, perhaps even cantankerous, but fiercely loyal to their community. In my fertile imagination I suppose they would have fought for the Duke of Monmouth in his ill-fated battle against King James II at Sedgemoor.

John Sparkes has set out the economics of Burtle farming and embellished it with some pen portraits of village personalities. One can only be struck by the relentless hard work of the village agriculture. The book emphasises how heavily dependent farming was upon family labour and how rare it was for any sons, let alone daughters, to stay at school beyond fourteen years of age. The span of Burtle

Above: The Rt. Hon. The Lord Biffen, past leader of the House of Commons.

farming and the levels generally, in addition to dairying, was narrow but it always included cider-making. Its strength was legendary and my father transferred that rough Burtle skill to his subsequent farm near Cannington. The real distinction of Burtle and the levels are the peat bogs. These began to be seriously developed in the 1870s. The world of peat will introduce the reader to a fascinating manufacturing terminology; mumps, turves, hyling, ruckles and unridding. With a glossary such as this who can doubt that Burtle was a world of its own.

The peat digging created a lunar landscape and superb habitat for wader birds and marsh flora and fauna. John Sparkes, who spent some time at Slimbridge, writes with feeling on the natural world which has been his heritage as a farmer's son. In a charming book, these passages are the most compelling.

There is also a message for the reader. It concerns the sanctity of rural life. Burtle was a tight-knit society, making its own pleasures - the Silver Band and the Harvest Home and supporting a strong sense of community.

Inevitably many of those features are disappearing but many could be retained if general authority were more sympathetic. It is not just a matter of putting on our Barbours and marching, it is a question of preserving village schools and having planning regulations that aid small scale village employment. The countryside is more than a weekend recreation for the urban wealthy.

The book is a cry for the sustaining of traditional values, John Sparkes reminds us "the countryside... is a consequence of many generations of man's activities". Go to Burtle and you will see why.

INTRODUCTION

Villages and village lives have been the subject of many interesting books since the advent of Gilbert White's *History of Selborne*. Some have an historical connection, others have beautiful scenery, streets of delightful old thatched cottages like those nestling in wooded valleys amongst the heather clad hills of West Somerset which so entranced those literary giants, Wordsworth, Coleridge and Shelley.

Villages on the Poldens have a character of their own with attractive cottages built with the local blue lias stone, largely offset by the insertion of incongruous modern houses in almost every piece of land capable of taking one or more. Despite this it is still possible to obtain attractive views within some of them.

The settlements on the levels of the Brue Valley appear to have little of great architectural or historical interest other than the Fish House and Manor Farm at Meare and possibly Burtle Farm. People travelling through could be forgiven for not taking a second glance. However when the veneer is peeled away from the surface of the peatland, the most amazing evidence of 6,000 years of man's activities is revealed, including what are probably the oldest man made roads and trackways in the world!

The independent disposition of the people who live on the levels has been fashioned by the harshness of their lives until relatively recent times and the enforced isolation during winter floods. In many ways they reflect the environment amongst which the old families have survived and developed, when one looks below the surface it is to discover a fiercely independent breed to be likened to the 'Fen Tigers' of Norfolk. Many villages have their characters but I would lay odds that few other villages of its size in England could equal the number of characters that have come out of Burtle over the years.

Although not a native of Burtle I have always felt drawn to that little settlement perched on its sandbank in the middle of the peat moors. Over the years I have received so much pleasure from my association with the people and their activities that I have felt a compulsion to commit my observations to paper in the hope that it will enable others to enjoy the 'Burtle Experience' with me.

C. S. John Sparkes

Aller Moor is kept as an overflow reservoir area to relieve the pressure on the banks of the Rivers Parret and Tone in times of flood.

Withies are grown on West Sedgemoor south of the Polden Hills, peat is dug in 'the Vale of Avalon' on the Northern side.

CHAPTER 1

Where on Earth is Burtle?

Somerset, so well known as the home of cider and Cheddar cheese, offers a greater variety of countryside than any other county in Britain, from the acid uplands of Exmoor, the sandstone of the Quantocks and the limestone of the Mendips to large lowland areas of alluvial clay and peat. The peatlands, cradled in the huge saucer-like centre of the county, are bisected east to west by the limestone Polden Hills. Much of the peatland lies below sea level.

Some 15,000 years ago, the whole area was covered by a deep layer of ice. About 10,000 years ago the ice was melting and, as a result, the sea level rose to cover the central Somerset basin. Alluvial silt was deposited by the tides within that area of inland sea. As the clay built up, the water became brackish, encouraging the growth of reeds. By 5,000 BC huge reed swamps were developing and the rivers eventually filled the lowlands with fresh water.

The surrounding country was heavily forested, providing the inhabitants with one of their most important raw materials – timber. Clearing the timber allowed cultivation of cereals and grazing for cattle and sheep. Game, wildfowl and fish were in abundance. Their diet balance would have benefited, as improving agricultural skills enabled them to grow pulses and cereals.

To the south and west of the Poldens is a large area of low-lying peatland, now known as West Sedgemoor. Watered mainly by the catchment area of the acidic Blackdown Hills, the water quality ensures that these peatlands retain a very high acidity. Until the advent of the pumping stations this low-lying land was an enormous swamp with occasional sandbanks originally deposited by the floodwater from the River Parrett and its tributaries – the Tone, Isle, Cary and Yeo. There are also a few small hills, such as Burrow Mump with its little church, dedicated to St. Michael, perched on the summit. This was the land of Alfred where he took refuge from the Danes, hiding on the small islands and protected by the treacherous peat bogs surrounding them.

Today, these moors are comparatively well drained with a patchwork of fields interlaced by miles of drainage ditches called rhynes, pronounced 'reens'. The summer grazing is good with a high concentration of dairy cows. The farmsteads are mainly built on the slightly higher ground just out of reach of the winter floodwaters.

Withies (osiers) are still grown to supply the local basket making industry. Although reduced from its heyday, the interest in high quality, hand-crafted products has given the industry a new lease of life. An unusual crop grown in large quantities in the past but now restricted to a few acres, are teazles, used for raising the nap on woollen cloth.

To the north of the Polden Hills lies the other half of the Somerset Levels, flanked to the west by the Bristol Channel and by the Mendips to the north and east. Looking down from a vantage point the appearance is quite different to that of West Sedgemoor.

The peat growth started to slow down some 1,500 years ago, digging started about 1,000 years ago. Since then, huge areas have been excavated, originally for fuel but more recently on an industrial scale for the horticultural market.

Alkaline water from the surrounding limestone hills, filtering through the peat, considerably reduces the natural acidity. This results in a fertile soil capable of supporting a wider range of fauna and flora than is normally associated with peat soils.

People have lived on the Somerset Levels for over 6,000 years. The Meare lake villages, a couple of miles from Burtle, were a discovery of international importance. These men of the mists constructed an intricate network of sophisticated timber trackways to link the raised parts of the moors. The best known are the Abbot's Way c.2,500BC (The 'main road' from Westhay to Burtle) and the Sweet Track, c.3,800BC. There are many more potential sites around the area which will no doubt be excavated at some future date.

Peat has a wonderfully preservative quality for some materials, particularly timber. Arthur Bulleid's excavations of the Glastonbury lake village and the two Meare lake villages which started a hundred years ago, have explained the surprisingly sophisticated prehistoric lifestyles and activities of the various tribes in considerable detail. There is also plenty of evidence of trading contacts with various continental and Mediterranean communities.

A range of cereals were grown on the islands and the foothills around the levels and ground for bread. Pigs, sheep and cattle were farmed on the firmer land. A visit to the museum in the old Tribunal building in Glastonbury is an illuminating and worthwhile exercise.

The moors can have a moving, ethereal quality, with the mists playing ghostly tricks. It must be remembered that the region is very flat which assists the unusual

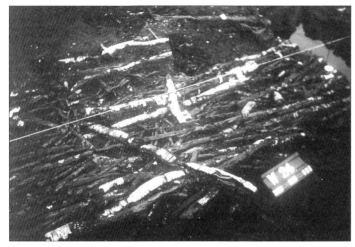

These tracks were discovered when it was decided to widen the Glastonbury Canal which involved a diversion and the building of a new bridge. Many different methods were employed to construct the network of prehistoric walkways that are present throughout the levels.

The excavation and recording is extremely painstaking and thorough. The timber soon deteriorates and crumbles when exposed to the air.

Many different methods of construction were employed by the track builders.

One of several dugout boats that have been discovered over the years. The picture was taken in 1906 by the The Griffin's Head, Westhay, now demolished. Here is the text used on a postcard at the time.. The boat was found in September 1906 and is dated about 350BC.

Interesting and Valuable Discovery: *A man Named G. Wall. whilst digging a ditch in the Shapwick turf moor recently, made a most interesting discovery of an old boat embedded in the turf. In digging the sides of the ditch he came across a piece of wood protruding into the ditch. Having recently visited the Glastonbury Museum and seen the ancient British boat unearthed some time ago at the lake village, curiosity prompted him to further investigate, with the result that he found it to be the nose of a boat. After further digging through the solid peat the whole of the boat was revealed. It is almost entire except where the part protruded in the ditch. No doubt others must have come across the same obstruction when digging the ditch before, but had not the curiosity to investigate further, thinking it was only a piece of wood as is often found imbedded in the turf, and left it alone. The boat lay in a slanting position from stem to stern, the lower end being quite 14 ft. below the surface of the ground. It is a flat bottom boat, measuring 20 ft. 6 ins in length and 2 ft 10 ins in width at its widest part. It was hewn out of a solid trunk, and is a very interesting relic of bygone times. That it is prehistoric there cannot be much doubt from the depth at which it was found. It is lying at present in the stable of the Griffins Hotel, Shapwick, near where it was found, and is in the charge of Mr. G. Willcox, the landlord.*

The moors can have a moving ethereal quality, with the mists playing ghostly tricks. The region is very flat which assists the unusual patterns that the mist creates. The mist covered moors give the impression of a huge inland sea with the trees protruding and the knolls resembling small islands. Much as it may have appeared five to six thousand years ago.

How Prehistoric man may have lived, round huts on land just above the flood level.

John Speede's map of 1610 clearly shows that Burtle House, alias The Priory, alias The Farm was the only house in what is now Burtle, although there is a religious building shown toward what is now Chapel Hill Farm . The only overland access was from Mark over what was then the Bastion Bridge. The Pilrow Cut runs North through Mark and joins the River Axe near Axebridge.

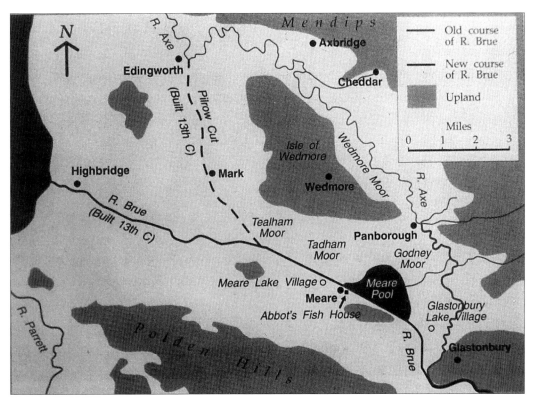

The River Brue and the Pilrow Cut were dug under the supervision of Glastonbury Abbey in the thirteenth century. The waterways were an essential method of transporting goods for trade and the above enabled the abbey to avoid paying tolls to their Bette-noir, the bishop of Bath and Wells.

patterns that the mist creates. Looking down from the hills the mists give the moors the appearance of a huge inland sea with the trees protruding above the mist and the knolls resembling small islands.

Another interesting phenomenon is when a thin layer of mist forms, as shallow as three feet. It can be possible to see a mile or more at ground level under the mist with the bases of trees and even cows' legs without bodies in clear view. Upon standing upright, vision can, again, be unrestricted with the bushes and the odd cow's head rising above it. When accompanied by some of the bird and animal calls it can truly be a spine-tingling experience.

A large proportion of the land lies around ten to fifteen feet below high spring tide level and is only protected from flooding at high tide by sand dunes and the river Parrett flood banks, said by some to have been originally built by the Romans. Flooding by fresh water is largely prevented in recent times by the numerous, large pumping stations in this part of the moors mainly built since the Second World War.

The main rivers are the Axe and the Brue, the latter with its meandering course from Bruton flows by Burtle on its way to the sea. In the thirteenth century, the passage of the Brue was diverted from its original course through the Bleadney Gap on its way to the Axe, providing a more direct route to the sea, via the estuary of the river Parrett, by the monks of Glastonbury Abbey. This must have been a daunting undertaking in terms of the scale of the project. The population reduction caused by the Black Death in medieval times reduced the need for food production and drainage came to a halt for several centuries. The prime mover was also removed from the scene by the dissolution of Glastonbury Abbey.

Many smaller drainage channels have been created in recent years and the water levels controlled by a series of pumping stations. The Pilrow cut linked the Brue with the Axe for boat traffic through Mark and can still be seen alongside the road when entering Mark from the Burtle direction. The Glastonbury Canal (or South Drain) was, for a period, the major supply route from the harbour on the Bristol Channel at Highbridge, to Glastonbury and beyond. It joins the River Brue at Cripps Corner, a couple of miles inland from East Huntspill (Bason Bridge).

A map of 1782 shows the only route in to what is now Burtle as the road from Mark passing over the Brue by way of the Bastion Bridge. The latter is also shown on a map of 1575 so it must be an ancient roadway, probably built when the river Brue was re-routed.

When the enclosures were at their height, mainly between 1785 and 1840 in this part of Somerset, drainage ditches were dug as boundaries on the peat land, in contrast to the boundary hedges being planted on the hill. In 1806, William White, surveyor, drew up the Brue Valley Drainage Plan. This covered a huge slice of the

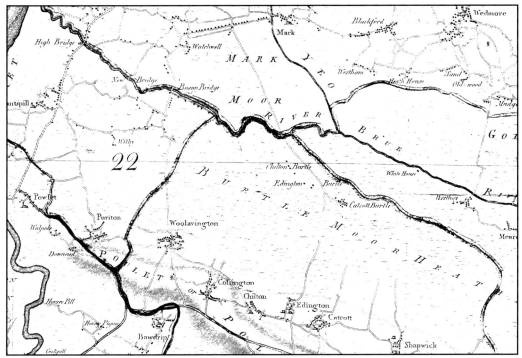

In 1782 there were about 20 houses in the three parts of Burtle. The roads to Edington, Chilton Polden, Catcott, Westhay and East Huntspill were not constructed until the major enclosures some twenty years later.

The diversion of the canal in around 1970 left the row of cottages on an artificial island. The site of the once extensive Edington Junction was between the canal and the Railway Hotel. The hugely enlarged inn is now The Tom Mogg.

Somerset Levels between the Poldens and the Mendips from as far East as North Wooton and Pilton right through to the sea. The map measures in excess of thirteen feet by five feet at eight inches to the mile! This was point when Burtle was linked to Westhay, Catcott, Edington, Chilton Polden and East Huntspill by the building of new roads.

The canal was excavated during this period, acting both as drainage channel and transport route. The gradual improvements and the, albeit slow, drainage must have been beneficial to agriculture. For the first time there could be an element of certainty in contrast to the previously relentless high water table which severely limited the potential land use. As with West Sedgemoor, there is also a strong dairy industry on the north side of the Poldens.

The indications are that, until the mid-nineteenth century, a busy boat trade operated throughout the moors. Most of the signs of these old activities have been destroyed by widening of the waterways in recent years. On the canal, midway between the Catcott-Burtle road bridge and the Shapwick-Westhay road bridge, was a large boat pool known as The Lock. Fine, cut stone wharves were dismantled for building stone as recently as the late 1980's.

Canals have public houses along their banks for the convenience of the boatmen and this one was no exception. Very little remains today but an old piece of doggerel gives us a clue to some of the names and their locations:

> My **Grey Horse** can beat the **Bear**
> and make the **Eagle** fly,
> Turn the **Flat Boat** upside down
> and drink the **Three Cups** dry.

The Flat Boat is believed to have been at the Lock along with a cottage and a farm. The Eagle could have been The Griffin's Head Hotel at Shapwick Station near Westhay. The remains of another old canal pub can be seen where the canal passes through Chilton Moor but the name has been lost. Some of these watering holes could only have been accessible by way of the canal when they were in use.

The canal company was eventually bought out by the railway company after its comparatively short commercial life in order to use the towpath as a route for its track. The landowners were very uncooperative and refused to release land for a route through the villages along the Poldens. Some of the boats were sold to local farmers and the materials used to construct farm buildings. Masts were sawn back to make wallplates as long as sixty feet in some cases, panels made good cowstall divisions. Sadly, little evidence remains today.

In the 1940's, a large cut known as the Huntspill River was dug to link the Glastonbury Canal to the Parrett estuary. As one nears the coast, the ground level rises where the sea overlaid the peat with a layer of alluvial silt. At the junction of the clay overlay and the exposed peat stands the Gold Corner pumping station, the largest in Europe when it was built. The whole construction was completed in very quick time, ostensibly to drain the moors for the improvement of agriculture. Years later it was officially admitted that the real purpose was to supply water to the Royal Ordnance Factory at Puriton. It is amazing what can be achieved when the chips are down.

The huge Gold Corner pumping station was the largest in Europe when it was built. The water is lifted about ten feet from the Glastonbury Canal into the Huntspill River, at that level it can be discharged near the mouth of the River Parret at low tide.

Even the vast Levels were being brought under control by the quarter of a million gallons per minute capacity of the new pumping station. Further, more exacting controls came with the building of more strategically placed pumping stations. No longer could it be said that the sea could reach up to Glastonbury as it was once reputed to do. The Gold Corner undertaking enabled the flood water in the South Drain (Glastonbury Canal) to be lifted the ten or twelve feet necessary to discharge into the sea, through the Huntspill River, at low tide. This led to the single, most significant improvement to the living standards of the people on the moors for two thousand years. Their lives were transformed and they no longer faced the perennial threat of severe winter flooding. On the other hand, some would argue that the floods brought great benefits by fertilising and consolidating the land.

Wherever you have two farmers you will receive at least three opinions!

I have presented this short account to explain the circumstances leading up to the creation of this unique village, situated amid an enormous area of peat, which is dotted with small isolated communities, each almost an island in its own right, is now accessible by, and, with easy access to, the outside world! The character of these villages is so different to the villages on the nearby Polden Hills, it was often said in jest that the third generation in Burtle developed webbed feet. There are no main roads across the peat moors and travellers had little reason to pass through the village unless there were business or family connections.

The settlement of Burtle is scattered around on a sandbank about one and a half miles long, east to west, by half a mile wide. Its location is more or less equidistant between Bridgwater, Highbridge, Wedmore and Glastonbury.

Burtle, too, used to have serious floods but they were not planned! The family in the water encircled cottage last lived in by Mrs. Hughie Norris would be accustomed to living upstairs in the winter and come and go by turf boat.

The Burtle Hoard

Courtesy Somerset Archaeological and Natural History Society

Mr W. Stradling lived the folly he built on Chilton Polden hill and is now known as The Priory. He was a keen archaeologist and antiquarian collecting numerous artifacts, many of which were incorporated into the structure of The Priory. In 1854 he presented a paper to the Somerset Archaeological and Natural History Society entitled 'A young turf-bearer's find in the turbaries'. Turbaries were the peat cutting areas. I feel I cannot do better than present the paper verbatim:

Many years are now passed, since a young friend of mine, by the name of Murch, entered his father's turbary (near Edington Burtle), with the determination of giving his assistance to the labourers, as a turf bearer, – a most arduous undertaking for one so young, and which I will endeavour to describe, as the process of preparing the peat, for fuel, is curious.

A pit, ten feet square, is commenced by the delver, with the turf scythe, with which he removes the top spine, as useless; he then proceeds to cut his brocks, which he does with the greatest accuracy; places them around the mouth of the pit, when the bearer, with the turf fork, lifts them into a barrow, and wheels them to the drying-place, where, with a scythe, he splits each brock into three. They then remain on the ground, until sufficiently dry to be placed into ruckles, or, the smallest kind of drying heaps. Those, in time, are formed into open tunegars, as they are termed; and lastly, they are ricked, in order to be carted to different markets.

A curious phenomenon, sometimes occurs in the turbaries. The delver, at the depth of eight, nine, and sometimes ten feet, and when within a foot or two of the clay, on which the peat rests, is suddenly lifted to the mouth of the pit, and steps off without difficulty or danger. A very old and experienced workman informed me "he had had several wind and water rides in his time, and that when wind caused the platform to rise, it went steadily up, and at the top he had only to pass his scythe through the mass, when the wind passed off, with a sound much like the drone of the bagpipe, and he gradually descended to the bottom, and resumed his work. When water was the cause, the ascent was more rapid, attended by a violent rocking motion, and the pit became useless".

Our young bearer felt much fatigued at the completion of what was his first and last day's work of that description; he was, however, well repaid; for whilst speaking to the delver, he espied in one corner at the bottom of the pit, what he imagined to be a log of black wood, and ordered it to be carefully removed. To his great delight, it proved to be a small square box, scooped in rather an oval shape within, and containing what I consider to be the most curious collection of British antiquities ever discovered in the turbaries of Somerset. The cist was unfortunately made of maple, and soon fell to dust; had it been of oak, or yew, it would have remained an interesting relic for ages yet to come. I will now endeavour to describe its contents:

* A knife unfinished, as it came from the mould, with the rough edge on.

* One that had been much used.

* A most beautiful specimen of nearly the same pattern.

* Another not so perfect:

* An armlet, with a ring for the finger to match.

* Two rings for the first or second joint of a lady's finger.

* An armlet, of a curious twisted pattern, with a finger ring to match.

* A torque, evidently, from its lightness, intended for the neck of a female.

* Part of a ring, much rubbed, and probably broken in order to ascertain of what metal the whole collection was made; which is of British brass.

* Four palstaves, or celts, without sockets; three having loops for thongs, the other without; all of different patterns.

I now come to what I consider to be the most interesting of the whole collection; it is of the same pattern as the Jogh-Draoch, or chain-ring of divination, discovered in Ireland, and which, Meyrick says, was worn on the third finger of the left hand, by the Arch-druid: the finger still held most sacred, and on which is placed the wedding-ring.

With all due deference to my archaeological friends, I will now risk my opinion as to those precious and truly interesting antiques. We know that from the number of oaks, yews, and other kinds of trees, which from time to time have been discovered in our once British lake, that forests were on its borders; in them, perhaps, the horrid rites of Druidism were performed. Might not, then, a British priestess, at a very early date, have lost this then most valuable cist from her canoe. The knives are precisely the same pattern as those of gold found in Ireland, which were supposed to have been used for sacrificing the victims in those barbarous days. The torque, armlets, and rings, convince us that she was one of high rank, and the Jogh-Draoch, I conceive, gave the Possessor the order of priesthood.

Some of my archaeological friends will exclaim - If this be your theory, how do you account for a priestess having in her possession the four palstaves? My reply would be, Might they not have been trophies, taken from the victims she had sacrificed? Others, I am aware, do not believe that any human sacrifices were ever made in Britain; but if we give up this chief, though inhuman rite, then farewell to Druidism, which from henceforth must be considered altogether fabulous.

NB: The methods of digging peat have changed considerably, throwing mumps out of a hole up to 10 ft deep would be very hard work indeed. As a consequence the terms used by peat diggers have either changed or Mr Stradling got some of them wrong which would be quite understandable. The find, known as the Burtle hoard, represents only a small proportion of the artifacts found in the moors over the years. This collection went to the Ashmolean museum in Oxford. It would be nice to think that these and other artifacts found in the peat moors could return to go on view nearer to the areas in which they were found. JS.

CHAPTER 2

History and Development of Burtle

The whole area is very flat, Burtle Hill is only eleven feet above sea level! The village rests on a sand bank, or 'birtle', originally laid down by the incursions of the sea followed by the floodwaters over many centuries.

Burtle has been almost an island community for most of its existence. The only exit from Burtle avoiding the floods during some winters was the route over the Bastion Bridge and the slightly higher alluvial clay of Mark Moor. As a consequence the villagers developed strongly independent qualities which have tended to set them apart from the villagers up on the surrounding hills.

Three hamlets – Chilton Burtle, Edington Burtle and Catcott Burtle – were the elements recently brought together to create the village of Burtle with parish status. In spite of, or maybe due to, the scattered nature of the settlement with its little nuclear clusters of dwellings, there has always been an extremely strong community spirit. For such a small population, of around 300, the number and variety of village leisure and working activities over the years is surprisingly wide.

The Augustinian Priory of Burtle Moor was started sometime early in the second half of the 13th century by a hermit who built himself a lodging on a piece land that was the property of the Abbey of Glastonbury and was held by Godfrey of Edington. It was situated on what was known as Sprawlsmede and was variously known as the Priory of the Holy Trinity, the Blessed Virgin and St Stephen of Burtle, Burcle or Sprawlsmede. The name Sprawlesmede somehow suggests the land and bogs that surrounded it. It was endowed by William of Edington, son of Godfrey.

In the private register of Abbot Walter de Monyngton of Glastonbury, made by order of the Abbot (1341-72) there is a series of six charters concerning the priory. This is now in the Bodleian Library. (Oxford) It is interesting to consider the names and appendices to them, they can easily be connected to local place names of today, William de Pedewell, Anthony de Bradeneye, Robert de Cadecot (Catcott) et al. Were they men of the "cloth" in the places that bear their names or were they merely born there and acquired their appendix when they moved away?

The Priory was to receive the eleventh part of any of the profit of his (Walter's) mills at Edington. To this was added five acres of land and cottage held by Hugh Buterstake, five acres held by William de Pedewell and Walter Sperling's cottage and croft and five acres of demesne.

Glastonbury Abbey owned the Priory but, although the area came within the Parish of Moorlinch, it was made very clear that the latter had no jurisdiction over it!

The priors of Burtle from the creation of the Priory until the dissolution in 1535 are as follows:

Walter	1275
Stephen	1276
Nicholas Drake	1312
Robert de cadecote	1343
Robert de Baltesborrow	1349
William de Fulbroke	1409
John Romney	1420
Thomas Bone	1463
John Faireman	1467
John Bennett	1488
Thomas Vele	?
William Badcock	1499
Stephen Stowell	1516-35

In Saxton's map of 1575 the only building shown is called Burtle House, this is almost certainly the oldest building in Chilton Burtle now known simply as 'The Farm'. There have always been rumours of it starting out as a priory, there appears to be a crypt and the building is certainly very old.

John Speede's map of 1610 and Blome's map of 1673 both show the addition of a religious building in a direction towards that of the present church. This church, dedicated to St Philip & St James, was built in 1839 by Miss Field of Edington at her expense. It was widely reported as having been built on the site of an old priory, although Frank Vowles told me, "I don't think the church is actually built on the site of the old priory, I've dug graves over most of the church yard for many years but I haven't ever found any signs of a previous building".

Chapel Hill Farm is situated almost midway between The Farm and the present church. There is no sign of a chapel now but there must have been some religious connection for it to justify the name. There is still a building between the farm and the road, now rather dilapidated, which served as a coach house for Miss Field's coach driver when she attended services at Burtle.

As the land originally belonged to Glastonbury Abbey, The Farm has always been known to have had an association with it, probably as one of its farms and/or a lodging house for pilgrims. The riddle is whether the original priory building was The Farm or was there another building erected close by it? Was the mapmaker of 1575 inaccurate? The cottages mentioned in the notes were most likely to have been close by the priory, an area known today as Little Burtle. Would it be stretching the imagination too far to speculate whether the old, small cottages near 'The Farm' today could be the originals?

There was a primitive Methodist chapel to the East by the Westhay Road, close by the First and Last public house, which has been demolished in recent times.

The present church was built by Miss Anne Field of Edington House on land donated by Earl Waldegrave. In August 1848 she conveyed 114 acres of land to the governors of Queen Anne's Bounty, the income from which was specifically designated for the use of **Burtle Church.** In July 1856 Miss Field gave a further 47 acres for the maintenance of the curate or incumbent of Burtle Church. In addition to the land she also gave and arranged the investment of large cash sums to meet running expenses and the vicar's stipend.

In 1933, the benefices of Burtle were combined with Catcott where there was no resident priest or vicarage. Although only two miles away, the Winter floods could no doubt present problems to the vicar travelling to Catcott. In 1974 the arrangement changed and Burtle was united with Shapwick and Ashcott and the vicarage was sold.

The vicars of Burtle:

1841-1842	Rev J. Cave Browne
1843-1844	Rev Mark W.W. James
1844-1864	Rev William Mathias
1864-1870	Rev E.C.Coney
1872-1882	Rev John B. Underwood
1882-1892	Rev A.J. Yarranton
1893-1912	Rev Thomas Lewis
1912-1937	Rev Leigh Philips
1937-1946	Rev A.S.N. Buchan
1947-1951	Rev D.B. Clatworthy
1951-1964	Rev A.C. Hoskin
1964-1974	Rev Frank E. Stubbings
1974-1995	Rev H. Leslie Baxter

Built in 1839 by Miss Anne Field of Edington,, Burtle church's exterior is fairly plain.
(M. Stone)

The interior projects a clean cut, unfussy simplicity that one might expect from its age.
(M. Stone)

Above: These buildings are said to have been used as a temporary coach house by Miss Field's coachman whilst she attended services at Burtle Church.

Left: Miss Anne Field, built the school in Burtle as well as the church.

One incumbent who was particularly well loved and still fondly remembered by the older generation, was the Rev Leigh Philips. He was a wonderful, caring personality but in later years developed an unfortunately serious association with alcohol. On one occasion, he travelled to Bridgwater on market day by train. Whilst there he had a few drinks, possibly with the encouragement of local farmers also attending the market! On the home journey he fell asleep, travelled, back to Bridgwater and once more out to Edington Junction before waking up. After another visit to town he managed to get as far as Gatcombe Farm, where he sat down under the wall and fell asleep. A couple of helpful young lads got a milk churn trolley and wheeled him back to the vicarage on it. In spite of his problems he is always remembered with warmth and affection tinged with a little sadness.

Miss Field also built the school and covenanted three acres of land, the income from which was intended to educate the children of, and, agricultural workers. It must be appreciated that this was well before the advent of compulsory, state aided, education. The field, situated diagonally across the crossroads from the church, was sold in 1957 to build a new kitchen in the school which, like many other village schools, it eventually closed its doors.

Soon afterwards, a remarkable man, Ron Atkinson acquired it to create the first school for dyslexic children in the country. During the hectic efforts to produce arms and machines during the second world war, he managed a production unit in which he had two brilliant designers - both were dyslexic! He realised that the condition could be an almost insurmountable barrier to people who had considerable talent. His son, Colin, was a past captain of Somerset County Cricket and, at the time, headmaster of Millfield. He no doubt drew on his son's experience to ensure the success of the project. So the old school thrives albeit in different clothes, providing some badly needed employment.

It seems wrong that Miss Field's intentions should no longer be honoured. Since the Church Commissioners took control of the property, buildings and land originally gifted to Burtle Church, the villagers of Burtle seem to spend all their spare time and energy raising cash to repair the building. Perhaps the circumstances of the transfer of ownership should be investigated. The integrity of the Church Commissioners has been the subject of very critical comment in recent years. Someone must have signed a piece of paper at some stage, did they have the authority to do this? How many parishes have suffered a similar experience, it seems to me that it is a subject deserving of closer investigation.

A charity known as Miss Field's gift, which provided a sack of coal to needy parishioners at Christmas and continued up until the second world war. This type of charitable arrangement was quite common in villages and, like many of them, the

Burtle one appears to have evaporated into thin air! No-one seems to know what happened to this charity, there could be a large capital sum accruing compound interest in a bank somewhere, provided that it has not been wound up.

There is a central registry under the auspices of the Charity Commissioners and **all** such charities should be registered in it. If the Charity Commissioners were more vigilant it might ensure that these benefits continue to be available to the community for which they were intended. Any registered charity which becomes inactive should be investigated as a matter of course so that any appropriate action can be taken. No doubt there are large sums of money sitting in banks countrywide just waiting to be claimed. Perhaps the banks should be made more responsible and be required to investigate these dormant accounts more vigorously, there is little incentive to do so as things stand.

The first farming on the levels started some six thousand years ago by neolithic man. Arthur Bulleid and Sir Harry Godwin have uncovered plenty of evidence to support these claims. In fact their lifestyles were surprisingly sophisticated, trading with Europe, even the Mediterranean countries. It is certain they did not have the level of bureaucracy and paperwork that we "enjoy" today! This is rather a pity as without written records it is not possible to establish whether they received any subsidies!

A primitive pig of the type probably kept by the prehistoric farmers of the lake villages. The pigs would largely exist by foraging amongst the woodlands for acorns etc; grain feed would be minimal it being needed for human consumption.

More seriously, these ancient farmers kept a similar range of farm livestock to those around today. Their arable endeavours produced mainly pulses and grain. The woodlands were being coppiced, some of the timber was used to build the trackways, some to make woven hurdles very similar to the woven wattle hurdles still available 6,000 years later! Ground game, fish and wild fowl were plentiful so they should have had a reasonable diet for the times. The main problems were those of health, rheumatism, ague and all those conditions associated with living in swampy conditions.

Most of the early land reclamation for agricultural use can be attributed to Glastonbury Abbey and the abbots. The monks always had a sharp eye to business and grazing land could substantially increase their wealth. This was particularly so when the local population could be more or less press ganged into the labour force necessary to carry through the drainage schemes. When the work was completed, the workers could then be charged more rent, often paid in eels, for the land they had worked so hard, and possibly charitably, to improve. A bit like the modern day rating system!

The first land to be made suitable for regular grazing and cultivation was that on the slightly higher coastal belt, only the highest of the peat beds could be used. One of the problems of draining the peat is that with the evacuation of the water the surface level is lowered, re-introducing potential flooding.

In spite of all this improvement, agricultural activities on the levels were almost completely dictated by the seasonal vicissitudes, continuing at a low level for several centuries, leading up to the enclosures and drainage schemes which started in the late eighteenth century. The rapidly increasing population helped to make these improvements viable.

The period between 1785 and 1850 was one of flux with gradual development of the subsistence agriculture following the Brue valley drainage scheme of 1806. Without today's pumping stations, the one in five thousand natural fall of the rivers made the lowering of the water table a very slow process. A map of 1782 shows a total of approximately 22 houses for the whole of what is now Burtle. As conditions improved with the advent of the enclosures effected by the excavation of drainage/ boundary ditches, from around 1785 and through the early 1800's, the road connections with Chilton Polden, Edington, Catcott and Westhay were constructed as part of the overall scheme. Before this point, farming activities would have been impossible on the lowest land which was underwater much of the year.

Most of the older, larger farmhouses and barns in Burtle are built of limestone, all of which would have to been hauled across the peat moors by horses or brought in by boat, as would the bricks used to build the smaller farms and cottages. On the lower land, little hovels were built using cut turf blocks reinforced by timber and plastered to give the walls protection from the weather. I heard of one of these being demolished in the 1970's although I have never seen one myself. This type of construction would not be able to resist flood water, giving them a relatively short life.

'The Farm' is one of the most imposing buildings in Burtle and the site is by far the oldest. The main house was probably re-vamped about 200 years ago. The portion to the right appears to be much older. (Colin Whitcome)

The oldest and most impressive farmhouse at Chilton Burtle, now known simply as 'The Farm', once had links with Glastonbury Abbey, about eight miles away. Legends of underground tunnels and secret rooms are traditionally associated with such ancient farm and manor houses. A rumoured underground passage to Westhay is unrealistic, the water tables would ensure it was permanently flooded. More believable, it is said that there is a crypt under the house where the old time monks were laid to rest.

Another, once impressive farm house with twenty two rooms was Burtle House Farm, about one mile away at the Eastern end of Edington Burtle. One of its features was a large window of unusual design. Sadly, the old house has been demolished, the substantial two storey barn adjoining it has been converted into a house. Another interesting claim I have heard is that the house known as Elm Tree Farm was originally built on Shepherd's Drove off the Catcott Road and in the late nineteenth century was dismantled and rebuilt in its present position.

The soils are mainly of two types, the greensand on which most of the village is situated is very fertile and fairly free draining. There have been many good gardeners over the years and it is maybe surprising no-one has developed a serious business growing horticultural crops. The village is almost completely surrounded by the low level peat, most of which has been dug for fuel over the centuries, thereby lowering the level and increasing its tendency to flood. To the western extremity of the village and raised just above the level of all but the most serious floods, there is a small extension of alluvial clay from the coastal belt, laid over the peat by the sea, contributing to the latter's final exclusion from the area.

Arthur Cox milking a cow in the traditional manner. The milker would walk up to the cow with a stool in one hand and a bucket in the other. He was the last man I knew to use the old fashioned wooden milking buckets. Milking could be a stressful job when the flies were busy in hot weather, it was also advisable not to stand directly behind any cow freshly out on young spring grass!

Dairy farming has been the traditional, economic mainstay of the area and most villagers would have a few cows. Sheep have never been kept in any quantity, liver fluke probably saw to that although many were once farmed at Mark, about three miles to the North. In the 1990's it is difficult to appreciate that, as recently as the 1950's, there were nearly forty Burtle people milking their own cows. Many families made a living by milking three or four cows supplemented by casual labour, a good garden and skilful use of a twelve bore shotgun. The milk collection would entail at least thirty pick up points for a total load of less than three hundred gallons.

During the summer months, cows were milked in the fields. The hand milker walked up to the cow with a bucket in one hand and a milking stool in the other. The cows were trained to stand wherever they were in the field, the milker sitting on the milking stool under the cow, milked straight into the bucket. The milking buckets, originally wooden ones in Burtle, were emptied straight into the churn, formerly the old conical seventeen galloners but latterly the more conventional and friendly ten gallon variety. In hot weather the latter would be immersed up to their shoulder in the water of a nearby ditch to cool the milk.

Stephen and Willie Pocock milking their cows opposite their Chapel Hill Farm, which their family occupied for over one hundred years. They lost their father when they were very young and their mother Elizabeth ran the farm for many years until they were old enough to take over. Note the turf cart which in this case is being used for the milk churns. (H. Willcox).

Transport to and from the Summer grazing, which could be several miles from home, was by horse and cart (milk float). Most farmers had a collie type cow dog, often tied somewhat precariously to the axle of the milk float when on the road. Pre 1950, thirty or more milking cows would establish the owner as being among the farming elite in Burtle.

Dodging the flies, the dirty, whip like tail and the occasional kick, a good hand milker could milk six to eight cows an hour. Cows that had just gone out to grass for the first time in the Spring had to be approached warily. An unexpected cough coupled with the laxative affect of the young grass could spell disaster to any person stood immediately behind!

During the Winter months, the cattle were brought into Winter quarters, usually, but not always above the Winter flood levels. Not all the houses were built out of reach of the floods and the Winters must have been sheer hell for some of the poorer families down on the peat. Although most of the peat areas had been dug at least once for fuel, thereby lowering the ground level whereupon it became very boggy, there were still a few fields that had raised peat beds that not been touched and could be as much as ten feet above the adjacent land. These stayed dry in the Winter and were ideal for outwintering cattle.

In 1922 and again in 1929 there were horrendously wet summers. This was probably the former when there was such a shortage of hay that many of the Burtle cattle were wintered on the Mendip Hills to ensure their survival. The turf boats were an essential part of everyday life on the moors and fulfilled a multitude of uses.

Cattle housing varied from the most primitive rough cut timber and corrugated iron sheds to good, purpose built stone and tile linhays (pronounced linneys) with hard floors. A linhay was usually a detached stone building which was often open on one side, in which hay could be stored and cattle fed in Winter. The story of Harry Selway, later in the book, who had a small holding nearly a mile off the Catcott road down the dirt track, Shepherd's Drove, is one such example of the hardships suffered by those living on the low land.

Some of the milk not required for liquid sales was used to make cheese and butter, some was processed in Catcott Burtle during the existence of the creamery in what was originally the school. The creamery bit the financial dust in the early 1920's, when road transport operated by Tommy Powell took over the transport of the milk to larger, nearby manufacturing centres at Bason Bridge and Highbridge. He collected milk locally and used the old creamery premises to cool it over night, benefitting from well water which emerged at a comparatively low temperature. From Bason Bridge the liquid milk would continue by rail to the cities.

Some of the Burtle farming sons and daughters trained as cheese makers although the number of individual farms making cheese declined with the restrictions introduced during the second world war. Curiously, so near the home of cheddar, the main cheese produced for the Highbridge cheese market was caerphilly destined for the South Wales mining valleys. One of the economic benefits of this cheese was the shorter period it needed to mature.

The coming of the railway greatly improved the dairy farmers' lot by enabling the quicker and wider distribution of farming products to the centres of population. Whatever the merits of the old canal, it was comparatively slow and therefore unsuitable for the transport of perishable produce. Moreover the train could usually get through the floods when the roads were under water.

Zig zag harrows were mainly used for harrowing in seed corn and for light cultivations, grassland was aerated and dung dispersed each spring with chain harrows.

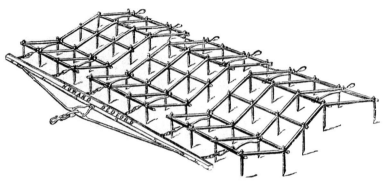

Ransomes were the first company to mass produce ploughs and the model shown was in regular use for over one hundred years without any substantial design changes

Some corn and other arable crops were grown for Winter feed. There were many casual, part time jobs that were associated with these crops. Hoeing mangolds, cow cabbage and kale were the sort of jobs that could be done by wives or outside of normal working hours by men in regular work. Farmers growing potatoes often had an arrangement with others in the village whereby a rank or two of potatoes could be grown in exchange for doing the hoeing work. There were many traditional means of bartering goods for services, some have survived to the present time.

In the Summers there was the hay to make, ditches to clear, arable work growing corn and mangolds and burning peat to cut and dry for use in the house and for sale.

A hay tedder similar to a model made at Glastonbury at the end of the nineteenth century and used on local farms. Designed to work at the speed of draught horses they could not tolerate the higher speeds of the Standard Fordson and other tractors. Much of the farm machinery of the day could remain in service for forty or fifty years with the help of a good local blacksmith.

Hay waggons were the pinnacle of rural craftsmanship, as much as 6 months labour went into the building of a good quality model. If properly looked after they could give up to one hundred years service..The peat land was treacherous when wet and overloaded waggons would cut through the grass spine surface, sinking up to their axles.

Hay and corn harvest were always busy times. It was not that a large acreage was grown but it was essential to gather it in good, dry condition in order to get through the Winter. In the early 1920's, after a disastrous hay making season, all except the milking cows were driven by road up to the Mendips for over wintering. There was just not enough hay to sustain them in Burtle. Most of the farmers cooperated in their efforts and welcomed some additional casual help at hay and harvest time.

One recipient of such assistance decided to show his appreciation to his helper by taking him down to the South coast for a day's fishing. They hired a boat at Beer and set out. Hours later there were no fish to show for their efforts so they decided to return to the harbour. Half way back they decided to have one last ditch attempt. The mackerel were biting and in no time they had more than they knew what to do with.

"Better mark the spot Bert", said Jack.

"OK", said Bert.

As they were getting into the car, Jack asked, "How diss thee mark thic spot, Bert?"

"I put a cross on the back o' the boat", said Bert.

"You bliddy o' vule", chastised Jack, "We might'n 'ave the same boat nex' time"!

One of the greatest advantages of the peat lands was in the event of a dryer than average Summer, water was always available not far below the surface and tremendous crops could be grown whilst farmers' grass crops on the nearby hill land soon 'burnt up'. Heavy crops could present a problem in themselves, causing considerable handling difficulties to the simplistic machinery of the day, thereby extending the drying time.

The lawsuit, a plaster cast with a moral, pointing out to farmers in particular that the main beneficiaries of legal action are usually the lawyers. While the farmers are arguing the lawyer is miking the cow!

In periods of wet weather the boot was on the other foot. The peat became too soft to work on, whereas the farmers on the hill could score with better results.

Haymaking was very dependent on the weather and ground conditions. Mowing with horses was an early morning job, often starting around three or four o'clock. The grass always cut easier with some dew on it and the temperature at that time of day was much kinder on the horses. The quality of the hay would be good if the weather was sunny and it was made quickly. A careless mowing leaving some uncut tufts would be greeted with "Leff a bit ta tie the hoss up to, I see!"

A typical hay time scene, the women did the lighter work such as raking in the hay around the field edge and the final cleaning up. It was hard work but people always seemed to have time for a chat and a tip of the cider jar. Meals were usually taken out to the field and became a social occasion.

The swathes had to be turned and tedded (fluffed up) in order to allow the air to dry it. Some of the early hay tedders, particularly one made at Glastonbury, were highly dangerous to use. The machine consisted of a rapidly revolving shaft, driven by the ground wheels, with a series of transverse wooden arms with rows of spikes set in them. These adjusted to a suitable height to pick up the hay and toss it into the air behind the tedder. As it settled gently down the looser consistency encouraged better air circulation and aided the drying process. There was little protection for the driver seated on the early machines and on uneven ground the flails could catch the ground and break up, pieces flying in all directions like shrapnel. Those that remained on farms into the 1950's were mainly destroyed by towing at speed behind tractors!.

Labour was cheap and plentiful, the outside swathes were laboriously hand raked into the field to be in reach of the machines. Particularly heavy swathes were even tossed and spread by hand in an effort to equalise the drying time. Clean raking with a horse drawn hay rake ensured nothing was missed or wasted.

A haymaking gathering out side the First and Last, probably to replenish the cider jars on route to the hayfield. The landlord, Arthur Norris, is leaning against the cart talking to Arthur Cox, with the cart to the right was a hardware salesman, a Mr. Binding who worked for a Mr. Nicholls who had a shop in Bridgwater. Further along the road we can see the chimneys of a bungalow and the Ebenezer Primitive Chapel both demolished soon after last war.

The hay could be gathered in by a variety of methods depending in part on the distance from the hayfield to the rick yard. Where there was a patch of higher ground above the Winter flood levels in an off field a rick would sometimes be built on the spot. This would often have to be retrieved by boat when the time came to use it.

Hand pitching onto horse drawn wagons was a dusty, slow and uncomfortable business. Hay loaders which were connected to the rear of the wagon and operated by their ground drive wheels were an improvement and also saved labour.

The wagons were unloaded either by hand pitching straight up to the rick maker or by using a clip pole. This was a system probably borrowed from the marine world, a vertical, mast like pole some forty to fifty feet high, in two sections that socketed together like the sections of a fishing rod, would be set into a hole adjacent to the rick and steadied by four guy ropes to steel pegs, a bit like the modern day radio mast. A cross spar resembling the boom on a ship's mast was suspended on ropes from pulley blocks fitted to the head of the pole. The heel end of the boom was

In fields at some distance from the homestead, hayricks would be built on a staddle of brushwood on a higher part of the moor in an effort to keep the hay above the winter floods. Often, the only way to fetch the hay was with the indispensable turf boat, no doubt much hay would be lost in a bad winter. Surplus hay would be cut with a hay knife, tied into trusses of around a hundred weight (fifty Kilos) and sold to W.H.Coate & Co. in Bridgwater who had a contract to supply the army. This provided much needed winter work for locals. (M. Moxey)

Almost every farm had a chaff cutter which was used to chop hay and straw into short lengths for bedding or fodder. Some businesses were based on buying and chaffing fodder for army horses. The feed was mechanically fed through the trough and guillotined by three sharp curved blades bolted to the spokes of the cast iron wheel. They were very dangerous and caused the loss of many fingers and worse.

The Clip Pole replaced the hard work of pitching hay by hand.

fastened to a steel ring which fitted around the pole, allowing the boom to revolve around it. A rope was passed around a pulley near the base of the pole up to one on the heel of the boom, along it and over a third pulley on the free swinging end. This end of the rope was attached to a set of grab forks which operated much like the self closing coal scoops used for unloading the coal boats in Bridgwater docks. When the horse on the other end of the rope pulled, the tension caused the forks to close, grabbing a substantial wad of hay. As the horse continued forward the hay was lifted to a height which allowed the boom to swing over the rick and the hay released by a tug on a trip rope. This method was a quite quick, efficient and labour saving. It could be a very boring job constantly walking backwards and forwards, leading the horse, usually given to the most junior worker present.

Horse-drawn hay sweeps were often used as a good, fast way of bringing the hay from the field to the clip pole, elevator or hand pitchers. These sweeps were the fore runners of the modern tractor buck rake, like a gigantic, coarse comb laid horizontally with the teeth facing forwards. At the rear corners of the 'comb' a second frame with a pair of handles was connected by two pivots. The sweep was pulled along the windrows, gathering up the hay. Arriving at the rick the machine could be discharged by a sharp upwards tug on the handles, the "comb" revolved on its points, leaving the hay behind. In the thirties, engine driven chain elevators began to appear and gradually took over.

Corn cutting usually came hard on the heels of hay making. To avoid waste, the perimeter ten feet around the outside of the field was hand cut by scythe and the sheaves tied by hand using some of the cut corn straw as a bond. The binder, drawn by two horses, was brought in and the serious cutting started. The sheaves now had to be stitched (stooked) by picking them up in pairs and leaning them together in double rows of eight to twelve per stitch. Corn cut with a binder was occasionally not quite fully ripe, in any case there was often grass and other plants growing in amongst the corn which had to dry before it could be ricked. In a very wet period, the grain could sprout when still in the stitches causing terrible problems, sometimes completely ruining the crop.

In addition to the single varieties a mixture locally known as dredge consisting of several or all of the following, horse beans, peas, barley and oats. As each variety ripened at different speeds the stooks often had to stand for several days to dry. The resulting crop when rolled or milled, was a reasonably balanced feed for milking cows, reducing the need to buy in expensive supplements.

Haymaking was such a non-stop frenzy of activity in Westhay! Bob Rogers and Geoff Parsons taking a 'breather'. Note the horse drawn hay tedder in the background. (H. Willcox)

Once the hay and corn ricks had been built, which was quite an expert job in itself, they had to be thatched as protection against the elements. Burtle's freelance spar maker and expert thatcher was Met Watts. He would spend many hours in the Winter and Spring months, cutting his raw materials from the pollarded withy trees which are so common on the levels. The 'pollarded' trees were coppiced every four to five years, some seven to eight feet above the ground, out of reach of browsing cattle. The one to two inch diameter wands, were split into four sections lengthways with a spar makers hook. The ends would be deftly pointed, two sharp clouts on the block with the back of the spar hook about two inches apart near the centre, a sharp twist and folded to resemble a large wooden hairpin. It looked quite simple, indeed it was, once one had made twenty or thirty thousand!

There was a great deal of pride involved in all the various stages of work on the land, critical eyes would be cast over the corn ricks awaiting the arrival of the threshing machine sometime during the Winter. Were the centres hard, the corners sloped out sufficiently and the thatch a good finish and at the right angle to shed the rain?

The perils of ploughing on the Somerset levels. (Courtesy of Lance Jordan Photography Ltd.)

Ploughing, in particular, attracted critical eyes, observation being colloquially termed 'hedge farming'. Casual mention of dead hares found in the field was countryspeak for crooked furrows. It was an old wives' tale that hares could only run in a straight line and that running down crooked furrows they beat their brains out or broke their necks on the furrow walls! Arthur Cox of Burtle House Farm once ploughed an acre of land with horses in three hours twenty minutes, a record at the time. An acre usually took a full day!

The threshing itself provided more work, a few lucky ones would 'sign up' for the whole threshing season, travelling throughout the villages within a workable radius of the threshing machine's home base. The old steam traction engines had a maximum road speed of about six miles per hour. It often took a full day to pack up on one site and set up on the next. In spite of their size and weight the ground traction of the steam engines was poor. Some farmyards were difficult to manoeuvre the clumsy threshing machines into, especially if the ground was wet and soft, even worse if sloping.

The procedure was that the five to six ton threshing machine on its solid steel spoked and rimmed wheels was juggled into place alongside the rick. Larger rick

Ern Lee with his threshing tackle at Westham before his return to Burtle to take over from his father, George Lee. The tractors are a 'high' Fordson Major and an Oliver, a very good tractor imported from the USA. Ern was quite a pioneer, note the baling of the straw.

yards might have a double row of ricks the right distance apart to enable two ricks to be threshed from one position avoiding some of the time consuming moves. The huge traction engine belt pulley was lined up with the much smaller pulley on the thresher, a highly skilled exercise. Unless perfectly aligned the enormously long drive belt would not stay on the pulleys.

Additional casual help would be enlisted from those in the village who normally helped the farmer whose corn was being threshed. A full team would number a minimum of ten workers. These would be the engine driver who was in overall charge, a driver's mate whose duties included keeping the engine coaled and watered.

The bond cutter's job was to feed the machine via the threshing drum having removed the twine from the sheaves. The two men on the rick fed the bond cutter, if the sheaves were not presented exactly to his liking, his displeasure would quickly be made plain!

At the front of the thresher the bagger weighed off the grain into the enormous West of England sacks, ready for the sack carrier. He often carried sacks weighing as much as two and a half hundred weights (125K) up the granary steps to the corn bins. Fortunately, a simple machine, a sack lifter, was used to winch the heavy sacks to a convenient height to enable them to be taken on the shoulder or back.

Mealtimes gave a much needed break, the cider jars were always kept within easy reach and some workers could drink a couple of gallons in hot weather.

The trussing machine was located at the rear of the threshing machine. The large, loosely packed bundles of threshed straw had to be transferred to the site of the straw rick originally by hand, latterly by mechanical elevator. At least one straw rick maker, probably two, would be on duty there. The dirtiest, least desirable job was that of clearing the dowse or cavings (husks) and a junior worker was normally instructed to attend! Mercifully, some enlightened engineer eventually designed a ducting system to blow the dowse to wherever it was required, thereby gaining the undying gratitude of a host of young workers.

Where an abundance of rats and mice were established in the rick a wire netting fence would be erected around the rick to prevent their escape. The children would have a very exciting time clubbing them with sticks in competition with the terriers and farm collies. During the last war, this was a legal requirement but it was not too strictly enforced.

On threshing days, the engine driver would have to start firing up the engine some two hours before the work began. It was common practice for them to cook their breakfast on the coal shovel thrust into the firebox. The smell on a frosty morning would be guaranteed to get one's digestive juices running riot! A plentiful water supply was essential to top up the boiler, and, as a precaution against possible fire caused by sparks from the engine.

If rain came, the work had to stop, the thresher and the ricks would be covered by heavy canvas rick sheets. One of the worst jobs on the farm was reckoned to be carrying a heavy sheet up a ladder with rain running down the back of one's neck. In spite of the hard graft the annual visit of the threshing team was always looked forward to with keen anticipation.

Wise farmers would keep an eagle eye on the threshing machine operators as the final half hour or so approached. It was not unknown for the shaker belts 'to come off', causing the threshing machine to retain as much as half a ton of grain within its bowels. A substantial 'bonus' could be gained by the operators when this was later recovered in another place, when the belt was replaced!!

The steam engines were gradually phased out during and soon after the second world war. Excellent new tractors were being imported from the United States, upstaging our more familiar, smaller Standard Fordsons. Two American favourites for use with threshing machines in the place of the old traction engines were the Oliver 90 and the Allis Chalmers, complimented by the British made Field Marshall. The latter was a single cylinder two stroke, the first diesel engined tractor around.

There were two methods of starting the Field Marshall, one by setting a decompression arm on to a spiral groove on the flywheel and turning like hell until the arm came off the end releasing the decompressor. In this case a warming fuse inserted into a special socket in the cylinderhead greatly assisted the 'not so strong'. The second used a special explosive cartridge inserted into the compression chamber and detonated by a sharp smack with a hammer. One interesting phenomenon was that the engine was reputed to be able to start and run in reverse and you had no certain way of knowing this until it was put in gear!

One day's combine harvesting today with three or four people would be roughly equivalent to one week's threshing with at least ten workers. This would not take into account the workers required to cut, stook, haul and rick the corn during the previous Summer. I actually took the first combine, a Massey 726 bagger, into Burtle in 1953 to cut corn on the glebe. Viv Moxey, a likeable character who farmed Glebe Farm in Robins Lane was instrumental in persuading several of his fellow farmers to 'give it a try'. The glebe was a large field on the Mark road with narrow, cultivated strips disappearing into the distance and growing every conceivable crop. No one farmer seemed to cultivate any two adjacent strips. As each ribbon of corn was cut, the combine had to be thoroughly cleaned out between each plot to ensure that each farmer was sure that he had not missed out! It must have taken as long to combine four or five acres as twenty five or more under normal circumstances. I often wonder how father made out the bill. He had bought all the twenty five inch ordnance maps to confirm that all the fields known as 'ten acres' were really twelve acres plus!! It is a fair bet that those Burtle farmers' bills took some working out!

Although the milk and dairies regulations, first introduced in 1929 were ridiculed as being over the top, they were a start toward hygienic milk production. The creation of the Milk Marketing Board in 1933, during the depression years, was a godsend to all dairy farmers whether or not they appreciated it. No other agricultural marketing co-operative has been anything like as successful in harnessing and managing the collective efforts of any section of the farming scene. For the first time ever, farmers and consumers alike knew the price at any time. It had powers well in excess of those vested in any of the other agricultural marketing boards which is probably the reason for its success over sixty years. In spite of being of a higher calibre than anything set up in Europe, it was sacrificed to the CAP.

A rough census based approximately 1950 shows that there were nearly forty milk producers in what is now the village of Burtle. Around three hundred, mainly shorthorn type cows, each producing an optimistic average of approximately five hundred gallons per year each. Fifty years later there are about five farms milking some four hundred friesian and holstein cows, each averaging over one thousand gallons per year! Bulk tanks have replaced the churns, the cost of the former did much to freeze out many of the small producers.

Although the farms are much larger today there are no outside employees. Father and son units milking seventy to one hundred cows are the norm. Erstwhile farm workers have had to find alternative employment, some had to move away to achieve this. Nonsensical planning regulations would not allow any diversification of businesses to be set up in the villages to create local employment. Fortunately, for them, the horticultural peat business was expanding apace and many turned to this as an alternative.

The march of time has transformed the farming scene. Over the last fifty years the Gold Corner pumping station has drained the land to a condition where tractors and implements could safely work on the peat land, even in dry spells during the Winter, not only in the Summer months.

Today, with flotation tyres on tractors and implements, almost anything is possible. In Burtle some of the higher peat land is ploughed, rotovated, cultivated, reseeded and even occasionally, planted to cereals. Enormous crops of silage and hay can be almost guaranteed now, the work being completed in a fraction of the time once needed. Maize grows to an enormous height at a tremendous rate, the main snag being the harvesting in a wet Autumn. Forays into growing massive crops of potatoes on a particularly low area of the peat near Burtle by "Pip" Gibbons

NEAR THE CROSS, BURTLE.

VOWLES, MINEHEAD
COPYRIGHT. 5.

Hill Farm is on the right, the last working farmers were Mr. And Mrs. Geoff Moxey who bought the farm in 1941 and built their retirement home in the walled garden in the foreground. In the distance, just to left of centre, is the old school with its little bell tower. It closed about 1890 and became a creamery under at least two companies for about thirty years. This was of great benefit to the Burtle farmers, under the first owners the manager was F.Bigg, later it was Seward Rice who lived in The Cottage on the Westhay Road at that time. The creamery closed in the early nineteen twenties probably due to the activities of a much larger operation at Bason Bridge. Tommy Powell continued to use the building as an overnight milk storage point as the cold spring water was ideal for cooling the milk. The band also used it as a practice room for several years. The building was recently demolished to make way for a new house. To the right of the old school building is a cottage that was once a public house, The Globe with William Tratt was listed as landlord and shopkeeper 1861 - 1866. Note the tree in the middle of the cross roads. The couple stood at the end of the farmhouse are Mr. Herbert and Mrs. Florence Frost who had a large family of mostly girls. Mrs. Frost died in childbirth in 1913 at the early age of thirty four. (M. Moxey) of Kent Farm, Shapwick have shown up a need for an underwater harvester, in the absence of which they are not much grown these days! His land has now been purchased by one of the conservation organisations and is covered by water for much of the year!

One Burtle farmer visiting another one Sunday morning in his car, drew up in the yard and said, "Hey Bert, I see vour of your old 'ens have stopped laying'.

"How's know that?" asked Bert.

"'Cos I just runned over 'em in the drive", answered the visitor.

Another farmer wanted to buy some land and was asked by the bank manager to prepare some financial forecasts. A sum of £200 in cash at the end of November caught the manager's eye.

"Oh, I usually take the missus up to London during the Smithfield Show", stated the farmer.

On the 25th of November the farmer rang the bank manager and advised him that he was going to need £500. "Oh, there's no problem", he said, "It's just that the wife can't go"

The present farming is mainly dairy with a some beef production. There are no longer the traditional hens, ducks and geese running around the farm yards which is probably just as well as foxes, which have become very common and bold, would soon see them off. Progress has made farming faster and easier physically but much less interesting and picturesque.

There was a rumor that a Westhay farmer who had won £8,000,000 on the lottery was heard to declare, "I shall just kep on varming til tis all gone"

A farmers' outing outside the 'Black Bull', previously known as The Mark Moor Inn and now River Farm. This could be a building with a long history as a hostelry, bearing in mind that this road was for many years the only established route into Burtle. It is also built on higher ground.

The Canal and the Somerset & Dorset Joint Railway

Peat land is a most difficult terrain on which to build roads, the maintenance thereafter can also be very costly. This being so, the alternatives were long, tedious journeys by horse and cart around the lengthy perimeter of the peat bogs, particularly during the Winter months.

If Joseph of Arimathea really did visit the Glastonbury area by boat, he would have had a tortuous route through the swamps. The contrast with his homeland must have presented quite a culture shock! The idea may not be so daft, there is evidence that the Mediterranean nations traded in the area at a very early date.

In mediaeval times most heavy materials were transported by boat via the rivers Brue and Axe, the latter was connected to the Brue by the Pilrow Cut through Mark. The most important trading organisation by far was Glastonbury Abbey and they had several inland ports as well as at Glastonbury itself. The Glastonbury Canal, or South Drain, was completed much later, in 1833. Waterways provided a means of moving heavy loads reasonably easily, albeit slowly through an otherwise difficult terrain. Moreover, it could have been possible for coastal boats plying their trade to navigate directly into them at the juncture of the Axe with the Bristol Channel. The considerable extra labour in double handling required to transfer cargo onto a second, smaller boat could be avoided.

The river Brue approached Glastonbury from the East along the South side of the Tor, it then turned north along what is now the Western boundary of the town, West to the Meare Pool and North through the Bleadney Gap, finally discharging into the River Axe.

Between 1330 and 1350, the monks of Glastonbury diverted the river into a new channel, from the Meare pool taking a more direct line to the present exit near the mouth of the River Parrett. Nevertheless, in 1606/7, terrible floods were experienced and the inhabitants of Glastonbury "feared a watery grave" There was an average of fifteen feet of water over the moors and considerable loss of life. Cradles in the area were made in the manner of small boats to prevent babies being drowned. The nearby village of Mark, on somewhat higher ground is reported to have had ten thousand sheep drowned.

The enclosures of farming land started in the late 18th century in this part of Somerset. The whole exercise was very piecemeal and complicated by curious old parish boundaries. As Burtle was not a parish in its own right but a part of several others, the applications were for a series of seemingly quite unconnected parcels of land, (and swamp!). As if this were not enough, most of it in turn came under the jurisdiction of Moorlinch, the local ecclesiastical centre.

In 1806 a major venture, the Brue Drainage Plan, drawn up by surveyor William White was approved. The Brue valley, stretching from Pilton to the sea was covered on a map 13 feet (4m) by 5ft 7" (1.65m) at 8" (.2m) to one mile. The necessary flood management arrangements were probably the forerunner of today's drainage boards. Part of this scheme included the digging of the Glastonbury Canal, or South Drain as it is alternatively known. As with the Huntspill River, there was a dual purpose in its creation.

The canal, no doubt, developed its own community and became a link between the people living on the moors and the outside world. Even in Summer there would have been some expanses of water, the Winter floods would have resembled an inland sea.

The Glastonbury canal existed as an important trade route for just over twenty years, until the Central Somerset Railway was completed and took over in 1854. There had been problems with the canal, peat is a curious substance and with its amorphous nature, tends to fill up waterways with little or no flow, from underneath and the canal had to be regularly cleaned to prevent the boats from grounding. In spite of its short life and the dredging problems, the canal carried a great volume of traffic. Before the building of the canal the Rivers Brue and Axe were the only waterways that could have been used to service the Glastonbury trade.

A train approaching Edington Station from the Glastonbury direction through the winter floods. Possibly pre 1890. (M. Moxey)

The railway companies had had a problem in finding a route for their track from the coast to the interior. The "Squires" on the Polden Hills would not co-operate, forcing the company to consider alternatives. The uncooperative landowners on the hill also owned land on the levels. The Bridgwater and Exeter Railway Company bought out the canal company in 1848 with the intention of using the towpath for their broad gauge track.

Building a rail track across the peat beds was a formidable undertaking as the land is very unstable. It is like a giant sponge, if you jump up and down the rushes twenty yards away will quiver and shake. (The rail track across Rannoch Moor in the north of Scotland presented similar difficulties. In that case the track was built on faggots of wood, the system used by the early inhabitants of the Somerset levels for their roadways, some five to six thousand years earlier. It is said that there is nothing new under the sun!)

Railway companies were fiercely competitive throughout the second half of the 19th century, employing many dubious strategies to out-do the competition. There were many curious alliances in spite of the deep emnities. The building of the railways countrywide required phenomenal labour resources. This often brought opportunities for the locals in rural areas to earn regular wages, for many, for the first time in their lives.

During the Autumn of 1850 a group of capitalists and manufacturers, prominent among whom were members of the Society of Friends, met to consider the feasibility of providing railway services to the mid Somerset area. The Bristol & Exeter Railway Company. with others, set up the Somerset Central Railway on July 1st 1852 and sold the canal to them. A meeting in the town hall, Glastonbury in June 1851 had already approved the proposals with "extreme enthusiasm".

The Central Somerset Railway raised capital of £70,000 by the issue of 3,500 shares of £20 each. In exchange for the Glastonbury Canal and Highbridge Harbour together with the "works therein", the Bristol and Exeter Railway received 400 paid up £20 shares, £8,000.

There were obviously some pretty sharp businessmen involved with the development of the railway. "The formation of the railway, involving, as it will, the abandonment of the canal for the purposes of traffic, will afford the means of using it for an improved system of drainage throughout the large tract of land intersected by it, whereby the value of the land will be greatly increased, and an additional source of revenue may be derived by obtaining powers for levying a rate upon the lands to be so benefitted".

To quote from an article in the Railway Magazine, February 1905, "The navigable waterway in existence between Glastonbury and Highbridge had already developed a very considerable trade but the canal was owned by the Bristol and Exeter Railway, and it was, therefore of importance that the property should, if possible, be purchased, to prevent any cutting of rates in the contingency of any misunderstanding with that railway." The ownership of the canal would enable the Central Somerset Railway to realise an immediate income from the canal traffic receipts. The Bristol and Exeter Railway had also tendered an undisclosed sum to indemnify them from any claim for repairs to the canal and associated property.

When the railway was built, the only option was the seven feet and half an inch broad gauge track as all the other railways in the county were of this gauge.

The work started on August 16th, 1852 as soon as the contractors had moved their plant to Glastonbury. I find this surprising in view of the much greater accessibility of the Highbridge end, although, on the other hand, the stone quarries were at the Glastonbury end. The line only crossed six roads on the level, three of these were turnpike roads, the other three were "green" droves. The whole twelve and a half miles, including sidings at Glastonbury, Ashcott, Shapwick, and Highbridge stations covered only eighty four acres. Presumably, as they are not mentioned, the sidings at Edington came later, when the Bridgwater branch was built and the station became Edington Junction.

A report of Autumn 1853 stated, "Works were proceeding rapidly, 200 men were employed at one point near the junction with the Bristol and Exeter Railway at Highbridge, it was anticipated that the whole line would be opened for traffic in less than a year. The engineer's report to the next meeting on February 26th 1854, confirmed that works were actively progressing towards completion, and, with favourable weather the line would be ready for traffic early in the Autumn of that year.

The line between Glastonbury and Highbridge was finally opened on August 7th 1854. A general holiday was celebrated with a procession over a mile long and a remarkable display of banners with symbolic mottoes. The directors were entertained at a civic banquet, standard practice in those days for such momentous occasions. It was, after all, a considerable achievement to build the track and all the ancillaries over a period of one week short of two years!

When the railway opened, some of the redundant canal boats were bought by "Squire" Durston who lived in Burtle House at that time. The timber was used for farm buildings and included masts of sixty feet cut back for wallplates. Canal barges would have no use for masts but small sea going craft could easily step their masts to enable them to pass under the odd (Highbridge) bridge on their journey in the direction of Glastonbury.

In 1858 the line was extended to Burnham on Sea, in 1859 the other end was extended to Wells. At the half yearly meeting of the Somerset Central Railway, held at Glastonbury on February 16th 1861, the assembly was told that it had been definitely decided that the narrow gauge should be laid, in order to provide for the traffic coming from the narrow gauge system with which, through the Dorset Central Railway, they were about to be connected at Bruton, and, said the report, it remains only to decide whether the line should be worked as a mixed gauge line or whether it should be worked exclusively on the narrow gauge, upon termination of the management lease in August next, for which the Bristol and Exeter Railway have given notice. A saving in outlay of £80,000 would be affected by converting the line to narrow gauge, as compared with the cost of laying down the mixed gauge; in spite of opposition from the big companies, it was recommended that the former proposal be the course adopted!

Later in 1862, the Somerset Central Railway merged with the Dorset Central Railway to form the familiar Somerset and Dorset Joint Railway. It was the ambition to establish a rail link directly between the Bristol Channel and the English Channel, an ambition eventually realised, in spite of the counter activities of other rail companies.

The first half yearly meeting of the new company was held at Blandford on February 27th 1863 when the report, ref the gauge, was unanimously adopted. The last link in the chain from the Bristol Channel and the English Channel occurred with the opening of the Somerset Junction to Blandford on Monday, August 21st, 1863.

The net profits in 1863 were £3,225, £7,500 in 1864, which was considered very satisfactory. It was reported that the import-export business through Highbridge had increased by 100% during the last six months. The fortunes of the railway continued to prosper until the great financial crisis of 1866, which resulted in two of the main lines in the country being thrown into chancery. The S & D was holding its own against its powerful broad gauge neighbours, when it suffered the seizure of a locomotive by a creditor, and a receiver was appointed to administer the affairs of the company.

The report of 1867 referred to the revenue being applied to meeting charges upon rolling stock and general line maintenance. Meanwhile, a rescue plan which it was hoped would meet the approval of the court of chancery was being prepared. The company had suffered a severe loss of reputation, loss of credit and was generally downgraded. The rescue plan must have been a good one, the company raised its head again in 1869 and once more entered a period of prosperity.

Authorisation to build the Edington Road Station to Bridgwater branch line was obtained in 1882, the lines of finance in place by 1888 and the line reaching

Bridgwater with a grand opening luncheon provided by the mayor on July 21st 1890. At this point Edington Road Station became Edington Junction.

When each phase of construction was completed, many local "navigators" became career railwaymen, introducing a whole new way of life, and one on which Burtle folks relied heavily for regular employment for many years. It also provided a stepping stone for many to earn enough money to enable them to progress from labouring to setting up in business on their own account.

Many of the farming families had no doubt been close to the breadline in the past. Now sons and even the fathers in some cases went to work, building the line and doing their farmwork outside of normal working hours. It would be fair to speculate that this extra income enabled the villagers to greatly improve their standard of living. Talking to the older generation, one wonders whether there was a man in the village who had not worked on railway at some point.

The rail track eventually ran from Burnham on Sea to Evercreech junction with spur lines from Edington (Burtle) Junction to Bridgwater and from Glastonbury to Wells. Wells, at one point with no railway station, finished up with three within a few years. Over a short period, the transport situation had been transformed, goods began to flow in and out of the region, creating a hitherto unknown level of prosperity.

A huge number of trucks were filled with burning peat for delivery all over the country. Coincidentally, most of the goods sidings had a pub close at hand, it was hard, thirsty work, hauling peat! The old canal had pubs at regular intervals along its length, although the track followed the towpath, few, if any survive today, probably due to their isolated situations being only accessible by the canal.

The peat industry was a major beneficiary with the opening of the railway. Distribution up to that date was largely limited to the range of a horse and cart. The upsurge in sales greatly increased the labour required, digging, drying, handling, hauling to the sidings etc. The whole population of the moors had work if they wanted it. Another major beneficiary was the rapidly growing Clarks shoe business in Street. Moreover, for the first time it was possible for individuals to travel to the nearby towns to obtain work.

Several excellent books have been written about the S&D, "slow and dirty" or "swift and delightful", depending on the personal point of view. Films have been compiled from footage taken before the fall of the Beeching "axe". Ivo Peters took what must rate as some of the best ever colour film of the west country railways in the 30's, 40's and 50's. John Betjeman was filmed made during a memorable trip on his favourite railway from Evercreech to Burnham sands. Percy Parsons, a Burtle man and a career railwayman, has written a super book of his memoirs of over fifty

Looking West at Edington Junction 1951, the signal box with the Bridgwater branch line peeling off to the left in the far distance. Note the milk churns on the trolley. (Mac Hawkins collection).

Looking East, 1951, with the three covered platforms, the crossing gates are across the Edington Road, the canal side cottages are on the right. It is difficult to realise that today there is barely a trace of once substantial premises. (Mac Hawkins collection)

By 1964 the Bridgwater branch line had been closed and most of the construction including 2 of the platforms has been removed. To the left is Station Farmhouse, to the right, the Station House that was bought by John Rice. (Mac Hawkins collection)

One of the last passenger trains in 1964, signs of dereliction are setting in: weeds on the platform. To the left is The Railway Hotel. (Mac Hawkins collection)

Percy Parsons, the Burtle author, with Mrs. Parsons, signing copies of his book, 'Lines on an S & D Branch', a fascinating account covering his fifty years as a railwayman. The West Somerset Steam Railway Company ran a special train from Bishops Lydeard to Minehead to celebrate the launch.

John Rice looking at 'his old S & D engine' on which he was fireman, when recently on loan to the West Somerset Railway from the North Staffordshire Railway.

years working on the railway.

The S & D Jt R has always engendered great affection from those who knew it, used it and railway buffs alike. It was never a very prosperous business in strictly financial terms, but it made many friends whilst providing a vital social function. Those who worked for the company looked upon its welfare as their own personal responsibility. There was a unique quality of life associated with it. After all, trains travelling over tracks obscured by the winter floodwater were a sight unlikely to be seen anywhere else. Another phenomenon was that this was reputed to be the only railway in England where the train went uphill in both directions! The explanation was that the line depressed into the spongy peat under the weight of the engine and would therefore be, temporarily, on the lowest point on the line!

Tales about life and working on the railway can be hilarious. Up and down the line everyone knew everyone, a new type of linear community grew up throughout its life. There were crossing cottages, even where the line crossed the "green" droves. Some of these cottages were incredibly small, yet large families were sometimes raised in them. Some housed railway retirees or widows, opening and shutting the crossing gates at least put a roof over their heads. It remains a mystery to me, how families could find room to grow up in such cramped conditions, they were presumably originally designed for single occupation.

Kindhearted engine drivers and firemen could arrange for a sizeable lump of coal to "fall off" whilst delivering the daily drinking water to the cottages. Occasionally things went wrong such as time when the lump of coal carried on down the bank and straight through the closed front door! At other times a greenhouse suffered a similar fate and a lady gatekeeper stood up behind a gooseberry bush a split second after a large lump of coal had passed over her head. All sorts of provisions, groceries' shopping lists would be dropped off on return journeys. Some of the cottages were quite a distance from the hard road and rather isolated, particularly in Winter.

John Rice recounts the occasion when his driver was given a chicken which they left, fully feathered, with his mother at her crossing cottage, picking it up oven ready on the return trip.

When Bill Vowles worked on the line he sometimes had to man the Edington road crossing gates in the evening. This could be done from the comfort of the bar in the 'Railway' Inn with the help of an alarm clock. One night, he had shut one gate and stopped to light a cigarette. Bert Whitcombe, a somewhat awkward villager, thinking he was about to return to the bar asked why he had only done half his job. "Cos I be only half expecting a train!" replied Bill.

Edington junction had a station master, a ticket clerk and three porters.

Cossington on the Bridgwater branch line had an incumbent, Mr Pepperal, whose daughter, Sheila, sometimes acted as ticket clerk and whose wife as clerk and relief porter. Bawdrip had a "halt", a covered waiting area but no staff. The station in Bridgwater employed about eight to ten staff.

Living in Cossington, I sometimes caught the 11 o'clock train to Bridgwater market on a Wednesday morning. Jimmy Warner, a local smallholder always took the train to market. One morning the train remained at the station blowing its whistle. After a few minutes the engine driver shouted to me, "Pop down on yer bike, boo-ey an' zee if Jimmy Warner be coming in wi' us today, wull 'ee?"

A stationmaster held a position of high esteem in village life, after all, he could be influential in the matter of job prospects! They do seem to have been strong characters and their memories linger long after they have left. Mr and Mrs Beakes are still fondly remembered for their presence in the station house in Burtle and their involvement with village life. Percy Parsons relates how, as a young man before the war, Mr Beakes asked him if he had a job yet. He went on to say that he had a job going and if someone else to whom it had been offered it did not take it up, he could have the job. Consequently, Percy spent his whole working life of fifty years on the railway!

When Mrs Mary Moxey, now a spritely 97, first visited Burtle to stay with uncle and aunt, Mr and Mrs Fred Tratt at Chapel Row, she arrived by train through the Winter floods. "It was just like driving through the sea" she said. "When I arrived at the Edington Station, the platforms were almost like little islands. If there had been a train going back I would have got straight onto it and never stayed! Lois Beakes, the stationmaster's daughter, organised a boat and I was ferried to where I was staying".

Mr Pugh followed Arthur Beakes. John Walton was the stationmaster in the 1950's and, true to tradition took a keen interest in village affairs, in particular, organising a concert party, the Burtle Venturers. More of this in a separate section.

The characters from the railway days are almost legendary, a few must have a mention. As at any one time as many as twenty Burtle villagers worked on the railway, between them and their quirky senses of humour, it would possibly provide sufficient material to justify its own volume.

Geoff Moxey worked on the line for many years and in common with others, when he got to the age of sixty, he had to have a medical examination. Afterwards, the doctor said, "Well Moxey, there's a lot of work left in you yet!".

"Yass", said Geoff, "and that's where tis gonna bide!".

Once, when working on the West Pennard stretch, the foreman had him in the office. "Major xxxx is of the opinion that you may have been liberating some of his pheasants," said the foreman, "but I told 'un you would'n dream of doing such a thing, would ee?".

On another occasion, whilst Geoff was having his breakfast before going to work, he noticed the starlings were after his pears on the tree against the house. At that moment his collie dog chased the neighbour's cat up the tree, frightening away the birds. He chained the dog to the tree and went off to work. The cat, stranded up the tree, kept the birds off the pears until he returned home to pick them that evening!

The railway huts with a good fire on a wet day could provide the time to dream up a lot of practical jokes. They often had rabbit wires, packs of cards, etc. secreted in various nooks and crannies all ready should a wet spell set in!

In 1954, Clarks Shoes, of Street, sponsored a special train from Glastonbury to Burnham on Sea to celebrate the centenary of the line. Clarks were major users of the S & D railway until nationalisation and its attendant bureaucracy at which point the company went over to road transport. (J. Rice)

Up until 1944, the trains were the standard mode of transport to Doctor Morgans and Girls' Grammar Schools in Bridgwater. Buses were introduced that year to take over. The problem for the Railway was that its station was on the North Eastern extremity of the town and the schools just outside the Western fringe, leaving the students with a two mile hike to complete the journey.

With the nationalisation came bureaucracy, spewing out of distant offices and originated by faceless wonders who had never heard of the Somerset and Dorset Jt. Railway. These little lines were an embarrassment and not considered worth the effort to continue with them. It is possible there were also some old scores to be settled. Goods were diverted away from the friendly little line and all sorts of stupid ploys such as arranging the timetables so as **not** to connect with the mainline trains, used to devalue it. It was inevitable that on its own it could be proved unviable as could any other enterprise treated in such a manner. In fact, the policies of British Rail could well be a case of shooting themselves in the foot, as can many other decisions by bureaucrats affecting rural services. The whole system, nationwide has been struggling and dug themselves into a hole from which they are having great difficulty in escaping. Almost every river in the world has tributaries, without which they would be of little account. It is too late for BR to realise that railways also need their tributaries if they are to succeed.

The railway anticipated Dr Beeching, closing the Bridgwater branch line in 1954. The rest of the line was closed in 1966, much to the sorrow of the locals who felt that they had lost an old friend as well as a whole way of life. After so many years of its own, peculiar, community spirit, linking as it did, the moorland settlements, it could be likened to closing down an unusual, linear, village stretching from Burnham On Sea to Evercreech.

The Turf Trade

The whole area, sometimes known as the Vale of Avalon, is a vast peat bed. The peat was laid down between approximately 5,000 BC and 500 AD. Many raised bogs with the peat as deep as ten metres were interspersed with lakes and meandering waterways. All but the highest would be submerged by the Winter floods most years.

Widespread peat digging for fuel started around 500 AD, the inhabitants would have rights to dig peat for burning granted to them by the major landowners. One of the largest of the latter was Glastonbury Abbey, they no doubt extracted some sort of rent or service in return. Some rents were reputed to have been paid for with eels, a regular harvest on the moors.

It is believed that the Romans were the first to seriously reduce the flooding of the moors by building up the sea walls and river banks, there by preventing ingress by all but the highest tides. The peat beds are in turn, overlaid by the clay silt along the coastal belt. There is abundant evidence of Roman pottery firing at the point where the inland edge of this clay belt meets the exposed peat. It is likely that the Romans

The Turf carts with their distinctive design outside Rowland Moxey's Railway Hotel which was built on the site of an earlier canal side cider house around 1855. In 1871 the landlord was George Moxey whose son, Rowland, born in 1870 was later a turf dealer and landlord of The First and Last, eventually taking over the Railway in 1900 and running it for about 25 years. Note the two handled quart cider cup which by tradition was passed around those present.(J. Heal)

The Griffin's Head at Westhay beside Shapwick Station, now demolished, was where much of the Burtle burning peat was loaded to rail and no doubt much cider was drunk. Seated is landlord George Willcox with his wife stood on his left. Sat on the barrel, Tom Willcox with his sister Ester stood on his left. (H. Willcox)

Turf cutting for domestic fuel was an essential activity for most villagers, any surplus could be sold to earn extra cash. In the photo; back row, Seward Rice, Mr. Packer, Mrs. Packer, Mrs. Freddie Coombes, Sylvia Millett (nee Coombes), Fred Tratt and Reg Norris. Front row; Fred Coombes junior, Alf Highnam, Charlie Norris, Freddie Coombes senior and Wilf Parsons. The cider jars were always kept handy!

Most of the able bodied men would dig peat at some time during their working life. Note the design of the turf barrow in the foreground. (M. Moxey)

used the peat to fire their kilns, possibly placing them among the first to use it as fuel.

The practice of peat digging became commonplace by about 1,000 AD. The inhabitants of the moors would have the right to dig peat fuel only for their personal use, not for sale. These rights still exist in Burtle although they are no longer exercised. The vicar has the right to dig peat for fuel as did the tenants of Glebe Farm. Most of the peat land has been dug over several times by hand. Each digging would reduce the levels by some two to three feet, exascerbating the drainage problems. In wet Summers, only the higher peat beds would be accessible for more than a few weeks.

As landowning became more widespread and with it, the freedom, additional income could be generated by selling some extra production. Turf dealing could be a full time occupation or a part time extra for farmers. Likewise, there were a mixture of freelance turf cutters and those that were employed. It was mainly seasonal and very hard work, occupying most of the Summer months. There was a great sense of pride in the methods and tools used, the latter were different to those used in other parts of the country. A man turning up with the wrong tools could well be sent away and denied work.

Serious commercial production started around 1870 by Alexanders of Shapwick who were also corn and hay merchants. Their production fell into three categories, fuel, firelighters and peat moss litter. In the early 1900's some horticultural production started but it was not until 1935 that the volume overtook extraction for other purposes. Where one pioneers successfully, others soon follow and the historically worthless peat of the moors was soon dubbed "black gold". The potential was so great that, among others, Fisons Agricultural division became very involved, buying out Alexanders. It was a great boost for local employment.

There is no doubt that considerable fortunes were made by local families who otherwise would have struggled to make a good living. There is the tale of four of the local "peat barons" visiting the motor show, dressed "country cut". On the Rolls Royce stand they were discussing which model they would prefer, amongst themselves, when a representative came up and asked them to move along. Little did he realise that any one of them could probably have signed a cheque and bought the whole stand there and then! Mercedes were the eventual beneficiaries, just to rub the salt in.

Over the centuries, all the peat land in the Burtle area has been dug at least once, but with the depths of the beds being less than those further East toward Westhay, Shapwick, Meare and Godney, they have been largely worked out. There is very little peat digging in Burtle today. Strict planning controls were introduced after the

Rowland Norris, Freddie Coombes, Wilf Parsons and Reg Norris in the turf ground,1925. (M. Moxey)

More peat diggers on Westhay Heath; Steve Hardwick, Tom Willcox, Bob Rogers and Jack Willis. Tom's brother, Alfie, was the schoolmaster at Burtle for some years. (H. Willcox)

second world war and many owners lost their hitherto automatic rights to extraction.

Ashcott and Shapwick Stations were the main centres for putting turf on rail to the cities and the haulage using horses and carts provided much employment, the Griffin's Head and Railway Inns no doubt benefitted greatly. Many of the turf dealers had regular rounds servicing the local villages and towns with house to house calling. The turf would be "expertly" packed into a "willy butt", a traditional, locally made farm withy basket. I say expertly advisedly, the vendors would have made wonderful window dressers, being able to make a proverbial pint look like a quart! When Geoff went to the basket maker to order a new one, he was asked, "Wot zackly doo 'ee want?"

"A big little 'un", said Geoff.

"I knaws what you mean", responded the basket maker. "Big around the top, deep sides but with a gurt rise in the bottom 'o 'un so as 'ee on't 'old too many!"

Frank Norris, who had the Crown Inn at Catcott for many years was one of the first to become motorised with a Model-T Ford truck. With this he was able to extend his deliveries to an area previously too far distant for the traditional horse and cart. There were still others delivering by horse and the especially designed turf carts up into the 1950's. It is only in recent years that a pub has been considered more than a part-time business and several of the local landlords did a bit of peat dealing to make up their incomes.

Many of the peat fields were almost inaccessible on foot, let alone by horse and cart. The local answer was the turf boat. The narrow beam and the flat bottom allowed it to be navigated along the rhynes and even some of the drainage ditches. These boats could propelled from within it by a punting pole with a forked metal end and known as a pound or pround. Where conditions permitted, more turf could be conveyed by towing the boat from the bank.

The number of operations between virgin ground and turf ready for the fire was considerable. Any scrub had to be cleared and the width of the 'bench' usually four feet, by almost any length within reason would be measured out. The top layer with the live roots and top soil would be taken off to a depth of a foot or more down to the peat proper. This was known as 'unridding'. The next step was to mark lines in the surface of the exposed peat with a turf scythe, delineating the size of the peat blocks (mumps). This was 'stroking' the benches. The turf scythe would then be plunged into the peat along the lines to the full depth of the blade, this was marking the benches. Where the water table was high, a special tapered mump was cut to countract the water pressure and assist the extraction of the first ones. The accuracy with which the 'old timers' could do this was marvellous to watch.

By West Heath Farm on the Edington Road, 1923, now known as Mallards. Left to right; Sylvia Coombes, Mrs. Coombes with Eileen (who later became the very popular landlady of the Railway Hotel which is now the Tom Mogg) with some neighbours no doubt checking that everything was alright in true Burtle tradition. (M. Moxey)

One man would be 'throwing' the mumps up onto the higher ground where a second man would 'bear' these to an area far enough back so as to spread them out without interfering with the working. Each mump had to be presented in exactly the right way every time. The bearer would be expected to cut each mump into three slices, called 'slitting'. The slitting had to be done in line with the grain of the peat mumps, otherwise the turves would disintegrate into dust when they dried, thus the reason for correct presentation of the mumps in the first place. The turves would be left on their edge to fulfil the first stage of the drying process. When the top edges were dry the turves were pulled end over end to expose the damp under edges to the sun, known as 'pulling up'. The next drying stage was 'hyling', fourteen turves were assembled like the houses of cards built by most of us when young and designed to permit maximum circulation of air. The turves were left in the hyles until almost dry at which point they would be built into 'ruckles', the familiar, beehive shaped, eight feet high heaps by which time the peat was relatively safe from the elements. When thoroughly dry, the ruckles would be hauled home to make a turf rick within easy reach of the house. An increasing volume was also being loaded to rail for delivery to all parts of the country.

Since 1935, the extraction for horticulture continued to outstrip that for fuel.

Production in 1954 is estimated to have been 16,000 tons, 1966 65,000 tons, 1976 113,000 tons, 1985 195,000 tons and peaking in 1990 at 250,000 tons. The depressions left by the industry are forming large expanses of open water and reedbeds. Fisons have donated about 1,000 acres to the conservation cause and many other sections have been purchased to compliment and extend the many nature reserves.

The account of a day in the peat field with Arthur Baker and Geoffrey Moxey which follows will help the reader to appreciate and understand the conditions and procedures. It is an experience that will never be repeated.

Aerial view of flooded, worked-out peat diggings.

A Day in the Field

It was seven o'clock on a beautiful late May morning. I had arranged to meet Arthur Baker and Geoffrey Moxey in order to film peat digging in the way it used to be done in the days when it was dug solely for fuel. The sun's heat was already dissipating what remained of the morning mist.

Geoff Moxey and Arthur Baker setting off to the turf ground.

The moors at this time of day have a mystical quality, sounds carry for great distances and yet one feels a sense of intimacy with the natural world. The whole place is alive with the songs of an amazing range of birds of woodland, water and the open moors. Many a townsman would be enraptured by an experience that countrymen take for granted. This is not to suggest that the latter are unaware of what is going on around them, they would immediately notice an unusual bird's song or other noise. The cadence of the willow warbler, the trill of the dabchick and above all, the fluting call of the curlew create a magical atmosphere.

On the dot of seven, Art and Geoff arrived on their bicycles with their tools strapped to the crossbars. Arthur was a quiet, stocky man whose easy, relaxed movements belied his seventy five years. Geoffrey, who owned the field, was a much larger, burly and robust figure some fifteen years Arthur's junior.

We opened the gate into the peat field and put the bikes out of sight behind the hedge. As I had quite a collection of photographic equipment I drove the car down the informal track worn by countless wheeled vehicles bringing home the peat over many years.

The field had been dug over much of its surface leaving a variety of levels, each of which had a different character. As I drove down the left hand side of the field against the rhyne, the first one hundred and fifty yards on the right was a shallow lake. Where the earth protruded above the water small birch trees had become established, around the edges sallow were reaching for the sky. Birch, closely followed by sallow, are the first to recolonise the areas that have been dug and it is amazing how quickly this occurs. Amongst the infant trees there grew some of the most luxuriant moss I have ever seen, ideal for the lining of hanging baskets.

Past the shallow pond we came to a couple of acres of pasture land in which grew a wonderful variety of marsh plants including orchids. On the far side grew a thickened hedge where alder and oaks had also become established with wild honeysuckle threading its way to the sun. The track continued alongside an area of mature woodland which held a rookery. The gridline from the Hinkley Point power station presented an intrusion from a high tech economy although the rooks had made use of it by nesting in the pylons! The woodland was carpeted with nettles and dog's mercury. Beyond the wood lay the site where the peat was being dug for fuel.

A clearing of about an acre and a half was sandwiched between the woodland and a drainage rhyne at the end of the field. It took the form of a strip about one hundred and fifty yards long by fifty yards at one end tapering down to about thirty yards at the other. Half way along there was a drainage gully connecting the rhyne with the pit from which the previous year's peat had been extracted. At the end of the drain by the pit a tripod had been erected using poles cut from the adjacent woodland. Suspended on ropes from this was a five gallon oil drum cut to resemble a large scoop. Onto this was fastened a rough cut handle about ten feet long. This apparatus was known as a "laval", used to scoop the water from the pit and lift it the two feet necessary into the drainage gully from whence it ran into the rhyne. "I've knowed four acres two foot deep cleared this way", informed Geoff. A demonstration soon convinced me that it would be possible, but considerable application would be required. A simple but effective answer to a common problem.

We reached the place where the action was to take place and Art started to empty his bag. Out came a collection of tools, several spade like but with subtle variations in design, with hand cut handles beautifully polished with years of use. The tools, with cutting edges honed to perfection, were carefully laid out on the ground ready for use. It was amazing how much came out of just one bag. Arthur said "If you do zee a bloke wi' a bag on a bike 'tis likely he came from Westhay but it weren't always tools that were in 'un!"

Scooping the water with the 'laval', a primitive but effective construction to drain flooded digging areas.

By now the sun had warmed the morning air and the mist had cleared. Insects were getting on the wing, the dawn chorus was decreasing to a murmur and merging with other daytime sounds. Art and Geoff opened their haversacks and each took out a quart bottle of cider and had a good swig. "We'm ready to start now," said Art. The bottles were put in the water in the bottom of the pit to keep the cider cool.

Before covering the various stages of the peat digging it is as well to acquaint the reader with the basic layout of the peat digging area. The virgin ground is known as the "high", the narrow strip from which the peat is being cut is known as the "benches" and finally the "low" from which area the peat has already been extracted. In this case the benches were about thirty five yards long.

Arthur selected a piece of batten from his collection of tools and using the marks notched into it, carefully measured back four feet from the edge of last year's pit and set a line parallel to its face, thereby setting the width of the new benches. He then selected a flat bladed, spade-like tool with razor sharp edges running to a point which he called a turf scythe. Standing with his back to the pit he proceeded to make a vertical cut along the line plunging to the full depth of the blade with each stroke.

This was known as "marking out the head," the dimensions of the benches were now established.

The next step was to remove the layer of top soil and throw it into last year's pit using ordinary garden spades. The surface was carefully cleaned off and levelled, this stage is known as 'unridding'.

Arthur Baker 'marking' the 'benches'.

Arthur took up his turf scythe, and used the sharp edge to scribe five lines about eight inches apart along the length of the benches. Next, he made similar lines across the benches, in this case at nine inch intervals. This is 'marking' or 'stroking' the benches. The turf scythe is then used to make vertical cuts in both directions along the lines thus forming the 'mumps'. Considering this was all done by eye, the result was immaculately uniform and straight. "Practice do make master, I s'pose", said Arthur in reply to my comment. He worked with a rhythm and balance that could only be achieved as the result of years of practice, the deceptive ease with which he worked belying his seventy five years!

We were now ready to start 'drawing' the mumps, Arthur informed me. A mump is the block of peat that is extracted, measuring seven inches vertically, eight inches by nine inches in the horizontal. Having a specific gravity similar to water each mump would weigh around eighteen to twenty pounds. A man was expected to dig several thousand in a day.

Arthur put down his turf scythe and picked up his turf spade. This was similar to the turf scythe but had more set in the handle. The purpose of this was to enable the blade to be used horizontally without having to bend quite so low as would have been the case with a straighter handle.

I had noticed that when he was marking along the benches, he made three of the incisions with his back to the pit and the remaining three he made facing the pit. I thought that this was in order to avoid falling backwards into it, but Arthur explained that this was necessary, particularly when the water table was high, as the pressure of the water could make the mumps difficult to extract. Apparently, when using the turf scythe, the cut is not precisely vertical and by turning around the row of mumps were slightly wedge shaped at that point, helping to overcome the suction and easing the 'drawing' of the mumps.

Arthur toiled away with the graceful rhythm of a man in control of his work, driving the spade under each mump and in one deft movement depositing it on the 'high'. He commented, "The idea is when you got 'un on the spade, you get rid o 'un as soon as you can!" When ground conditions were bad it used to be the practice to drop the mumps on a mump board to avoid churning up the surface.

Geoff Moxey 'slitting' the mumps.

Bearing' the mumps is the next process, where they are put into neat rows at some distance from the face of the benches. As a bench may be three or four mumps deep, more space is required to lay them out in a single layer than the area taken up by the bench itself. Once on the high, the mumps are always kept the same way up. This is to facilitate "slitting", an operation using a piece of equipment from which the modern lawn edging tool was surely derived. Geoffrey, who had been bearing the mumps, proceeded to cut each mump into three. When the peat was laid down the layers form a grain and if cut the wrong way the turves would disintegrate into dust when dry. Geoffrey explained, "You have to make six 'ranks' plus the head rank as more space is needed than before the mumps was dug from the benches.

What's more the ranks have to be far enough back on the high to take more mumps as they'm dug". This explained to me why he was arranging them so far back from the benches. The purpose of the head rank being put the other way was, "to kip 'em up together when they'm slitted".

Depending on the depth of the peat, the water level etc. the digging would be three, four or five mumps deep. When the mumps were 'slitted', this was as far as the work could go until they had had a chance to dry out.

It was now time for a break with some bread and cheese and an onion, washed down with a 'drop 'o scrumpy'. I was regaled with tales of long ago days in the peat fields, the hard work and miserable wages, even the women were expected to play a full part. By now the sun was high in the sky, the earlier cacophony of bird song had subsided and given way to the hum of insects on the still air. One of the most rewarding experiences I know is to sit quietly and allow nature to present its floor show. Birds lose their normal timidity, a wren venturing within a few feet and, almost casually, delivering its surprisingly powerful song. The peat moors are incredibly fertile, sustaining a very wide range of flora and fauna. I spent a few minutes filming some plants and insects.

I was jolted back to the modern world by Arthur.

"Time we made a move", he said.

I got up, rather reluctantly, and followed them over to where some digging had taken place earlier in the season.

"The fust job we gotta do", said Geoffrey, "is to pull up the mumps I slitted t'other day"

A week's sun had dried them out quite well. Starting at one end he began rolling the turves back towards him on their edges through one hundred and eighty degrees so that the bottom edges were now exposed to the sun. Another week of good weather would get them ready for the next stage.

"We be going to show 'e how to hyle 'em now," said Arthur. This is the next step in drying. Fourteen turves are used build a small structure similar in principle to the system used by children to build houses out of playing cards. It is not as easy as it looks and several attempts were necessary before my efforts passed Arthur's inspection!

"Pulling 'em up and hyling used to be the job of the women and kids, yurs ago", said Geoffrey. "Nowadays, we do the digging fust thing in the morning, before it do git too hot". Now, being considered competent at hyling, I was led along to the final stage.

Confronted with a large, beehive shaped pile of turves, I was about to be shown how to build a 'ruckle'. Laying the dry turves on their flat, a circle about four feet

The 'turves' are built into weatherproof 'ruckles' which finishes the drying process. These will be later transported and built into a turf rick near the house.

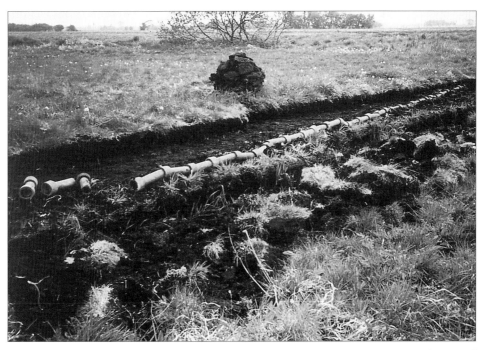

The whole of Westhay Heath was piped with these small bore clay pipes with loose collars, made by John Browne and Co. Bridgwater.

across was formed on the ground. The centre was filled with more turves and then a second layer and so on, keeping the exterior vertical for the first four feet, then gradually pulling them in to form a rounded, weather tight top. The turves will stay in the ruckles until they are brought in to be built into a turf rick near the house, from where they can be easily retrieved for use on the fires.

I made a number of visits to the turf ground over that Summer and enjoyed every minute. Spending time with Arthur and Geoffrey in their secluded corner of the peat moors, absorbing the atmosphere and listening to the moorland sounds was an experience I shall never forget.

Frank (Brammer) Groves hauling peat to his shed on the Catcott Road. (M. Moxey)

Sadly, Arthur died soon after and I was never able to make the improved version of the film as I had intended. He was a perfectionist in every thing he did and I feel very privileged in having had the opportunity to share at least part of that Summer with him. Geoffrey continued digging for a few years with the assistance of a younger helper, Garry Bishop, who had recently returned to live in Burtle.

Miscellaneous Commercial Activities

Over the years there have been a number of pubs and cider houses in the village. In fact, if you include the farms that made cider, there must have been almost a drinking house to each family. The only pub to have a full license until relatively recent times was the Railway Hotel, the present Tom Mogg. The other centre of liquid cheer to survive, and servicing the opposite end of the parish, is the Burtle Inn.

Among those that have fallen by the wayside, the building almost completely disappeared, was the one in Chilton moor, most probably built to service the canal trade. The site is a good fifty yards from the bank, on a slight rise. Today it appears to be a most lonely spot but there used to be several more cottages and smallholders' houses by the Chilton Moor bridge. The only access was over fields or by the canal. Not much firm information is available, the name or landlords.

Midway between the Catcott river crossing and the Shapwick/Westhay one is a wider stretch of canal known as the lock. There was a canal pub at this point, possibly called the 'Flat Bottomed Boat', quite appropriate in view of the regular shallowing of the canal. At this point there was a farm and a cottage, the latter presumably for the lock keeper. It is only a few years since the cut stone was removed from the wharves for building purposes. The railway changed from the North side of the canal to the South side at this point.

On the Mark Road over the river bridge, for centuries called the Bastion Bridge, and some quarter of a mile along the way is a large, old farmhouse. This was for many years The Mark Moor Inn and then 'The Black Bull'. This could well have been the first pub in the district, as for several centuries that was the only road route into Burtle. There used to be a community clustered around the bridge location, at least three or four cottages there have been demolished. A Thomas Fear was landlord from 1861 to 1883, Isaac Tratt who succeeded him was replaced by Mrs Esther Tratt a little before the first world war. Sidney Westlake is recorded as landlord in 1919 but the pub closed soon afterwards and Mr Westlake farmed from there up to the second world war. He was followed by Hubert Triggoll and then up to the present by Vic Whitcombe who came from just down the road at Westhay.

Many years ago there was a murder at the Black Bull. A family called Larder lived in one of the cottages on the river bank, another family by the name of Watts also lived nearby. One night Watts was hit over the head with a bottle in a drunken brawl and subsequently died. The young Larder was tried for murder at Wells assizes and, luckily for him, was acquitted. Some years later, there was a violent falling out between the Larder father and son, during which the son was heard to

Most goods and services were available in the village, either in house or by visiting traders. This butcher's cart would cause a heart attack to a modern health and hygiene official!

Reg Arthur the blacksmith shoeing a horse outside the smithy. On the right is the Burtle Inn, in the distance the winter floods can be seen through the horses legs. The cottage on the left was once The Globe Inn. Churches Farm, opposite the Burtle Inn was the centre of several businesses run by the Grant family, first George and then Reg. Attached to the dairy farm was a slaughter house, a coal business and in 1898 George first obtained licence to sell postage stamps. (M. Moxey)

Looking in the opposite direction out the Westhay Road with the smithy on the right and on the left in what is now Ye Olde Burtle Inne car park, there used to be the twice yearly market known as the repository sales where locals could sell livestock and other goods by auction. (M. Stone)

Floods on the Westhay Road nearly reaching the First and Last door. The building has been greatly changed and reduced in size. Once four cottages on the right called Chapel Row, now converted into two dwellings.

Cattle taken out to drink from the floods on the Catcott Road. Across the water is the cottage last lived in by Mrs. Hughie Norris, the cottage with nearly 3 acres was withdrawn at £55 in the sale of the Hennicker estate. (M. Moxey)

Looking north up the Catcott Road towards the Burtle Inn. From the left Reg Grant, Mrs. Groves, Henry Groves, Rose Groves, in the turf boat, George Giblett, Victor Cox, Violet Groves, Frank 'Brammer' Groves. There were

often boat races across the floods on a Sunday mornings. (M. Moxey)

Reg Grant watering his cows on the Catcott Road. (M. Moxey)

High water at the Mark Moor bridge, known as the Bastion Bridge in mediaeval times.

The River Brue flooding over the banks looking upstream from the bridge. There were once several cottages on either side of the river.

shout, "I nearly swung vur you, you stupid ol' bugger!"

An ariel view of Catcott Burtle.

Although not strictly in Burtle, there was a pub in the Nidon Cottages, the first on the right as you enter Catcott from the moor road. This was a beer and cider house called the 'New Inn' and run by a remarkable woman called Mrs Elizabeth Hucker. In 1875 she is recorded as being a turf dealer, a very tough business for a woman to be in. 1883 shows her to be the landlady at the Crown Inn, Catcott but by 1889, John Badman is landlord of the Crown and Mrs Hucker becomes listed as a beer retailer, presumably the start of the New Inn. There is a story, unsubstantiated, that the local policeman, George Gould, eventually hounded her out of the place and then took it over himself! It sounds like a story of a woman who lost her husband at an early age but who was very determined indeed to succeed. In 1919, a George Hucker was listed as a farmer of Steel Farm, Catcott. This could have been her son, there do not appear to have been any other Huckers around at the time. They have both disappeared from the records by 1923 after a business career spanning at least 44 years.

Many years ago, there used to be a pub called The Globe by the cross next to the old blacksmith's shop. The last landlord I have traced was W. Tratt who was there in the 1860's.

Farmer With a Cornet Is Leader of the Band

Cream-washed cottages at Burtle, Somerset

OUR VILLAGE (25)
BURTLE

STRETCHING from the Mendip to the Polden Hills of Somerset is a level tract of low-lying moorland. Traversed by gleaming rhines and broad droves, dotted with little cream-washed cottages, and with Friesian cattle grazing on the lush meadows, it reminds you of a Dutch landscape.

In its heart lies the little village of Burtle, approached by a narrow roadway bordered with alders and pollard-willows. Yellow irises grow wild in the fields alongside.

INLAND SEA

At intervals by the verge are white posts to guide travellers when the road is submerged. In the winter the country often resembles an inland sea, hundreds of acres being under water.

The tarmac undulates and trembles perceptibly on its spongy bed of peat, the digging of which is a Burtle industry.

Burtle men have to be sailors on occasion, as goods are punted across country in flood time.

The brass band is an outstanding feature of the village of 400 folk, and

it accepts engagements for miles around.

Farmer Alan Moxey has been conductor since he formed it 30 years ago. He taught himself to play a cornet with the aid of a self-tutor.

ASKED TO BROADCAST

There are now 15 members who practise in a disused cheese room; they have been invited to broadcast by the B.B.C.

Mr. Moxey can tell you how he opened the "Abbot's Way" in three places and found it to be made of split tree trunks a pace apart, laid on clay beneath eight feet of peat.

He once found a line of rods six feet apart, buried in a peat-bed. He surmises that they may have been fishnet stakes used by lake villagers.

The Harvest Home is a noted Burtle event, attracting large crowds. A spirit of co-operative enthusiasm makes such affairs successful.

Burtle (and the Bridgwater R.D.C.) should be proud of the unusually attractive Council houses. They are really home-like, semi-detached with bow windows and are let at 7s. 3d. a week.

A newspaper cutting from 1937 showing a group of cottages on the Westhay Road, now demolished. Working lurcher dogs were common in the village then, no doubt to help to fill the pot!

Out on the Westhay road, the last building on the right and still known as 'The First and Last' was a popular venue for many Burtolians. Starting with Ralph Norris at the end of the first world war, members of the extensive Norris family ran the establishment until it closed in the 1960's. A beer and cider house it was the centre for a lot of merriment and spawned many practical jokes, Gus Meader, an architect, who came to live in the village was well known for his cartoons of local characters and events. As Harry Cox once told me, "I laughed so much, me ribs hurt for a week!" Before the Norris family, it was run by Frederick Tratt who left to go farming, in the 1890's by Rowland Moxey who left to take over the 'Railway Hotel' about 1900.

The Railway has had a long active life as one of the Burtle refreshment centres. It was originally built on the site of an old cottage, possibly a canal side beer and cider house, when the railway was constructed around 1852/4. One interesting landlord, listed in 1866 was a John Biffin, a family member of the well known politician, cabinet minister and leader of the house of commons. The Biffin (Biffen) family used to farm in Robins Lane at Chilton Burtle Farm. Harold Biffen was a Chilton Polden parish councillor for many years. In 1883 the landlord was a Thomas Ash, in 1919 a Thomas Ash turns up as landlord at the Burtle Inn at the age of 69. When Rowland Moxey left the 'First and Last' he took over the 'Railway' and ran it for over twenty years. He was followed by William Salway, in 1935 Mrs Salway, in 1939 by George Caple, then Norman Moxey for a while. Ray and Eileen Bates, then ran it for over twenty years. It was for many years a Holts' Brewery of Burnham house, until they were taken over by Starkey, Knight and Ford of Bridgwater. In turn they were taken over by Whitbreads and there was no opportunity to buy the place until Ray and Eileen were about to retire from the trade. Since then a succession of owners have extended the premises into a huge complex which is somewhat out of place in such a quiet backwater as Burtle.

We now come to the Burtle Inn rejoicing these days in the rather twee handle of Ye Olde Burtle Inne. This establishment is often believed to be the elder of the two remaining but the records discovered to date do not support this. In 1919 the Hennikers sold up the Catcott estate and most of Catcott Burtle was included in the sale. It was common place for pubs to have land attached to them and the landlords would make up their income by additional business activities such as farming or turf dealing. It was considered a very good house if the landlord could make an acceptable living from it alone. The Burtle Inn with twenty six acres and a range of farm buildings where the car parks are now, made £1,450, a very considerable sum in those days. The inn used to be the venue for twice yearly livestock auctions known as the 'Repository Sales'. William Coombs was the landlord in 1906 and a tenant of the Hennikers, and, at the time of the sale, Thomas Ash. William Coombs had moved into Hill Farm and become a full time farmer. George Lee bought the premises and land and stayed until the early 1930's when he built the farm next to the present post office and retained the land to farm with it. He was succeeded in turn by Stan Whitcombe, Herbert Carp, Sid Gardner and Dennis Walker. A businessman from Wells, Mr Palmer, had bought the pub from Sid Gardner when he quit. About 1960 he undertook a major and tasteful refurbishment and extension programme. In the days before the visitation of Dutch elm disease, elm was plentiful and cheap. The liberal use of this attractive timber together with innovative displays of farm carts and blacksmiths artifacts make it one of the most comfortable and attractive pubs for miles around the Poldens and moors.

Like all Somerset villages, cider has been made on many of the farms, mainly for local consumption. It has always been the tradition to offer visitors a glass of cider and a bit of bread and cheese. In spite of its innocuous appearance and deceptively benign taste, it must be remembered that it can be twice the strength of beer. It is not whilst the imbiber is sitting down that the affects become apparent but when he makes to stand up the knees refuse to respond. It always seems to be the knees that give up first. Farm workers used to have 'firkin', a small barrel from half a gallon up to a full gallon or more. The size usually denoted the importance of the farm worker in the hierarchy and would be filled each morning for him to take on to work. Double rations would be issued in the hot weather for haymaking and harvesting and, most probably, a nightcap to boot. Latterly, stone jars have tended to replace the old traditional firkin.

Screwing down the 'cheese' to get the last drop of cider out of the apples. Reg Burge of East Huntspill with his helper.

When cider was being made it was customary to visit the farms in order to ascertain the likely quality. One villager, reporting back to a friend after such 'tour of inspection' said that he thought it would be good this year.

"You had a sample, then", said Bill.

"Yass, I 'ad six or seven pints, mind I could 'ave 'ad a guts full if I'd been minded"!

In some parts it was customary to make a cider equivalent to 'small beer', a watered down version of the real thing, I very much doubt whether the Burtle lads would have stood for that. I have never found any evidence of it in this locality.

On another occasion, just after the first world war, during the epidemic of Spanish 'flu, old Jim re-appeared in the village with his cider jar after a lengthy absence.

"Wurs thee bin to"?, he was asked.

"I ant bin vurry well, you, I've bin in baid vur dree wicks," responded Jim.

"Diss 'ave the doctor in to zee'e"?

"Yass, 'e comed down two or dree times but 'e didn't zeem to know much, jus' kep' on saying I 'ad 'ens vlew out the winder."

When I was young, I used to visit my mother's old home farm near Stogursey. My grandfather used to make cider in a building at the back of the farmhouse. The local coal merchant, Tommy Chidgey, arrived with a load of coal on his horse drawn dray. When he had unloaded, he went out to the cider house for the usual hospitality session. About an hour later he came out to drive home. My uncles, in the meantime, had taken the horse out of the cart, put the shafts through the farm gate and replaced the horse in them. Tommy, in his befuddled state demonstrated an impressively fluent adjectival ability. I was whisked indoors rather rapidly so that I would not absorb such expressive word structures!

The cider quality could vary from 'mother's milk' to what is best described as 'liquid barbed wire'. Connoisseurs would declare their judgement on the quality and whether it would keep. Ironically, the better the brew the less likely is was to **keep,** popularity would see to that! Some cider drinkers would drink anything, others could be very fussy. The capacity of some individuals was legendary. I have heard stories of men drinking twelve pints whilst Big Ben struck twelve. A local postman reckoned that he hadn't had a drink unless he had drunk a gallon before eight am. It was said that he never missed a delivery in many years of service. On all the farms that he visited, he had a mug in the cider house and he was expected to help himself, without reference, as he progressed around the village.

Villages used to be fairly self sufficient with tradesmen and little shops. These were supplemented with regular rounds by bakers, butchers, ironmongers and other nicknacks. Gypsies would call selling clothes pegs, artificial flowers and the like. Indians purveying silks, ribbons turned up periodically with a suitcase that, judging by the amount contained, must have been the forerunner of Dr. Who's tardus! There was very little that could not be bought either at the door or from the shops. Orders sent in to the village shop via the postman or others would be delivered to the door, usually without charge.

Above: Burtle Post Office 1927 with Victor Cox as Postmaster. The old motor cycle has registration no. Y7441. The ladies cycle with acetylene lamp belonged to Nurse Lee (Aunt Bet) who is just coming out of the shop. Victor Cox sold the Post Office to Frank (Nacky) Lee who in turn sold it to Mr. F. W. Stone when Frank moved into Whites Farm. Victor took over the Ashcott Post Office. (M. Moxey)

Left: Burtle Post Office 1935/6, in the photo Miss Doris Lee (married Sid Gardener), Mr. Stone, Mary Stone. (M. Stone)

The new Post Office and village stores in 1939, purpose-built for Mr. Stone. (M. Stone)

In the 1860's, William Tratt was listed as Globe Inn and shopkeeper. During the 1870's and 80's, William Tratt is listed as a farmer, the move from shopkeeper to farmer was a step up the social and financial ladder. It is not until 1906 that George Grant in Churches Farm was listed as grocer, draper and post office although he got his license to sell stamps in 1898. His son, Reg, ran what must have been Burtle's version of a department store for many years. He was slaughter man, butcher, dairyman, farmer and coal merchant as well as taking on the other businesses from his father. It is not surprising that he divested himself of the shop and post office when the opportunity arose. Frank (Nacky) Lee followed Victor Cox into the Old Post Office in the early 1930's, sold the business to Mr Stone and moved into Upper Whites Farm at the top of Green Drove. We are urged to forget the old idea of jobs for life and to retrain for new careers, Burtle folk were doing this of their own accord years ago. Many jobs and businesses were considered just a stepping stone to something better. A pub with some land is a good example.

The Highnam family had a little sweet shop in the cottage on the corner of the Westhay road, still fondly remembered by the older generation.

Over the turn of the century a Miss Anna Ellen Cox had a grocery and drapers business, presumably stealing a march on Reg Grant! There would normally be a part time haircutter, whose back room became the venue for a social gathering and exchange of news weekends and evenings. Should there be no "barber" in Burtle, one would cycle in from Westhay or Catcott, borrowing a room from a friend in which to work. Most skills could be found within the community.

Blacksmiths operated out of the old smithy opposite the Burtle Inn for many years, although it is likely that the Burtle workshop was serviced some of the time by the Catcott blacksmiths, certain days each week as over some periods, Blacksmiths are not always separately listed. In 1897 Charles Coleman was the incumbent followed by Herbert Welland who learnt his trade at the old forge in Cossington. He came from a farming family in the Burnham district. At the turn of the century, Theodore Rainey appears on the Burtle scene, described as 'blacksmith'. By 1914 his rating has shot up to include machinist, wheelwright and general engineer. He was one of a well known family of blacksmiths who were of enormous size and strength. In nearby Catcott, several generations of the Martin family held sway, Jonas from 1860 to 1882, Robert almost up to the second world war. Various others followed, Frank Pole, Reg Arthur and Lenny Buttle who also appeared to be the landlord at the Royal Hotel in Catcott.

There was a brickworks near to Hill Farm Burtle Hill Farm. Burtle bricks were made of a poor quality clay, possibly recovered from the bed of the River Brue when it was cleaned out. They were mainly used for internal walls.

There was once a brickworks in the village somewhere around the area of Hill Farm and Burtle House. I am told that 'Squire" Durston of Hill Farm and later, of Burtle House set this up. I have an example of a Burtle Brick which is a rectangular tube a little bigger than a conventional brick, economical in material, a little like the continentals in design. It is not obvious where the supplies of clay came from, Burtle is on a sandbank. There was a claypit near Shapwick and a Brickworks Farm there. Alternatively, the clay could have been brought in from the Highbridge direction where there are beds of good material. One opinion offered to me was that when the River Brue was cleaned out at regular intervals this clay could have been used. However, the quality of the fired clay is not good, probably more suitable for interior walls, I would think it suspect in frosty weather.

A wholesale milk factory was created out of the old, defunct Catcott Burtle school in the early part of this century. It was, no doubt a big improvement on what went before. The Western Dairies Co. is first listed in 1906, manager F. Bigg. It appears as The Cream Dairy Company Ltd in 1914 and 1919, manager Seward Rice.

By this time a much bigger venture at Bason Bridge coupled with much improved road transport combined to squeeze out the local enterprise. It is a little sad to see in some old documents, mention Seward Rice, Factory manager and a few years later see him referred to as just labourer when his house is transferred to his wife's name in order to raise a mortgage. He spent the rest of his life working for the Coombs family at Burtle Hill Farm and peat digging.

An American rancher cousin was visiting his Burtle farmer counterpart and trying to explain how large his ranch was.

"I can get in my car and after driving all day I can still be on my own land," he insisted.

"I can sympathise with you", our man replied, "I had a car like that once".

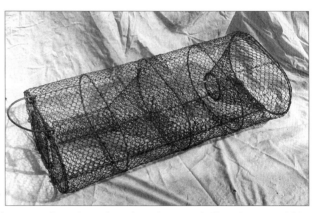

Eels formed an important part of the moorland diet for at least a thousand years. There were 3 main methods employed to catch them. A baited eel trap, this one made by Young Bros. of Misterton near Crewkerne, would be lowered into the river or rhyne and anchored to a peg. The second method was 'clatting' or 'rayballing' (reedballing?) where a quantity of large earthworms would be threaded on woollen thread and tied into a ball. This would be fixed to a 3 to 4 ft length of wire on the end of a long withy pole. The eels could be felt tugging and could be lifted out of the water and shaken off into an eel tub, often an old tin bath floating on the water.

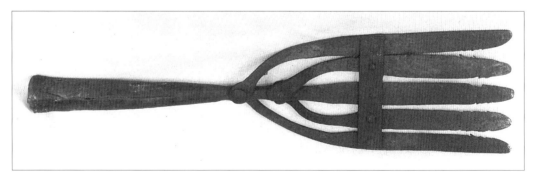

Eel spears usually made by local blacksmiths were the third method. The spear would be jabbed into the mud and the barbs prevented the eels escaping. This was called pecking and considerable expertise was necessary to be successful. When a boy, Geoff Moxey bought one for 1s.6d (7.5p) and caught enough eels to pay for it the first day.

Dennis (Vicar) Thorne with his catch of eels.

Somerset psychiatry, (Courtesy of Lance Jordan Photography Ltd, Wells).

From Bridgwater Mercury, Jan 1950:

PUBLIC INQUIRY AT BURTLE

References to "floating coffins and ghosts"

Petitions bearing signatures representing almost every household in the village in opposition to the compulsory purchase of land by Bridgwater Rural District Council were produced at a Ministry of Health public inquiry at Burtle village hall on Tuesday.

During the hearing of the inquiry which was to confirm the order of compulsory purchase of land for a building site there was mention of floating coffins in graves containing polluted water. A church warden objecting to building houses close to a burial ground said it would not be very nice to "look out on the dead and ghosts".

The inquiry was conducted on behalf of the Ministry by Mr. E.E. Hall. Mr. R.G. Ash (Messrs Christopher Rowe and Ash) appeared on behalf of the owners of the land, Mr. and Mrs. H.S.V. Norris of Burtle Farm to oppose the compulsory purchase.

Opening the inquiry, Mr. H. G. Blay, Clerk to Bridgwater Rural District Council, explained there were some 700 applicants on the Council's register for houses, 12 of which were for Burtle. Burtle is peculiar, in as much that it is in 4 civil parishes-- Chilton Polden, Edington, Cossington (?) and Catcott added Mr. Blay who went on to emphasise that the 12 applications were for Burtle alone.

The Council is satisfied that there is a need for additional houses in Burtle and included 4 in their post-war programme.

The Clerk went on to state that representatives of the various authorities concerned had toured the district in October and approved the site as free from objection.

An alternative site was rejected in favour of the site suggested because of the need for dealing with the drainage of existing houses, a problem which had faced the Council for many years. There had been many complaints about drainage and it was the Council's intention to deal with the problem with any future plans.

"Favourable Site"

It was not generally understood by the public the formalities of "clearing" sites before acquisition. The Council had to follow a procedure laid down by the Ministry and Planning Authority. New houses were needed in remote parishes, and, although agricultural needs predominated, every effort should be made to meet the demand whenever the occasion arose.

"This site appears to be as favourable as any in Burtle", said Mr. Blay.

The Council would much prefer to acquire land by agreement but it must be understood that we can only acquire land free from objection and approved by the Ministry. Many of the sites which councillors and owners suggest as alternatives and which the Council would wish to acquire, unfortunately do not meet the approval of the Ministry concerned.

Mr. R. P. Flaherty, the Council's housing manager, gave evidence of Burtle's housing needs, and said that 6 of the 12 applications were for agricultural workers and 6 for miscellaneous workers.

He had received many complaints of existing drainage which should be rectified by the new scheme.

Mr. F. R. P. Maile, the Council's Sanitary Inspector, referred to a survey of the rural district, and said that 20 houses in the district were considered unfit for habitation and beyond repair at reasonable cost. Those 20 houses accommodated 61 occupants, including married couples and families up to 8.

Details of specifications of the proposed drainage scheme were given by Mr. R. S. Nicholls, architect, of Messrs Gallannaugh and Nicholls.

Floods to come?

Mr. Arthur Tratt, church warden, opposing on behalf of Burtle Parochial Church Council, pointed out that several dry seasons had been experienced and floods were not like they used to be. "They will come again, however, and when they do the council houses will have trouble", said Mr. Tratt.

The church wants the houses to go up but they are anxious about the drainage.

When there had been burials he had seen the coffin swimming about the grave, not that they had not got the church drained, because they had a tunnel right under the road.

"To build council houses round a burial ground is not a very nice thought - looking out on the dead and the Ghosts. It would not suit my view", he declared.

The vicar, the Rev. D. V. Clatworthy, "People in the parish have a distaste to the idea of their relations being buried in a pool of polluted water. If we can have an assurance that the water running down the slope will not be polluted any further by building houses the Parochial Council will be satisfied", he added.

Mr. Nicholls replied that there would be very little pollution and it might be that the drainage level would be deeper than the churchyard.

Two petitions

Mr. Ash produced 2 petitions which he described as "remarkable documents" as they contained a total of 160 signatures representing, with the exception of 3 households, 1 member of every household in the district.

The grounds for opposing the site were that the amenities of the church would be severely predjudiced; the nuisance already caused by the overflow of drainage in Robin's Lane would be greatly increased and a bad corner would be made far more dangerous.

It was pointed out by Mr. Ash that if the land was taken away from Mr. and Mrs. Norris they would be left with a field of awkward shape. It was the home field of Burtle Farm - an important factor from their point of view, as it was situated higher than their remaining land and was used for stocking in the Winter. Mr. Norris confirmed that the home field was the driest of all his land, all his pasture land being liable to flooding. He alleged that complaints made to the Council had been ignored.

The inspector then left to inspect the site and promised to place his findings before the Minister.

N.B. The council houses on Robins Lane were eventually built so the site must have been deemed suitable!

KELLY'S DIRECTORIES

These directories are a valuable source of information on past commercial activities and general matters of interest. Starting in 1861 they were produced approximately every 4 years in great detail, county by county. A few examples are reproduced here. Burtle was not treated as a separate village until 1897, up to that date the records were merged into the villages of Catcott, Edington and Chilton Polden, making it more difficult to establish who was where with any certainty.

BURTLE 1897

BURTLE is an ecclesiastical parish, formed in 1846 from Edington : it is about 1 mile north from Edington Junction station on the Somerset and Dorset railway, and about 9 north-east from Bridgwater, in the Bridgwater division of the county, Witley hundred, Bridgwater petty sessional division, union and county court district, rural deanery of Glastonbury, archdeaconry of Taunton and diocese of Bath and Wells. The church of SS. Philip and James, erected in 1839, at the cost of the late Miss Field, is a building of stone in the Gothic style, consisting of chancel and nave, south porch and a western turret containing one bell : there are sittings for 250 persons. The register dates from the year 1839. The living is a vicarage, net yearly value £270, in the gift of A. R. Poole esq. and held since 1892 by the Rev. Thomas Lewis. The population of this district in 1891 was 292.

Parish Clerk, Robert Watts.

Letters through Bridgwater. WALL LETTER Box, Burtle, cleared at 4.30 & 6.20 p.m. Edgington, 3 miles distant. is the nearest money order & telegraph office

Durston John, Burtle house
Lewis Rev. Thomas [vicar]
Moxey Lewis
Tratt Mrs
Coleman Charles, blacksmith

Cox Anna Ellen (Miss), grocer & drapr
Cox Edmund, farmer
Cox Hubert, farmer
Durston William & James, farmers, Burtle Hill farm

Grant James, farmer
Lee Thomas, farmer, Chilton Burtle
Moxey George, turf dealer
Tratt Charles, farmer

BURTLE 1902

BURTLE is an ecclesiastical parish, formed in 1846 from Edington : it is about 1 mile north from Edington Junction station on the Somerset and Dorset railway, and about 9 north-east from Bridgwater, in the Bridgwater division of the county, Witley hundred, Bridgwater petty sessional division, union and county court district, rural deanery of Glastonbury, archdeaconry of Wells, and diocese of Bath and Wells. The church of SS. Philip and James, erected in 1839, at the cost of the late Miss Field, is a building of stone in the Gothic style, consisting of chancel and nave, south porch and a western turret containing one bell : there are sittings for 250 persons. The register dates from the year 1839. The living is a vicarage, net yearly value £270, in the gift of Mrs. Poole, and held since 1892 by the Rev. Thomas Lewis. The population of this district in 1891 was 292.

Sexton, Robert Watts.

Letters through Bridgwater arrive at Catcott Burtle, 7.30 a.m. & 6.5 p.m.; cleared at 6.10 p.m. Wall Letter Box, Burtle, cleared at 4.30 & 6.20 p.m. Friginton, about 2½ miles distant, is the nearest money order & telegraph office

Durston John, Burtle house
Lewis Rev. Thomas (vicar)
Moxey Lewis
Tratt Oliver
Cox Anna Ellen (Miss), grocer & drapr

Cox Edmund, farmer
Cox Hubert, farmer
Durston William & James, farmers, Burtle Hill farm

Grant James, farmer
Lee Thomas, farmer, Chilton Burtle
Moxey George, turf dealer
Welland Herbert, blacksmith

BURTLE 1906

BURTLE is an ecclesiastical parish, formed in 1846 from Edington and Chilton-upon-Polden: it is about 1 mile north from Edington Junction station on the Somerset and Dorset Joint railway, and about 9 north-east from Bridgwater, in the Bridgwater division of the county, Witley hundred, Bridgwater petty sessional division, union and county court district, rural deanery of Glastonbury, archdeaconry of Wells, and diocese of Bath and Wells. The church of SS. Philip and James, erected in 1839, at the cost of the late Miss Field, is a building of stone in the Gothic style, consisting of chancel and nave, south porch and a western turret containing one bell: there are sittings for 250 persons. The register dates from the year 1839. The living is a vicarage, net yearly value £270, in the gift of Mrs. Poole, and held since 1892 by the Rev. Thomas Lewis, who is also vicar of Catcott. The population of this district in 1901 was 243.

Sexton, Robert Watts.

Post Office.—George Grant, sub-postmaster. Letters arrive from Bridgwater at 7 a.m. & 6 p.m. & despatched at 6.10 p.m. week days only. Edington, about 3 miles distant, is the nearest money order & telegraph office

Wall Letter Box, near the church, cleared at 6.20 p.m. week days only

Public Elementary School (under the control of the County Council) (mixed), erected in 1839, and since enlarged, to hold 100 children; average attendance, 70; & has an endowment of 3 acres of land; Henry James Kidd, master

Bridger Harry Edmund, Burtle house
Lewis Rev. Thomas (vicar)
Moxey Thomas, Blagdon house

COMMERCIAL

Durston Sarah (Mrs.), farmer, Lilac farm
Durston William James Biddlecombe, farmer & yeoman, & chairman of Parish Council, Burtle Hill farm
Grant George, grocer & draper, & post office
Grant James, farmer
Lee Thomas, farmer, Glebe farm
Moxey Lewis, farmer
Pocock William, farmer, Chapel hill
Rainey —, blacksmith
Shephard John, farmer
Trott Oliver, farmer
Watts George, farmer
Western Dairies Co. (F. Bigg, manager), wholesale dairymen

BURTLE 1910

BURTLE is an ecclesiastical parish, formed in 1846 from Edington and Chilton-upon-Polden: it is about 1 mile north from Edington Junction station on the Somerset and Dorset Joint railway, and about 9 north-east from Bridgwater, in the Bridgwater division of the county, Witley hundred, Bridgwater petty sessional division, union and county court district, rural deanery of Glastonbury, archdeaconry of Wells, and diocese of Bath and Wells. The church of SS. Philip and James, erected in 1839, at the cost of the late Miss Field, is a building of stone in the Gothic style, consisting of chancel and nave, south porch and a western turret containing one bell: there are sittings for 250 persons. The register dates from the year 1839. The living is a vicarage, net yearly value £270, in the gift of Mrs. Poole, and held since 1892 by the Rev. Thomas Lewis, who is also vicar of Catcott. The population of this district in 1901 was 243.

Sexton, Theodore Rainey.

Post Office.—George Grant, sub-postmaster. Letters arrive from Bridgwater at 7.15 a.m. & 6.20 p.m. & dispatched at 6.10 p.m. week days only; no sunday delivery. Edington, about 3 miles distant, is the nearest money order & telegraph office

Wall Letter Box, near the church, cleared at 6.25 p.m. week days only

Public Elementary School (under the control of the County Council) (mixed), erected in 1839, and since enlarged, to hold 100 children; average attendance, 80; & has an endowment of 3 acres of land; James Henry Kidd, master

Durston Mrs. Burtle house
Lewis Rev. Thomas (vicar)
Moxey Thomas, Blagdon house

COMMERCIAL.

Durston Sarah (Mrs.), frmr. Lilac fm
Frost Albert, farmer, Burtle Hill frm
Grant George, grocer & draper, & post office
Grant James, farmer
Lee Thomas, farmer, Glebe farm
Moxey Lewis, farmer
Pocock William, farmer, Chapel hill
Rainey Theodore, blacksmith
Shephard John, farmer
Tratt Oliver, farmer
Watts George, farmer
Western Dairies Co. (F. Bigg, manager), wholesale dairymen

BURTLE 1914

BURTLE is an ecclesiastical parish, formed in 1846 from Edington and Chilton-upon-Polden: it is about 1 mile north from Edington Junction station on the Somerset and Dorset Joint railway, and about 9 north-east from Bridgwater, in the Bridgwater division of the county, Witley hundred, Bridgwater petty sessional division, union and county court district, rural deanery of Glastonbury, archdeaconry of Wells, and diocese of Bath and Wells. The church of SS. Philip and James, erected in 1839, at the cost of the late Miss Field, is a building of stone in the Gothic style, consisting of chancel and nave, south porch and a western turret containing one bell: there are sittings for 250 persons. The register dates from the year 1839. The living is a vicarage, net yearly value £230, in the gift of Mrs. Poole, and held since 1912 by the Rev. William James Leigh-Phillips M.A. of St. John's College, Cambridge, who is also vicar of Catcott. The population of this district in 1911 was 252.

Sexton, Theodore Rainey.

Post Office.—George Grant, sub-postmaster. Letters arrive from Bridgwater at 6.45 a.m. & 6 p.m. & dispatched at 6.20 p.m. week days only; no sunday delivery. Edington, about 3 miles distant, is the nearest money order & telegraph office

Wall Letter Box, near the church, cleared at 6.25 p.m. week days only

Public Elementary School (under the control of the County Council) (mixed), erected in 1839, and since enlarged, to hold 100 children; average attendance, 72; & has an endowment of 3 acres of land; James Henry Kidd, master

PRIVATE RESIDENTS.
Durston Mrs. Burtle house
Leigh-Phillips Rev. William James M.A. (vicar), Vicarage
Moxey Thomas, Blagdon house

COMMERCIAL.

Coombes Samuel, farmer
Cream Dairy Co. Ltd. (The) (Seward Rice, manager), who. dairymen
Durston Sarah (Mrs.), frmr. Lilac fm
Frost Albert, farmer, Burtle Hill frm
Grant George, grocer, & post office
Grant Lewis, farmer
Lee Thomas, farmer, Glebe farm
Moxey Lewis (Mrs.), farmer
Pocock William, farmer, Chapel hill
Rainey Theodore, blacksmith, machinist, wheelwright & general engnr
Tratt Oliver, farmer
Watts George, farmer

BURTLE 1919

BURTLE is an ecclesiastical parish, formed in 1846 from Edington and Chilton-upon-Polden: it is about 1 mile north from Edington Junction station on the Somerset and Dorset Joint railway, and about 9 north-east from Bridgwater, in the Bridgwater division of the county, Witley hundred, Bridgwater petty sessional division, union and county court district, rural deanery of Glastonbury, archdeaconry of Wells, and diocese of Bath and Wells. The church of SS. Philip and James, erected in 1839, at the cost of the late Miss Field, is a building of stone in the Gothic style, consisting of chancel and nave, south porch and a western turret containing one bell: there are sittings for 250 persons. The register dates from the year 1839. The living is a vicarage, net yearly value £230, in the gift of Mrs. A. R. Poole, and held since 1912 by the Rev. William James Leigh-Phillips M.A. of St. John's College, Cambridge, who is also vicar of Catcott. The population of this district in 1911 was 232.

Sexton, Rufus Norris (acting).

Post Office.—Mrs. Florence Elizabeth Grant, sub-post-mistress. Letters through Bridgwater. Edington, about 3 miles distant, is the nearest money order & telegraph office

Wall Letter Box, near the church

Public Elementary School (under the control of the County Council) (mixed), erected in 1839, and since enlarged, to hold 100 children; & has an endowment of 3 acres of land; James Henry Kidd, master

PRIVATE RESIDENTS.

Leigh-Phillips Rev. William James M.A. (vicar), Vicarage

COMMERCIAL.

Marked thus † farm 150 acres or over.

†Coombes Samuel, farmer

Cox Arthur, farmer

Cox Hubert, farmer

Cream Dairy Co. Ltd. (The) (Seward Rice, manager), who. dairymen

Durston Sarah (Mrs.), frmr. Lilac fm

Frost Herbert, farmer,Burtle Hill fm

Grant Florence Elizabeth (Mrs.), grocer, & post office

Grant Lewis, farmer

Heal Samuel, farmer

Lee Thomas, farmer, Glebe farm

Moxey Rowland, Railway inn

Norris Ralph, Burtle inn

Pocock William. farmer, Chapel hill

†Tratt Oliver, farmer

Watts George, farmer

Westlake Tom, farmer

Young Albert, farmer

BURTLE 1923

BURTLE is an ecclesiastical parish, formed in 1846 from Edington and Chilton-upon-Polden: it is about 1 mile north from Edington Junction station on the Somerset and Dorset Joint railway, and about 9 north-east from Bridgwater, in the Bridgwater division of the county, hundred of Witley, petty sessional division, union and county court district of Bridgwater, rural deanery of Glastonbury, archdeaconry of Wells and diocese of Bath and Wells. The church of SS. Philip and James, erected in 1839 at the cost of the late Miss Field, is a building of stone in the Gothic style, consisting of chancel and nave, south porch and a western turret containing one bell: there are sittings for 200 persons. The register dates from the year 1839. The living is a perpetual curacy, net yearly value £210, in the gift of Mrs. A. R. Poole and held since 1912 by the Rev. William James Leigh Phillips M.A. of St. John's College, Cambridge, who is also vicar of Catcott. The population of this district in 1911 was 232.

Sexton, Rufus Norris (acting).

Post Office.—Victor Cox, postmaster. Letters through Bridgwater. Edington, about 3 miles distant, is the nearest money order & telegraph office

Public Elementary School (under the control of the County Council) (mixed), erected in 1839, and since enlarged, to hold 100 children; & has an endowment of 3 acres of land; James Henry Kidd, master

PRIVATE RESIDENT.

Leigh Phillips Rev. Wiliam James M.A. (vicar), Vicarage

COMMERCIAL.

Marked thus † farm 150 acres or over.

Cox Albert, farmer. Lilac farm

Cox Arthur, farmer

Cox Hubert, farmer

Cox Victor, grocer, & post office

Frost Herbert, farmer,Burtle Hill fm

Grant Lewis, farmer

Heal Samuel, farmer

Lee George, Burtle inn

†Lewis John, farmer

Moxey Allan, farmer, Glebe farm

Moxey Clifford, farmer

Moxey Rowland, Railway inn

Pocock Stephen, farmer, Chapel hill

Sweet William, farmer

†Tratt Oliver, farmer

Westlake Sydney, farmer

BURTLE 1927

BURTLE is an ecclesiastical parish, formed in 1846 from Edington and Chilton-upon-Polden: it is about 1 mile north from Edington Junction station on the Somerset and Dorset Joint railway, and about 9 north-east from Bridgwater, in the Bridgwater division of the county, hundred of Witley, petty sessional division, union and county court district of Bridgwater, rural deanery of Glastonbury, archdeaconry of Wells and diocese of Bath and Wells. The church of SS. Philip and James, erected in 1839 at the cost of the late Miss Field, is a building of stone in the Gothic style, consisting of chancel and nave, south porch and a western turret containing one bell: there are sittings for 200 persons. The register dates from the year 1839. The living is a perpetual curacy, net yearly value £250, in the gift of Mrs. A. R. Poole, and held since 1912 by the Rev. William James Leigh Phillips M.A. of St. John's College, Cambridge, who is also vicar of Catcott. The population in 1921 was 225.

Sexton, Reginald Norris (acting).

Post Office.—Victor Cox, postmaster. Letters through Bridgwater. Edington, about 3 miles distant, is the nearest money order, telephone & telegraph office

Public Elementary School (under the control of the County Council) (mixed), erected in 1839, and since enlarged, to hold 100 children; & has an endowment of 3 acres of land; Alfred Wilcox, master

Leigh Phillips Rev. William James M.A. (vicar), Vicarage

COMMERCIAL.

Marked thus † farm 150 acres or over.

Coombs Ivor, farmer,Burtle Hill frm

Cox Arthur, farmer

Cox Hubert, farmer

Cox Ralph, farmer, Lilac farm

Cox Victor, grocer, & post office

Durston Mrs. Rt. smallholder

Grant Alfd. smallholder

Grant Lewis, farmer, Burtle farm

Heal Samuel, farmer

Lee Frank, farmer

Lee George, Burtle inn

Lewis Jn. farmer

Moxey Allan, farmer, Glebe farm, Chilton Burtle

Moxey Clifford, farmer

Pocock Stephen & Wm. farmers, Chapel hill

Salway Wm. Railway inn

Sweet William. farmer

†Tratt Oliver, farmer

Westlake Sydney, farmer

Young Albt. A. farmer

101

BURTLE 1931

BURTLE is an ecclesiastical parish, formed in 1839 from Edington and Chilton-upon-Polden: it is about 1 mile north from Edington Junction station on the Somerset and Dorset joint railway, and about 9 north-east from Bridgwater, in the Bridgwater division of the county, hundred of Witley, petty sessional division, rural district and county court district of Bridgwater, rural deanery of Glastonbury, archdeaconry of Wells and diocese of Bath and Wells. The church of SS. Philip and James, erected in 1839 at the cost of the late Miss Field, is a building of stone in the Gothic style, consisting of chancel and nave, south porch and a western turret containing one bell: there are sittings for 200 persons. The register dates from the year 1839. The living is a perpetual curacy, net yearly value £250, with residence, in the gift of Gilbert R. Poole esq. and held since 1912 by the Rev. William James Leigh Phillips M.A. of St. John's College, Cambridge, who is also vicar of Catcott. The population in 1921 was 225.

Sexton, Charles Norris.

Post & Telephone Call Office. Letters through Bridgwater. Edington nearest M. O. & T. office

Coombes Mrs. Lucinda
Leigh Phillips Rev. William James M.A. (vicar), Vicarage

COMMERCIAL.

Marked thus † farm 150 acres or over.
Coombs Ivor, farmer, Burtle Hill frm
Cox Arth. farmer
Cox Hubert, farmer

Cox Ralph, farmer, Lilac farm
Durston Rt. (Mrs.), smallholder
Grant Alfd. smallholder
Grant Lewis, farmer, Burtle farm
Heal Herbt. farmer
Heal Samuel, farmer
Lee Frank, shopkpr
Lee George, Burtle inn
Lewis Jn. farmer

Moxey Allan, farmer, Glebe farm, Chilton Burtle
Moxey Clifford, farmer
Pocock Stephen & Wm. farmers, Chapel hill
Salway Wm. Railway inn
Sweet Wm. farmer
†Tratt Oliver, farmer
Westlake Sydney, farmer

BURTLE 1935

BURTLE is an ecclesiastical parish, formed in 1839 from Edington and Chilton-upon-Polden: it is about 1 mile north from Edington Junction station on the Somerset and Dorset joint railway, and about 9 north-east from Bridgwater, in the Bridgwater division of the county, hundred of Witley, petty sessional division and county court district of Bridgwater, rural deanery of Glastonbury archdeaconry of Wells and diocese of Bath and Wells. The church of SS. Philip and James, erected in 1839 at the cost of the late Miss Field, is a building of stone in the Gothic style, consisting of chancel and nave, south porch and a western turret containing one bell: there are sittings for 200 persons. The register dates from the year 1839. The living is a perpetual curacy, net yearly value £250, with residence, in the gift of Gilbert R. Poole esq. and held since 1912 by the Rev. William James Leigh Phillips M.A. of St. John's College, Cambridge, who is also vicar of Catcott. There is a Methodist chapel. The ownership of the land is divided. The population in 1931 was 209.

Post & Telephone Call Office. Letters through Bridgwater. Edington nearest M. O. & T. office

PRIVATE RESIDENT.
Leigh Phillips Rev. William James M.A. (vicar), Vicarage

COMMERCIAL.

Marked thus † farm 150 acres or over.
Boyer Jn. farmer
Coombs Ivor, farmer, Burtle Hill frm
Coombes Wm. farmer
Cox Arth. farmer
Cox Hubert, farmer
Cox Ralph, farmer, Elm Tree farm
Durston Rt. (Mrs.), smallholder
Fewings Jn. farmer

Grant Alfd. smallholder
Grant Lewis, farmer, Burtle farm
Grant Lucas Geo. farmer, Hurst frm
Ham Herbt. farmer
Hayes Leonard, farmer
Heal Samuel, farmer
Lee Geo. farmer
Lee Wm. Frank, farmer, White's frm
Lewis Jn. farmer
Moxey Allan, farmer, Glebe farm, Chilton Burtle
Moxey Clifford, farmer
Norris Arth. First & Last inn

Pocock Stephen & Wm. farmers, Chapel hill
Salway Wm. Railway inn
Shepherd Geo. farmer
Shingleton Wm. farmer, Liberty frm
Stone Fredk. Wesley, shopkpr. Post office
Tratt Fredk. turf dlr
†Tratt Oliver, farmer
Webster Fras. L.R.C.P. & S., L.M. Irel. physcn. & surgn. (attends thurs)
Whitcombe Stanley, Burtle inn

BURTLE 1939

BURTLE is an ecclesiastical parish, formed in 1839 from Edington and Chilton-upon-Polden: it is about 1 mile north from Edington Junction station on the Somerset and Dorset joint railway, and about 9 north-east from Bridgwater, in the Bridgwater division of the county, hundred of Witley, petty sessional division and county court district of Bridgwater, rural deanery of Glastonbury archdeaconry of Wells and diocese of Bath and Wells. Electricity is available. The church of SS. Philip and James, erected in 1839 at the cost of the late Miss Field, is a building of stone in the Gothic style, consisting of chancel and nave, south porch and a western turret containing 1 bell: there are sittings for 200 persons. The register dates from the year 1839. The living is a perpetual curacy, net yearly value £323, with residence, in the gift of Gilbert R. Poole esq. and held since 1937 by the Rev. Alexander Strachan Ness Buchan, who is also vicar of Catcott. The ownership of the land is divided. The population in 1931 was 209.

Post Office. Letters through Bridgwater. Edington nearest M. O. & T. office

PRIVATE RESIDENT.

Buchan Rev. Alexander Stachan Ness (vicar), Vicarage

COMMERCIAL.

Marked thus ° farm 150 acres or over.
Boyer Jn. farmer
Burtle Inn (Herbt. Edwd. Carp)
Coombs Ivor, farmer, Burtle Hill farm. Chilton Polden 212
Coombes Wm. farmer
Cox Arth. farmer
Cox Hubert, farmer
Cox Ralph, farmer, Elm Tree farm

Durston Rt. (Mrs.), smallholder
Fewings Jn. farmer
First & Last Inn (Arth. Norris)
Grant Alfd. smallholder
Grant Lewis, farmer, Burtle farm
Grant Lucas Geo. farmer, Hurst frm
Hayes Leonard, farmer
Heal Samuel, farmer
Lee Geo. farmer
Lee Wltr. Frank, farmer
Lee Wm. Frank, farmer, White's frm Chilton Polden 3
Lockyer Frank, farmer, Cottcot Burtle farm

Moxey Allan, farmer, Glebe farm, Chilton Burtle
Moxey Clifford, farmer
Pocock Stephen, farmer, Chapel hill
Railway Inn (George E. Caple)
Shepherd Geo. farmer
Shingleton Wm. farmer, Liberty frm
Stone Fredk. Wesley, shopkpr. Post office
Tratt Arth. Edwd. farmer, Watts fm
Tratt Fredk. turf dlr
°Tratt Wltr. Oliver, farmer
Webster Fras. L.R.C.P. & S., L.M. Irel. physcn. & surgn. (attends thurs)

CATCOTT 1883

CATCOTT is a village, and was anciently a chapelry in the parish of Moorlinch, but is now a parish of itself: it is 3 miles south from the Edington and Shapwick stations on the Somerset and Dorset railway and 7 east-north-east from Bridgwater, in the Western division of the county, hundred of Whitley, union and county court district of Bridgwater, rural deanery of Glastonbury, archdeaconry of Wells, diocese of Bath and Wells. The church is an ancient stone structure in the Norman style, with chancel, nave and a tower containing 2 bells. The register dates from about the year 1500. The living is a donative, yearly value £100, in the gift of Aldborough Henniker esq. and held by the Rev. Edward Williams M.A. of St. John's College, Cambridge, who is vicar of and resides at East Huntspill. The Wesleyans have a chapel here, and there is a Primitive Methodist chapel at Burtle. The charities are of £60 yearly value. A Henniker esq. and John Latch esq. are the chief landowners; the former is lord of the manor. The soil is rocky marl, loam and clay. The chief crops are wheat, beans and oats. The parish contains 2,265 acres; rateable value, £3,127; the population in 1881 was 550.

Parish Clerk, John Pople.

Letters received from Bridgwater at 9 a.m.; dispatched at 5 p.m. The nearest money order office is at Edington

Here is a National school (mixed), erected in 1842, capacity 128, average attendance 57; Thomas Lambert Blackwell, master

CARRIERS TO BRIDGWATER.—John Gillard, mon. wed. thurs. & sat.; Charles Acreman, wed. & sat

Fletcher Frederick
Henniker Miss, Elmsfield
Sherriff Capt. Daniel
Warren Mrs

COMMERCIAL.

Acreman Charles, carpenter & carrier
Acreman Edward, turf dealer
Acreman John, farmer
Acreman William, shopkeeper
Acreman William, wheelwright
Arthur Joel, turf dealer
Arthur William, carpenter
Badman James, farmer
Badman John, beer retailer
Badman Joseph, shopkeeper

Bartlett John, turf dealer
Bartlett Robert, turf dealer
Bawden Richard, shopkeeper
Coombs Frederick, farmer
Darch George, baker & shopkeeper
Durston Christopher, *Royal inn*
Durston Ira, turf dealer
Durston James, farmer
Durston John, farmer
Durston Oliver, farmer
Fisher Joseph, haulier
Gillard John, carrier
Gillard Samuel, *King William*
Groves Edmund, turf dealer
Groves Frederick, farmer & turf dealer
Hooper Henry, farmer

Hucker Elizabeth (Mrs.), *Crown inn*
Hull Frederick, turf dealer
Hurford Charles, farmer
Hurford James, farmer
Jones Robert, turf dealer
Lister Henry, farmer
Martin Robert, blacksmith
Moxey Robert, farmer & turf dealer
Norris Joseph, shopkeeper
Packer James, stonemason
Pole George, turf dealer
Tratt Frederick, farmer, Burtle
Tratt Frederick, farmer, Longlands
Tratt William, farmer, Burtle
Vowells George, farmer, Westbrook
Warren Joseph, farmer

EDINGTON 1883

EDINGTON, a village, formerly a chapelry in the parish of Moorlinch, is now an ecclesiastical parish, having the river Brue on the north, 2¼ miles south from Edington Road railway staion, and 6½ east-north-east from Bridgwater, in the Western division of the county, hundred of Witley, union and county court district of Bridgwater, rural deanery of Glastonbury, archdeaconry of Wells, and diocese of Bath and Wells. The church of St. George was rebuilt in 1879 at a cost of £2,500, and consists of chancel, nave and turret containing 2 bells: there is a stained east window in memory of the late Miss Field; also a west window in memory of the late Miss Field. The register dates from the year 1813. The living is a vicarage, annexed to to that of Chilton Polden, joint yearly value £120 with residence, in the gift of the vicar of Moorlinch, and held since 1878 by the Rev. Matthew Benjamin George Reed Lucas M.A. of Corpus Christi college, Cambridge, who resides at Chilton Polden. A district church was erected by the late Miss Field in 1839 at BURTLE, which is 3 miles north from Edington: it consists of chancel and nave, with a bell turret. The living is a perpetual curacy, yearly value £320, in the gift of G. S. Poole esq. and held since 1871 by the Rev. Andrew John Yarranton B.A. of St. John's College, Cambridge. The population in 1881 was 300. There are charities of £32 annual value. Edington House is the seat of Mrs. Westmacott. The representatives of the late Frances Countess Waldegrave (who are owners of the manor), Mrs. Westmacott, Captain John Alex. Fownes Luttrell R.N. and William Vale esq. are the chief landowners. The soil is sandy, and the subsoil is peat and stone. The chief crops are wheat, beans, barley and oats; there are also numerous orchards. The area of the parish is 2,167 acres; rateable value, £3,792; and the population in 1881 was 435.

Parish Clerk, William Moore.

POST & MONEY ORDER OFFICE & Savings Bank.—John Darch, receiver. Letters received through Bridgwater at 4.35 a.m.; dispatched at 8.40 p.m. The telegraph office is at the railway station

There is a sunday & week day school at Burtle Hill; the latter has an endowment of three acres of land, one-sixth of the income arising from which is given away in clothing

Church School, Burtle, to hold 63; average attendance, 31

National School, Burtle hill, to hold 75; average attendance, 50; Harry Coleman, master

Railway Station, William Marks, station master

Burridge Miss
Luttrell Capt. John Alex. Fownes R.N.,J.P
Norris Thomas, Pines
Vale William
Westmacott Mrs. Edington house
Yarranton Rev. Andrew John B.A. Burtle

COMMERCIAL.

Ash Thos. *Railway inn*, Edington station
Cox Charles, grocer & draper, Burtle hill

Cox Edmund, farmer, Burtle
Cox Jesse, farmer & turf dealer
Darch George, shopkeeper
Durston John, farmer & butcher, Burtle hill
Durston John, farmer, Hill farm
Durston John, sen. farmer, Burtle moor
Gardener Joseph, turf dealer
Godfrey Edwin, turf dealer
Godfrey George, cooper

Godfrey William, turf dealer
Grant George, shopkeeper
Grant James, farmer
Granville Henry, stone mason
Harvey William, shoe maker
Jennings John, farmer
Jennings Thomas, farmer
Moxey George, turf dealer
Moxey George, sen. farmer
Nicholas James, farmer

Norris Alfred, farmer
Pocock Elizh. (Mrs.), farmer, Chapel hill
Pollard William, farmer

Rugg John Warren, farmer
Snook David, farmer
Tratt Joseph (Mrs.), farmer

Vale William, farmer & landowner
Watts Anthony, farmer, West Burtle
Webb Richard, farmer

CHILTON POLDEN 1883

CHILTON POLDEN (or CHILTON-UPON-POLDEN) is a village, 2¾ miles south-west from Edington railway station and 5½ east-north-east from Bridgwater: it was formerly a chapelry in the parish of Moorlinch, but is now constituted a distinct parish, in the Western division of the county, hundred of Whitley, union and county court district of Bridgwater, rural deanery of Glastonbury, archdeaconry of Wells and diocese of Bath and Wells. The church, dedication unknown, is a plain stone building, having chancel, nave, north aisle and a turret with 1 bell. The register dates from the year 1813. The living is a vicarage, annexed to that of Edington, joint yearly value £114, with residence, in the gift of the vicar of Moorlinch, and held since 1878 by the Rev. Matthew Benjamin George Reed Lucas M.A. of Corpus Christi college, Cambridge. Here is a Congregational chapel. There are charities of £4 9s. 2d. annual value. Many rare specimens of ferns are found on the moor, which is much frequented by botanists: occasionally ancient British remains of relics are found on the peat moor. Lady Cooper, who is lady of the manor, J. C. Carver esq. and Col. C. K. Kemeys-Tynte are the chief landowners. The soil is sandy; subsoil, peat and stone. The chief crops are wheat, barley, oats and beans; there are also many good orchards. The parish contains 1,844 acres; rateable value, £3,017; the population in 1881 was 397.

Parish Clerk, Richard Batten.

There is a National school, erected in 1875, to hold 114; average attendance 70; John Quinn, master

POST OFFICE.—William Emery, receiver. Letters arrive from Bridgwater at 4.24 a.m.; dispatched at 9 p.m. The nearest money order office is at Edington

Biffen Mrs
Campbell George
Carver John J.P
Carver Miss
Durston Thomas
Jones Miss
Lucas Rev. Matthew Benjamin George Reed M.A. Vicarage
Young Charles

COMMERCIAL.
Biffen Charles, farmer
Biffen John, farmer
Campbell George, surgeon
Crossman Joseph, butcher
Edgar Frank, farmer
Edgar William, farmer
Emery Joseph, gardener
Emery Wm. shopkeeper & letter receiver
Fear Edward, farmer
Gibbs Robert, stone mason
Godfrey James, farmer
Groves Charles, sen. farmer
House Alfred John, boot & shoe maker
Langdon & Moffatt, tailors
Langdon Henry, *White Hart*
Laver John, farmer
Lawrence Charles, saddler
Lee Thomas, farmer
Moore John, plumber
Pitman John, farmer
Plece & Nicholas, wheelwrights
Rowe John, *New inn*
Rugg Francis, wheelwright
Tucker William, farmer
Tucker William, sen. farmer
Watts Isaac, blacksmith
Way Sidney, farmer
Wood Walter, shopkeeper
Young Charles, surgeon & medical officer & public vaccinator, No. 5 district, Bridgwater union

CHILTON-SUPER-POLDEN, CHILTON BURTLE, AND CHILTON SEDGEMOOR ALLOTMENTS,

WITHIN 6 MILES OF THE TOWN AND PORT OF

BRIDGWATER, SOMERSET.

Particulars, Plan, and Conditions of Sale

of the MANOR OR LORDSHIP OF CHILTON POLDEN, with

FARMHOUSES, FARM BUILDINGS,

AND NUMEROUS DETACHED CLOSES OF

MEADOW, PASTURE, TURBARY, & ARABLE LANDS,

CONTAINING ALTOGETHER

404 acres, **3** roods, **17** perches,

Which will be offered for Sale by Auction at the

ROYAL CLARENCE HOTEL, BRIDGWATER,

ON

Thursday and Friday, the 11th and 12th days of June, 1896.

Commencing each day at 12 o'clock, by

MR. ROBERT SQUIBBS

IN 98 LOTS.

The ABOVE ESTATE consists of DETACHED PIECES of

FERTILE MEADOW PASTURE, AND ARABLE LANDS,

mostly adjoining good roads. A large number of the Lots are detached, and OCCUPYING IMPORTANT POSITIONS in or near the CENTRE OF THE VILLAGE of CHILTON POLDEN. Several of the Lots contain

VALUABLE BEDS OF STONE AND CEMENT SHALE.

The ESTATE extends

from CHILTON BURTLE southwards through CHILTON MOOR and the Centre of the Village to the Northern Slope of Cock Hill, and every Lot is conveniently situated for

AGRICULTURAL PURPOSES.

In addition there are NUMEROUS LOTS in the CHILTON POLDEN RIGHTS in KING SEDGEMOOR, adjoining the Cary Valley River or SEDGEMOOR MAIN DRAIN, and NEAR TO THE VILLAGE OF WESTONZOYLAND. There are also several

BEAST LEAZES OR RIGHTS OF STOCKAGE IN THE CHILTON DROVES.

The Estate is divided into Small Lots

according to the detached character of the property,

AND OFFERS MOST EXCEPTIONAL ADVANTAGES TO INVESTORS OR SMALL OCCUPIERS.

Save and except a small portion of the property at Chilton Burtle which was occupied by the late Mr. E. Fear up to a recent date, the whole Estate has been for many years past in the occupation of Mr. William Tucker, whose family have occupied the principal portions of the property for many years past.

The respective Lots may be viewed on application to Mr. William Tucker, who has kindly consented to shew the same.

Printed Particulars with Plan may be obtained gratis on application to the Auctioneer—

R. SQUIBBS,
No. 7, King Square,
Bridgwater.

or to

Messrs. BAKER, FOLDER & UPPERTON,
SOLICITORS,
14, Lincoln's Inn Fields, London, W.C.

ALL THAT COMFORTABLE

FARMHOUSE, OUTBUILDINGS & PREMISES

Situate at Chilton Burtle,

and numbered 55 on the Tithe Survey. The

DWELLING HOUSE

is stone-built and tiled, and comprises, on the Ground Floor, Parlour, Sitting Room, Kitchen, Laundry, Cheese Room, Cider Cellar, Dairy and Offices, with three Bedrooms over.

About two years ago the Vendors laid out a large sum of money in the erection of a most substantial set of

Cow Stalling, Stables, Chaff Houses, Cart or Trap House, Piggeries, &c.,

Suitable for

CARRYING ON A 20 TO 30 COW DAIRY.

This Lot is sub-let to Mr. Wm. Biffin, Dairyman.

AND ALSO ALL THAT

Farmhouse, Outbuildings and Premises

Numbered 60 on the said Tithe Survey, and formerly in the occupation of the late Mr. Edward Fear.

Amongst the Outbuildings there is a Useful

STONE-BUILT AND TILED WAGGON HOUSE, STABLE, &c.

The respective properties occupied by Mr. William Biffin and the late Mr. Edward Fear form together a compact block standing on a slightly elevated position with a sandy subsoil, and contain altogether

16 acres 3 roods 9 perches

(be the same more or less) of

Meadow and Orchard Land,

The whole being described in the Tithe Survey as follows :—

No.		Description.			Quality.			Quantity.		
								A.	R.	P.
55	...	East Burtle	...	...	Meadow	...	...}	3	1	10
	...	Do.	...	...	House, &c.	...	...}			
56	...	Do.	...	...	Meadow	...	...	1	2	28
57	...	Do.	...	...	Orchard	...	...	1	0	21
58	...	Do.	...	...	Meadow	...	...	2	1	32
59	...	Do.	...	...	Do.	...	...	4	0	0
60	...	Do.	...	...	Orchard	...	...	1	1	25
	...	Do.	...	...	House, &c.	...	...}	2	3	13
61	...	Do.	...	...	Meadow	...	...}			
							A.	16	3	9

This Lot is bounded by Lands belonging to W. Brice, Esq., Rev. T. Lewis, and adjoins "Robins Drove" and Chilton Drove.

The Henniker Estate Sale

As Burtle was the outpost of three villages, there was no single estate and lord of the manor who dominated the whole scene since, possibly, the dissolution of Glastonbury Abbey. The major landowners on the hill had various parcels of land on the levels and the Henniker estate at Catcott owned a large slice of Catcott Burtle, upon the death of John Granville Henniker, JP, the estate was sold by auction by Stiling, Ker & Duckworth in September 1918.

Most of his land in Catcott Burtle was turbary or peat and this lay mainly in the block known as the five hundred acres, to the east of the Catcott Broad Drove, now the Catcott Road. The droves all have names such as Shepherd's Drove, Upper and Lower Ropes Droves, Batchkey Drove, Skimmers Drove, Lady's Drove, Jane's Drove and Stubbylawn Drove. Some of the fields were a mile or more off the hard road and would be difficult to access in wet Summers and covered with several feet of water most Winters.

In common with many rural areas where the road verges were wide enough to allow it, small "longacre" cottages were built and after the passage of a certain period, became the legal home of the occupants. The squires however, usually claimed the ownership of the verges and it would have been difficult for the people living in them to fight such a claim. Consequently, Squire Henniker had each cottage numbered and started charging rent, often as little as one pound a year, again the hapless occupants would have little option but to pay it.

At the sale some twenty of these properties were sold by the estate who no doubt pocketed the money. It was tough on the occupants, some of whose ancestors probably built them at their own expense. Along the verges were separate tiny patches of ground which had been used as vegetable gardens, a necessity to supplement the time's low incomes, these too, were in the sale, usually linked to a cottage but sometimes as much as half a mile from It.

All the land measurements are in acres, roods and perches. For the uninitiated there are four roods to the acre and forty perches to the rood. These terms have largely died out in these days of decimalisation and the advent of hectares, or hectacres as an old friend of mine insists on calling them!

The large variation in prices paid is interesting and the bidding for some lots must have been hotly contested. Peat land varied from about seven pounds an acre to as much as twenty. The small cottages actually sold at auction ranged from fifteen pounds with some land included but several were withdrawn and no doubt sold privately afterwards. At that time there were about eight cottages on the Catcott side of the Catcott rail crossing but the only one left today is the 'eighteen pounder' owned by the Groves family.

The main concentration of dwellings in Catcott Burtle was on the higher ground near the Burtle Inn where the land averaged forty to fifty pounds an acre. The Burtle Inn with twenty six acres was bought by Frank (Nacky) Lee on behalf of his brother, George, for one thousand, four hundred and sixty pounds, a considerable sum in those days especially when one considers that the land was scattered around in small pieces on the peat land of the 'five hundred acres'. The milk factory, previously the school, was bought by Reg Grant for seven hundred and fifty pounds whilst a block of three cottages adjoining (now two) were bought by Tom Clark for one hundred and thirty pounds. The two cottages on the corner of the Westhay Road also known as Grail House and latterly as Cherry Tree Cottage was occupied by Samuel Rice but bought by Henry Grove, who was using one as a store, for sixty five pounds. The cheapest lot of the day was a piece of garden ground on the Westhay Road at five pounds for a little under a quarter of an acre bought by S. Rice.

Some of the land and premises were not bought by the tenants at the time of the sale, there being a lot of cross purchasing, and one can only conjecture at how many old scores were settled and at the atmosphere in the village as the purchasers took possession of their newly acquired properties from the hitherto tenants! The Catcott section of the sale took place the following day.

In the Estate of JOHN GRANVILLE HENNIKER, Esq., J.P., deceased.

PARTICULARS of a

Valuable Freehold Estate

Comprising a Total
Area of about 1,400 ACRES,

CONSISTING OF

DAIRY FARMS,

Small Holdings, Licensed Premises, Dwelling-Houses, Cottages
and Closes of Rich and Productive Pasture, Meadow,
Orchard, Arable and Accommodation Land,

Divided into 166 LOTS, together with the

**DONATIVE TITHE of £40 per annum, the ADVOWSON
and the LORDSHIP of the Manor of Catcott,**

COMPRISING THE

Catcott Manor Estate

Situate at CATCOTT and CATCOTT BURTLE and EDINGTON, SOMERSET,

Close to the Important Market Towns of Bridgwater and Highbridge, and which will be

SOLD by AUCTION by

MESSRS.

STILING, KER & DUCKWORTH

At the "Royal Clarence" Hotel, Bridgwater,

ON

Wednesday and Thursday, the 11th & 12th September, 1918,

At 2 p.m. on WEDNESDAY and at 11 a.m. on THURSDAY

In Lots as set out in these Particulars or as may otherwise be determined upon, and on the
days herein Specified or otherwise, and subject to Special and other Conditions.

These Particulars, with Plans and Conditions of Sale, may be obtained of the Auctioneers,
The Mart, Bridgwater ; or of

Messrs. RUSSELL, SON & FISHER,
Solicitors, 3, Serjeants Inn, Temple, E.C. 4.

Dated Auction and Estate Agency Offices, The Mart, Bridgwater, 10th July, 1918.

BIGWOOD & STAPLE, PRINTERS (opposite Parr's Bank), BRIDGWATER.

CATCOTT MANOR ESTATE.

PARTICULARS.

First Day's Sale.

LOT 1. All that **Fully Licensed Public House,**

Known as the **"BURTLE INN,"** together with the FARM BUILDINGS, GARDEN, LANDS and PREMISES belonging thereto, situate at Catcott Burtle, in the Parish of Catcott, comprising and containing A26 1r. 13p. as follows.

Tithe No.	Ordnance No.	Description.			Cultivation.			Quantity. Tithe.			Ordnance.
								A.	R.	P.	A.
pt. 82	pt. 104	Burtle Inn	...	...	House, Garden & Orchard			0	2	22	·637
69	96	In the 500 Acres	...	...	Pasture	...	...	9	0	0	12·999
87	110	Long Ground	...	...	Meadow	...	...	3	2	12	3·488
97	126	In the 500 Acres	...	...	Pasture	...	...	2	2	0	2·016
107	137	Ditto	...	...	Ditto	...	...	1	0	0	·880
130		Ditto	...	...	Ditto	...	...	0	2	0 }	
131	136	Ditto	...	...	Ditto	...	...	0	2	0 }	2·021
132		Ditto	...	...	Ditto	...	...	0	2	0 }	
147		Ditto	...	...	Ditto	...	...	0	3	0 }	
118	116	Ditto	...	...	Ditto	...	...	0	2	0 }	2·792
119		Ditto	...	...	Ditto	...	...	2	2	0 }	
153	143	Ditto	...	...	Ditto	...	...	0	2	0 }	1·472
151		Ditto	...	...	Ditto	...	...	0	2	0 }	
								A22	3	34	A26·335

The House contains : on the ground floor—Bar-room, parlour, kitchen, cellar, covered-in pump and furnace-house. Upstairs are four good bedrooms.

The Buildings consist of cellar, two-stall stable, capital barn, two cow-stalls (to tie up 14 and 9), two pig-styes, etc.

An open cart shed and also a shed at the end of the Barton belong to the Tenant.

The long open shed adjoining one of the cow-stalls does not belong to the property.

The Burtle Inn and Lands are in the occupation of Mr. Ralph Norris as a Yearly (Lady-day) Tenant with other Lands under a written Agreement.

Apportioned Tithes 10/10.

LOT 2. All those Three Closes of **Pasture Land**

Situate in Catcott Burtle "In the 500 Acres," being Tithe Nos. 63, 64 and 65, and Ordnance Nos. 82, 83 and 84, and containing

A9 1r. 30p.

These Lands are also in the occupation of Mr. Ralph Norris under the aforementioned Agreement.

Apportioned Tithes 3/4.

LOT 3. All that Close of **Pasture Land**

Situate in Catcott Burtle, and known as "In Burtle Ground," being Tithe No. 56 and Ordnance Nos. 33, 36 and 78, and containing

A14 3r. 0p.

as in the occupation of Mr. Ralph Norris under the aforementioned Agreement.

Apportioned Tithes 7/4.

LOT 4. All that Close of **Meadow or Pasture Land**

Situate in Catcott Burtle "In the 500 Acres," being No. 61 on the Tithe Map and No. 80 on the Ordnance Map, and containing

A8 0r. 15p.

as in the occupation of Mr. George Lee as a Yearly (Lady-day) Tenant under a written Agreement.

Apportioned Tithes 3/6.

3

LOT 12. All that

Barton, Farm-Buildings, Garden and Premises

Situate in Catcott Burtle, together with the several Closes of Meadow or Pasture Land situate "In the 500 Acres," and containing A25 1r. 26p. as follows:

Mr R G Moxey

£900

Tithe No.	Ordnance No.	Description				Cultivation			Quantity. Tithe			Ordnance.
									A.	R.	P.	A.
78	pt. 100	Cox's	...	...	...	Garden	...	...	0	1	10	·235 (about)
73 72 pt. 75	pt. 103	Watt's Ditto Globe Hotel (site of)	... ...	... ...	... ...	Orchard Barton, &c. Wagon House	... ...	... ...	0 0 0	2 1 0	27 0 1	·813 (about)
104	132	In the 500 Acres	...	...	...	Pasture	...	...	3	2	5	1·560
95	121	Ditto	...	...	...	Ditto	...	...	4	0	0	3·674
96	125	Ditto	...	...	...	Ditto	...	...	1	2	0	1·633
91	116	Ditto	...	...	...	Ditto	...	...	2	0	0	2·282
88	114	Ditto	...	...	...	Ditto	...	...	5	0	0	6·452
119	112	Ditto	...	...	...	Ditto	...	...	4	2	0	5·961
									A21	2	38	A25·112

as in the occupation of the Reps. of Mr. Robert Moxey, as Yearly (Lady-day) Tenants, with other Lands, under a written Agreement.

Apportioned Tithes 9/9.

LOT 13. All that ## Cottage, Garden and Premises

Situate at Catcott Burtle, as in the occupation of Mr. Samuel Rice, together with the COTTAGE adjoining, now occupied by Mr. Henry Grove as a store house, being Tithe Nos. part 81 and part 80 and Ordnance No. part 99. Mr. Rice holds as a Yearly (Lady-day) Tenant at a rent of £4 a year and Mr. Henry Grove at a rent of £1 5s. a year. Tenants paying Rates.

The Store house and furnace adjoining the Cottage occupied by Mr. Rice belong to the tenant.

Mr H Grove

£65

LOT 14. All that ## Garden and Storehouse

Situate at Catcott Burtle, being Tithe No. 78a and Ordnance No. part 100, as in the occupation of Mrs. M. A. Clarke as a Yearly (Lady-day) Tenant at a rent of £1. Tenant paying Rates.

Mrs M A Clark

£10

LOT 15. All that

Building (formerly the School House), Ground and Premises

Situate at Catcott Burtle, as in the occupation of the Cream Dairy Company, Ltd., and used as a Milk Factory, being part Tithe No. 76 and part Ordnance No. 100, held under lease for a term of 21 years from Lady-day, 1904, at a rent of £10 10s. a year.

The Company also pays the following acknowledgments, which are sold with the Lots concerned, viz. :

1. 5/- a year in respect of a small piece of garden belonging to the garden of the cottage in the occupation of Mr. William Coombs (Lot 16) and

2. 10/- a year in respect of site of well sunk on Tithe No. part 71 and Ordnance No. part 101 and containing about 4 perches as referred to in Lot 11. The grant to sink a well is for a term of 20 years from Lady-day, 1905.

The wood and iron buildings, added to the original brick building by the Cream Dairy Company, Ltd., from time to time, are the property of the Company.

A right-of-way to Tithe Nos. 71a and 71 and Ordnance Nos. 102 and 101 (Lot 11) extends over the roadway leading to these premises.

Also with this Lot All that Close of

Meadow or Pasture Land

Mr R G Grant

£750

Being Tithe No. 89 and Ordnance No. 115 and containing

A7 2r. 39p.

held by the Company under a Yearly (Lady-day) written Agreement at an annual rent of £10.

Apportioned Tithes 3/8.

5

CHAPTER 3

Village Social Development and Activities

Surprisingly, in view of the scattered nature of the parish, there has always been a strong sense of co-operation with a wide range of communal activities. Although life must have been very hard, the older Burtolians, enjoy talking about the fun they had, playing practical jokes, attending the various village functions and over a pint of cider in either the Railway, Burtle or First and Last pubs. They would arrange a celebration at the drop of a hat! There cannot be many villages with such a universal sense of humour.

In spite of the adverse environment of the moors it is more or less expected that people should live to a ripe old age. Burtle has probably had more than its share of centenarians, and plenty more have made the mid-nineties. Old George Clarke kicked off the ball to start a football match on his hundredth birthday, Mrs Allan Moxey and her sister in law, Mrs Kate Stradling (nee Moxey) both passed their century in recent years. A typical response to a comment on this longevity of Burtle people, was that when the church was built they had to shoot the first three to get the cemetery started!

One explanation offered of the apparent longevity was that they never wore themselves out. A man on his bike, and everyone in Burtle had a bike, was bound to meet another man on his bike, they would always stop to have a chat. After a while one or the other would take out his watch and comment "Hardly wurf going down thur now, not enough time fur thic job, better goo 'ome fur dinner!" And off home they would go. Perhaps if, in this frenetic age, we could find more time for a chat, we would be living in a happier world.

Villages are often associated with family names particular to that village. Burtle is no exception with about seven families who have dominated the scene over the last couple of centuries. Even when young people have moved away to the surrounding villages, Burtle seems to draw them back like a magnet later in life.

This stability provided the continuity necessary to establish and maintain the quality of community spirit. A great pride existed in those committing years of their time, often backed by cash sponsorship, to the various activities and organisations in the village.

In the 1891 census the old family names keep cropping up, how they ever squeezed those large families into some of the tiny cottages it is difficult to imagine! At that time there were sixty people living in Chilton Burtle, one hundred and forty one in Edington Burtle and one hundred and seventy one in Catcott Burtle, a total of three hundred and seventy two. The oldest person was a Phebe Lee who lived down Green Drove who was ninety one, ie. born in 1800. There were 32 Coxs, 31 Tratts, 28 Norris's, 27 Watts's and 25 Moxey's. Today, many of these family names are absent from the village although most have decendants through marriage. There were 11 by name of Grove and 11 named Groves who were insistant on not being lumped together, claiming different ancestry.

Some of the families now have several branches in the village, one section denying any family connection with others of the same name. The reasons for this might well be an interesting subject to research - everyone in Burtle had a bike! The Lee family is a case in point where some of the Groves, (or was it Grove?), changed their name to Lee by deed poll. The reason is not clear, maybe it was to gain an inheritance, alternatively it could also be that the family had some past deed or connection they wished to avoid! Some families have been in the village for so many generations that the original connections have been lost in the mists of time.

During the Winter floods the villagers' main link with the outside world was by boat. These were in the form of a flat bottomed punt, pointed at both ends and principally used to ferry the peat blocks along the rhynes from the peat fields to a point accessible by a horse and cart. In the Winter these turf boats doubled up as shooting punts, wildfowl formed an important part of the diet and income of the locals in those days.

Although there were villages within two or three miles, these must have seemed like 'vurrin parts'. Burtle folk became expert at developing their own entertainment. The villagers can be fiercely independent, expressing firm but honestly held views, on all manner of subjects.

Today there is much discussion about the loss of village community spirit. The latter is usually strongest where there is a history of stability of the population. Successive generations with the sons almost "inheriting" the communal responsibilities when relinquished by the fathers. Burtle families who have been in the village for many generations, have contributed greatly to these traditions.

The Burtle silver band was founded in 1907 and still flourishes over 90 years on.

Almost every child growing up in Burtle learnt music and to play a musical instrument. There have only been 4 bandmasters in that time, drawn from three generations of the Moxey family.

Burtle has only recently become a parish in its own right, having represented outposts of three of the Polden villages, Catcott Burtle, Edington Burtle and Chilton Burtle. The first practical step towards unity was probably when Miss Ann Field of Edington built the church and the school in 1839, in the centre of what is now the village of Burtle. People living in Catcott Burtle still have the right to be buried in Catcott churchyard and there used to be a path from the edge of the moor directly up to the church yard in order to transport the coffins which, in wet Winters would have been ferried by boat to the end of the path. Mr and Mrs Mark Pollard were married by boat on boxing day 1912.

Catcott Burtle used to have a school which was closed in the 1880's, the pupils transferred to the comparatively new school in Edington Burtle.

One strange fact is that the Moxeys originated from two sources, Newton St Cyres near Crediton, Devon, and the other from Romsey in Hampshire. The chances of two independent families of the same name settling in such a small village from such diverse origins must be so remote as to suggest that they must have had some earlier connection. In the early 1800's, it is surprising to realise how far some families moved. Doing business with someone a hundred miles distant must have presented many difficulties. How did they know that a farm or whatever was available? Before the railways, a hundred miles represented several days travelling light, much longer when removing goods and chattels. It must have been a most daunting prospect.

The main, non commercial activities were the Harvest Home, Revels and the Burtle Silver Band

One of the difficulties with this chapter is the separation of business from past-times eg. shooting and eel trapping. Although both were a pleasurable activity, many families relied on the addition income it brought in. In the distant past, eels were an alternative to cash and some rents were paid in eels.

In the early 1970's there was outrage on the moors when the water board started confiscating any eel traps the bailiffs found. A petition was set up and received tremendous support. Correspondence was received from other areas with the same problem such as Norfolk. Tempers were running high, it was felt that an ancient right was being rescinded. The campaign attracted the attention of television and the programme was followed by many messages of support.

Apparently, a bill, mainly concerned with salmon fishing had been passed in parliament. A sneaky paragraph had been added un-noticed, requiring anyone trapping eels to now buy a licence. The rivers board claimed that the rod fishermen wanted the eels protected, a clear case of tradition being overthrown by the board's newly acquired income from the sale of fishing rights. The ownership of some of these rights could well be open to question. Adjoining landowners' rights tend to be bulldozed aside by such monopolistic bodies.

Vigorous campaigning eventually led to a compromise, the board would not confiscate eel traps provided they were not causing a hazard in the drainage channels. The numbers of those seriously trapping eels has reduced as the older generation decreases.

Some years ago, a visitor to the village, a high flier in the world of big business, was strolling down to the Burtle Inn for a drink. Old George who was well known for his ability in eel trapping, was sitting on the bench outside enjoying a pint of cider.

"Could you catch me a couple of pounds of eels for tomorrow?", asked the visitor.

"No trouble" replied George, "they be a pound a pound."

In the morning the visitor collected and paid for his eels.

"I've got some friends coming down, could you get me five or six pounds for Thursday?"

"Get 'ee however many you do want", confirmed George.

The visitor duly collected his eels and asked whether there was any limit to the quantities of eels he could catch. George inferred that quantities presented no problems to him, he could always call on friends to help him out. You could make a good business out of this said the visitor, with yourself as the co-ordinator, you could send the eels up to London where they would make good money. When you become established, you could start smoking eels and send them far and wide, making a lot of money.

"Why should I want to do that?", asked George.

"Well, you could always sit in front of the pub, in the sun, drinking your cider!", said the visitor.

Burtle Band

Farmer Allan Moxey bought a second hand cornet for £2, a transaction which had a resounding affect on village life. Starting with members of his family he proceeded to gather a group of villagers together who liked the idea of learning to play musical instruments. This was the birth of the Burtle Silver Band.

Above: The original photo of Burtle Silver Band. George Lee on the drum.

Left: Alan Moxey the founder of the band. (Pat Moxey)

By 1907, the players had become proficient enough to appear in public and the band began to take on a round of engagements. With Allan Moxey as band master and a fair percentage of the male villagers participating when they could spare the time, they travelled surprising distances. An elderly lady from the midlands, a regular visitor to Weston Super Mare in the 1920's clearly remembered sitting on the sea front listening to "Mr Moxey's Band". Regular bookings at harvest homes, village fetes, flower shows and other events soon became a considerable commitment by people who already had plenty on their plate. In spite of haymaking, harvesting and other demanding work the band prospered.

By now the players were appearing in snappy uniforms which no doubt elevated the band into the ranks of the surrounding town bands. The original dress reminded one of army officer uniforms, the band was obviously going places!

Christmas gave the band an ideal opportunity to visit and entertain their many supporters in the village. With the abundance of cider, readily available in most Burtle homes, carol playing could take as long as three weeks to complete the village circuit! It was quite difficult to see that no-one got 'lost' along the way during the evening.

So great was the enthusiasm, most youngsters were taught music and to play a variety of instruments. Gradually, girls were accepted into the band and the social life no doubt improved in direct proportion. There is little doubt that some of the boys' interest was maintained, or even improved by their inclusion!

Transport in the early days was by bicycle and horse and cart, later by charabanc. Harvest Homes were one of the favourite playing venues, there was practically unlimited food and cider at these functions. What affect this had on the music is not recorded but as the audience were probably in a similar state, it did not make much difference. The Harvest Homes and other functions attended had to be within a reasonable distance, cows had to be milked and other chores finished before setting off. The band started playing in the procession to the marquee before lunch, striking up again in the afternoon. Farming members had to rush back home to attend to the afternoon milking, calf feeding etc. The chances were that the band were also engaged to play in the evening, necessitating a rapid return to the Harvest Home and a very late night.

Allan Moxey was a large, burly and charismatic man with a good natured, bluff manner. The earliest known photo of the band was taken in 1907 and pictured some thirteen members in the uniforms fashionable at the time. Practice nights were held in a variety of places, the cheese room in Burtle Farm, the old creamery, village hall etc.

The membership, mainly from the village, grew as the young protegees came up

Norman and Vivian Moxey, both ex-bandmasters.

The band practice was held in a variety of premises, this was in the hayloft over the vicarage stables. In the picture; back row, 1) David Porter, 2) John Luxon, 3) Jenny Winne, 4) Joan Luxon, 5) Carol Moxey, 6) Ken Porter, 7) Kay Thorne, 8) Jim Moxey, 9) George Baker, 10) Doreen Baker (née Court), 11) Steve ?, 12) John Court, 13) Norman Moxey, 14) Dave Loud, 15) ? , 16) Pat Moxey, Fred Wride. Seated 1) ? , 2) ? , 3) Gladys Court, 4) Angela Whitcombe, 5) ? Porter, 6) Ken Stainer, 7) ? , 8) ? , 9) Jackie Whitcombe.

The band and the friendly society join forces to raise money for Bridgwater hospital, taken at The Farm in the late 20s. (Mrs. I. Storey). The little girl is Ruth Pollard by her father.

The band's 70th anniversary party in the village hall.

Jim Moxey has spent many hours teaching young recruits

A young line up at a band concert in the village hall.

George Baker whipping up enthusiasm at a band concert and party for adults and children alike.

Waiting for Father Christmas.

Sid Lock from Langport played Santa at both band and senior citizens parties for many years.

Sid and Charlie Tratt afterwards. Sid used to donate the presents for the children himself.

Presentation to Mrs Lucy Moxey (Aunt Luce), Alan Moxey's widow, on her 100th birthday.

Carol, Jim, Norman, and Pat, Carol's father.

to scratch. Almost everyone in the village seems to have played in the band at some stage. It is difficult to imagine any other ongoing activity which could have a more cohesive influence on village life.

As the festivities could easily over-run the rather restrictive drinking laws that prevailed in those days, it was standard practice to detail the local bobby to ensure that the law was not broken, well, not by too much! As the evening's entertainment was drawing to a close, local farmers and others would stagger out of the tent under the weight of many pints of cider, probably reretting their over indulgence when getting up early the next day to do the milking!

Opposite: Westhay Revels, 1936. In the top hats: Edgar Moxey, son of Roland, and Tom Willcox.

The Revels

Most villages had friendly societies, a form of brotherhood designed to look after the needy. Stewards were appointed and each would be presented with a staff of office. These were often passed down from father to son, a stewardship was considered a great honour. Small, regular payments were gathered to provide a fund to assist in cases of severe hardship. At least once a year there would be a procession through the village, elaborate banners were carried and there might well be some music. Another activity was known locally as 'the revels', some of the older folk can still remember the carnival atmosphere that prevailed. It appears that it was rather like a local version of a fair holiday, all but essential work being set aside for the day.

In Burtle the revels took place at the beginning of September. Various regular standholders set up their stalls in their recognised spots. Mrs Betty from Bridgwater always had a pitch selling cockles, mussels and whelks beside the Burtle Inn. There were simple swings and roundabouts, set up across the road from the pub and traders selling all manner of wares.

Some villagers travelled around the village, stopping regularly at houses on the way. The professed reason was to wish everyone well but I suspect the real reason was to sample the cider available in almost every house, to confirm its quality, of course!. No doubt the tempo of the festivities was suitably elevated as a result! Many of those in the procession found it difficult to complete the circuit. The revels were certainly the annual highspot of many of the villages around the area.

The Burtle Venturers

Rural communities have always delighted in putting on shows in their local village halls. Villagers on the stage in the village halls, dressed in funny clothes, seem to lose any inhibitions even when doing the daftest things! It is also surprising how much talent turns up on occasion, good singing voices, tellers of bawdy tales and the priceless, veiled references to some of those present in the audience. The latter were always sure of a roar of laughter from the audience.

It is not surprising that Burtle should put on such a show under the expertly enthusiastic direction of John Walton, the then station master. Rehearsals were held in the hall for several weeks prior to the presentations. A concert has advantages over a set performance such as a play or a pantomime in that each act could be rehearsed in isolation from the others.

The acts were a mixture of individual and collective effort, some of which were very innovative, others old chestnuts that were more or less expected by the audience. Amongst the latter, I well remember the age old sketch of the old tramp, played by Bob Ireland, sitting on a park bench. Various characters would join him on the seat and soon start scratching. It was possible to eventually get the whole audience scratching like mad, whereupon the tramp would stand up and mimic the audience scratching. At this point the audience realised how they had been fooled and howl with laughter.

With the combined effort and the honing of the whole concert into an enjoyable evening's entertainment, it seemed sensible to put on a number of performances. A round of the local villages was arranged, a coach booked and a full house was almost guaranteed. The profits went charity, we all had a good time.

A good compere was a great help, Bob (Phooey) Ireland from Chilton Polden was outstanding. An excellent musician with his own dance band and a born comic, he could well have succeeded on the professional stage. He was a large, rotund figure with big, beaming features. His normal opener was to thrust just his face, with a few days stubble, straw hat and chewing a piece of straw through the curtains to ask "'Ow be on you?"

Others from Burtle who gave a lot of time and talent to the operation were Eileen Bates, Helen Puddy, Frank and Stella Robinson. There were also the helpers in the background such as Charlie Tratt who always supported any thing in the village. As well as Bob Ireland, there were a few others who had always had an affinity with Burtle. Ken Smith, Heather Fry from Stawell and myself from Cossington. Ken was and still is a first class accordionist, Heather was decorative and had a great sense of fun, I fancied myself as a tenor vocalist, (I was probably the only one that did!) and a general mucker in.

One person, also with an affiliation to Burtle, was our piano accompanist Dot Warner from East Huntspill. In spite of being disabled, she rarely missed rehearsals and was an excellent example to anyone whose resolve may have been wobbling.

Children always featured prominently and one of the star turns for me were the children on the hand bells. John Walton was a very keen bell ringer and had a beautiful, large set of hand bells. His tuition and enthusiasm shone through, with highly polished stage performances.

Burtle Harvest Home

Harvest Homes have always been a highlight of the rural year. They are not to be confused with harvest festivals which are primarily religious. The harvest home is a gigantic binge with surrounding ancillary activities, funfair, side shows and stalls, originally for the farmers and their helpers. The scale escalated to encompass the whole village and eventually to become a major event for all the villages in the area. Those at East Brent, Mark and Wedmore are the best known in this region. Over a thousand diners are seated at some of them. Most of the smaller ones have fallen by the wayside, the costs today are crippling. A marquee alone can cost well into four figures.

Burtle harvest home was started up after the first world war, originally with an element of thanksgiving. It prospered until the second world war, when, like most social activities, it fell by the wayside. After the war it restarted with the efforts of such as Ern Lee. Burtle Harvest Home, sadly, fell away in 1970. Those in charge were not getting any younger and many of those that would normally have stepped into the breech had been obliged to move away to earn their living. To organise an event on this scale needs almost complete co-operation from the whole village community.

The preparation, planning and fund raising, started months before the event. Once the date was fixed so as not to clash with any other, the marquee had to be booked. Dances, whist drives, skittles competitions and other innovations would be held to raise the large sums of cash needed to stage the event.

The morning started with a procession led by the band marching with a standard bearer, followed by a procession of carnival type carts, decorated bicycles and children in fancy dress. Meanwhile, the food was being prepared in the Marquee by the ladies. The huge joints of meat were placed in the care of carvers who took a

Pre-war Harvest Home procession approaching village from the First and Last, about 1930 (I.Storey)

The children in fancy dress and with decorated bicycles would compete with each other. The entrance to Catcott Burtle Farm is between the hay ricks in Petherams Farm and the cottages on the right which have been demolished. (I. Storey)

British goods are the best', the early 30's were a very difficult period for farming and a lot of effort went into promotion at every opportunity.

Line up after the procession in the field. On the left with the Douglas motor cycle Tom Fisher, next to him Bill Vowles. The steam showman's engine on the distant far right belonged to W. Jones & Sons. The village nurse (Aunt Bet Lee) was part of the community and grew up in the village.

Farmers in the village would have a float in the procession, here are Geoff and Evelyn Moxey with Frank Lee in his tractor, 1970.

Ray (Col.) Cox leading the Harvest Home procession, 1970.

Celebrating the first heart transplant.

Joyce Hill with 'Burtle Lighthouse'.

More surgery - Burtle style!

great pride in their job and often undertook this task at other Harvest Homes. The meat was served cold, the vegetables hot, on tables running the length of the tent by an army of helpers.

Cider was available in unlimited quantities, often beer as well. Spirits and consumption rose side by side! The celebrations would continue throughout the day and night. Music at the Burtle Harvest Home would be provided by the Burtle Silver Band whose members would also join in the celebrations.

The fancy dress competition.

The local bobby would normally make an appearance towards the end of the evening to ensure that the boistrous revellers did not get out of hand. On one occasion a local farmer reeled out of the marquee at the end of festivities.

"How be you getting home?" the arm of the law asked him.

"Oh, I've got me car in the vield", he replied.

"Bloody good job," said the copper, "thee's 'ould never make it on voot!".

In the field would be a funfair and sideshows, dancing and drinking in the tent and a huge evening attendance could be expected if the weather was good.

Many cows would be milked late in the afternoon, some probably not at all! Heads would be still be a bit dodgy the following morning and any recalcitrant cows would receive short shrift! Otherwise, life in the village would be quiet for a few days after the big event.

Saturday Lunch Club

It is only in the last 25 - 30 years that pubs have developed into the gin palace restaurants we accept as the norm today. Many establishments in this part of Somerset were simply beer and cider houses. They would probably sell 10 pints of their locally or home made cider to one pint of beer and absolutely no wines or spirits; well not officially! Local workmen, some way from home or with a liking for company, would take in their bread and cheese lunch and chase it down with a pint or three of cider.

In Burtle, in the 1960's, something unusual was being born. Every Saturday, during the hour or so around mid-day observers would notice a general migration of the men in the village towards the Burtle Inn. Some would be in vehicles, some on bikes and more on shank's pony. They would have one thing in common, they all headed into the pub clutching bags containing a wide variety of food. Bill Vowles, Charlie Tratt and Arthur Baker all made their weekly pilgrimage on bicycles, as they had been doing for years. Some of these machines were the old twenty eight inch wheel variety, family heirlooms in themselves. Others like Geoff Moxey only had a short step on foot. There were some who travelled from much further afield. The Duke brothers from Birmingham had a couple of holiday caravans on the site of an old cottage on the bank of the River Brue out by the Mark Road bridge. Lenny, Lou and Freddie used to be amazingly regular visitors along with their wives and families.

With this background, it is not surprising that in Burtle this custom developed into something that would be unthinkable today. The Saturday lunch club sort of evolved in the mid 60's. It is difficult to say who really started it, or when, it was more or less a spontaneous development, suddenly we realised it was there. Landlords were nearly all local people in those days, very few pubs did food other than pasties and pork pies. Den Walker at the Burtle Inn was no exception. The custom of bringing in one's own lunch for consumption on the premises developed in to a communal affair. More and more brought in food which was heaped up on one or more tables with everyone helping themselves from the gastronomic pool. As well as the normal bread, cheese and onions there were chitterlings, hocks, pigs trotters and home made goodies of every description. A particular delicacy, much appreciated, were eels, cooked to one or other of the local recipes. One day Den Thorne persuaded some holiday makers to sample them, saying that they were freshwater herrings! The visitors declared them delicious but when they discovered they had been eating eels they were most upset!

Saturday lunch club regulars, Geoff Moxey and Jack Richards from Chilton Polden.

More regulars, Lionel (Doctor) Burroughs and Arthur Baker.

Harry Warman from Ashcott telling one his tales. Harry was a huge man in every respect, 6ft 5ins and over 20 stone in weight, he lived well into his 90s.

When Dennis (Vicar) Thorne auctioned items for club funds personal items had to be kept out of sight!!

Bill Vowles wondering who tied the cucumber into a knot!.

Dennis and Bill demonstrating brain surgery Burtle style!

Right: Home from the 'Railway by Burtle 'taxi', Arthur Baker and Connie Vowles.

Burtle attracted a numbers of people from outside the village who became what might be described as adopted sons. A leading light in the Saturday lunch club, an immigrant from the Forest of Dean was Bill Reece who lived a few miles away at Cossington. Bill had had a promising career in cricket and football with Gloucestershire and Wolverhampton, snuffed out by the war. He was a charismatic man's man who genuinely delighted in the companionship of the country characters who were particularly abundant in Burtle. Bill had gained a Bsc the hard way and was a manager in the huge British Cellophane Co in Bridgwater a fact he always played down. A friend of his from Bridgwater who also delighted in the mid-day assemblies and a lovely bloke to boot was Cliff Fursland, a TGW steward in Bill's place of work. Another extrovert who slotted into the picture was Harold Hill from Birmingham who, after holiday visits to the village and having been pensioned off following a serious back injury, decided to settle in the village. Almost all Burtle residents and associates acquire nicknames and Lionel (doctor) Burrows from Chilton Polden and Dennis (vicar) Thorne, were close to the action.

It soon became such a lively social gathering by 1970, the interest turned it into a spectator sport! The bar trade was greatly increased by those coming to witness the phenomenon. Rustic humour flew through the smoke laden air, the wit was usually sharp and to the point. One visitor confided that if you wanted to find an idiot in Burtle you would have to bring him with you! To the entre- preneurial folk of Burtle, it was natural that such a regular crowd should be harvested on behalf of some good cause. A regular weekly raffle of a joint of meat, provided at a special price by John Richards, the village Postmaster, butcher and shopkeeper soon began to accumulate funds towards a Christmas party for the senior citizens. One interesting factor was that some of the regulars were in their eighties and even nineties. Good fellowship flourished across the widest age spectrum imaginable. Unlike the chattering classes writing political columns, there was no class discrimination in Burtle. Everyone was accepted for what they were, incomers who were prepared to muck in and become involved quickly became integrated into the community. However, woe betide those who tried to take over, that characteristic independent nature still prevails today.

Only in a country area could the interest in people, families and occupations, who married who, who **should** have married who, where and what they did, be such a sustaining topic of conversation. Anecdotes by the score, snippets of information which could leave one wondering about the participants in past scandals and wishing that someone would fill in the gaps in the stories obviously known by the older blokes present.

The Christmas Party

The first senior citizens' party was held in the village hall in about 1968. Members of the lunch club, assisted by their wives and even teenagers all pitched in to cook some enormous turkeys and all the associated Christmas fare in their homes and transport it to the hall. It was a big undertaking, starting quite early in the morning. Eileen Bates, landlady at the "Railway", and Helen Puddy headed the band of lady cooks who worked wonders in somewhat cramped conditions. An enormous pile of presents were purchased and all worked together to wrap and label them. Every pensioner in the village, regardless of whether they attended the party, received a most worthwhile present.

Some of the younger car owners had a list of the party goers requiring transport and did the rounds, from mid-day there was a growing hum of conversation as old friends renewed their acquaintance. The village band playing carols gave the occasion just the right atmosphere. The wide range of drinks were all provided by the lunch club and the volume withstood the most determined efforts of some of the more practised drinkers! The whole operation was masterminded by Bill Reece, ably assisted by some twenty members of the club, all of whom were decked out in aprons and fetching chefs' hats. I bet most of the wives were muttering "If only!"

The attention lavished on the diners could not have been bettered by the most expensive restaurant, the food arrived on the tables hot and in generous portions. The "wine waiters" paid constant attention to their liquid needs. Mr Ponsillo who farmed down Green Lane, joined forces with some Italian friends in the area to make some excellent red wine. Ern (Jumper) Lee, the local cider maker, supplied copious quantities of his product. Crackers and balloons were supplied in plenty, the sight of Freddie Coombes at the age of ninety, fly kicking at a head high balloon was indelibly impressed on my mind. The overall atmosphere was wonderful, Burtle folk were always experts at celebrations. After the meal, a professional entertainer took the stage, followed by a visit from Father Christmas in the person of Mr Locke from Langport who did a splendid job. Mr Locke had a very soft spot for Burtle and would have been most upset if he had not been invited to perform his annual ritual.

The festivities would draw to a close around five o'clock, the pensioners ferried home, other presents and meals delivered to absentees and sick people who were also visited by Santa Claus. Meanwhile, the clearing up would be carried out by the rest of the club. There were always a few bottles and food that needed clearing up! By the time we were due to vacate the hall everyone was feeling the pace but enjoying a festive mellowness befitting the day's activities.

Above: The Christmas parties were a great event and the chefs' hats were worn by all the helpers.

Right: Harold Hill, an incomer who could be life and soul of the party and active member of the Lunch Club.

Below: There were nearly as many helpers as diners. Back row; 1) Harold Hill, 2) Bill Reece, 3) Alan Reece, 4) Den Elson, 5) Bill Vowles, 6) Mrs Higins, 7) Colin Burrows, 8) Geoff Moxey. Middle row; 1) Eileen Bates, 2) Connie Vowles, 3) ?? , 4) Betty Kitchen, 5) Des Higgins. Front row; 1) Tom Brewer, 2) Mrs. Dennis Thorne, 3) Lionel (Dr.) Burroughs, 4) Evelyn Wilton, 5) Mrs. Walt Cook, 6) Cliff Fursland. Foreground; Dennis (Vicar) Thorne and Mrs Whitcomb.

Left: Den Thorne was always good for a laugh, entertaining the guests!

Right: Jack Whitcombe always did his share.

*The Lunch Club 'committee'. 1) Bill Vowles, 2) Alan Moss, 3) Bill Reece, 4) Charlie Talbot,
5) Jack Whitcome, 6) Harold Hill, 7) Des Higgins.*

A Problem with a Landlord!

Whilst Den Walker was landlord at the Burtle Inn the pub came up for sale. It seems strange today that although the price was reasonable at £4,500, the Walkers were unable to raise the finance to purchase it. This was an eye opening reflection on the generally low currency of pubs in the commercial world. The premises were eventually bought by a Mr Palmer, a businessman from Wells. He completely refurbished the bars and built a splendid new restaurant on the Northern end of the building on the site of the old pigsty. The work was tastefully executed, masses of natural elm timber exuded a aura of polished rusticity. The Walkers did not wish to become involved in the sale of food but the owner increased the rent to cover the cost of the new restaurant etc. Eventually the inevitable happened, Den and Hella Walker gave up the tenancy and moved to the Royal Hotel, Catcott and subsequently to the Ashcott Inn.

The general appearance and facilities at the pub were head and shoulders above any others in the district. Very little food could be bought at any other pub for miles around in those days. One exception and one of the first, Eileen Bates at the Railway had just started a steak supper to order on Saturday nights, cost £1.5s - £1.25p to you youngsters! It was perhaps to be expected that such a quality premises as the Burtle Inn had become, should attract the attentions of potential tenants with gastronomic aspirations. It was thus that the village's peace and tranquillity was shattered with the arrival of Wing Commander Garry Coles DFC etc. The upmarket approach soon alienated the regulars, farmhouse cider was removed from the bar and the sales of gin probably quadrupled. On one brief visit, I was met with the unusual sight of Ray (Colonel) Cox drinking a pint of beer instead of his customary cider. My query was answered in a loud, clear and beautifully delivered Burtle dialect, " Thic bugger awver thur 'ave took off the cider and I baint coming in yur no more". What is more he never did.

The Saturday lunch club moved down to the Railway Inn, it is difficult to say whether they jumped or were pushed. The Burtle Inn became a country gin palace and not many locals ever went there for several years.

A New Home

Ray and Eileen Bates made us wonderfully welcome at the more basic but infinitely more homely Railway Inn. Not only was the raffle run by the club during the lunchtime gatherings, Ray and Eileen continued to sell the tickets at other times considerably swelling the club's funds. Many people who did not regularly attend the lunch club, bought tickets every week through friends who did. Others made a point of calling in to purchase tickets over the bar. The sums raised became very substantial, well over £1,000 per year.

All sorts of dodges were used to raise cash, an impromptu auction by Dennis (Vicar) Thorne was an occasion when everyone carefully ensured that their more treasured possessions were tucked out of sight. I once had to buy back my lunch box which had been inadvertently left on the table! The best defence was to bring along something specifically for the auction.

Eventually, the time came for Eileen and Ray to retire from the pub after many years. Up until that time, the Railway had always been a tied house, that is it belonged to the brewery and therefore they had to toe the company line. At one time, Ray and Eileen would like to have bought the place but the brewery was not interested. Holts in Burnham on Sea were the brewery and Gerald Holt, the owner was an excellent naturalist and a very keen shot. Mr Holt used to come to Burtle wildfowling, his party repairing to The Railway afterwards. This was a popular visit, drinks were free during his occupancy! Starkey, Knight and Ford of Bridgwater took over Holts brewery and the pubs, they in turn were taken over by the much larger company of Whitbread. Along the line the policy changed and, too late for Ray and Eileen, the premises were up for sale.

There is always a period of apprehension before the arrival of a new landlord but we need not have worried. Rex Carpenter was an ex copper from Kent, with wife Trish and a seemingly endless, young family. Rarely could a family have integrated into a new village so perfectly and quickly. The lunch club was in clover and continued without a hiccough. Then came the tragedy. One of the children had had their bicycle stolen from outside the pub and Rex and Trish set off to Glastonbury with a carload of children to buy a replacement. On the way home, they were waiting at Cockhill on the A 39 to turn right down to Edington and Burtle when an articulated lorry ploughed into the car. Rex and two of the children were killed, Trish was critically injured. The whole village was devastated. During their short presence, the Carpenters had captured the hearts and minds of the whole community.

The next owner was Richard Lane who bought the pub as a speculative venture and did quite a lot of work on the building and extensions. To be fair, Richard went along with and probably enjoyed the presence of the lunch club when his other business interests enabled him to be present. Among his developments was a new restaurant and an enlarged skittle alley.

Within a short time, the pub was sold to Ron Fox, a retired airline pilot, and wife Hazel. It was their first venture into the licensed trade but they made a pretty good fist of it. They loved having the lunch club and gave it a lot of support. The club continued to prosper, and, there was as yet, no sign of decline in its popularity.

Ron and Hazel had so taken to Burtle that when a house they liked came up for sale, they bought it. The pub was once more on the market. The new owners were Alan and Nita Roberts who were a little perplexed by the phenomenon of the lunch club. Nevertheless, they gave it guarded support, particularly Nita. Club numbers had reduced as some of the older members passed on and some younger ones had married and moved away. For several years the Christmas lunch had been in the skittle alley and then in the new pub restaurant. Most of the original organisers and helpers now qualified to become beneficiaries and the village hall venue needed a lot of labour. The party continued to be held in the now enlarged and much upgraded skittle alley.

Alan and Nita embarked on a massive programme of extensions in the late '80's during the boom period. The now enormous premises could hold and feed several hundred people at a time, trade relied very largely on cars, mini buses and coaches.

Among the visitors to the lunchclub were the occasional oddballs. One such was a chap recently moved into a cottage in Edington. He had been a clever engineer, working on helicopters but had developed a taste for cider and, we imagine, had thereby lost his job. He would turn up in what could most charitably be described as fancy dress. Old uniforms, funny hats and tooting on cardboard horns usually associated with childrens' Christmas parties. His wife must have had a terrible time, he would nick anything from his home to sell for cash in order to buy cider. He was a thin, wispy sort of build with a straggly ginger beard and soon acquired the nickname of 'catweasel'! There was no harm in him, he was more to be pitied. Cider can be a good servant but an extremely bad master when not under control. He eventually disappeared from the district, last seen in a Salvation Army hostel in Bristol.

The Summer Outings

With the best will in the world and even taking into account the healthy thirsts and appetites on hand in Burtle, the cash was no longer exhausted each year by the Christmas party alone. It was decided to run a Summer outing with everything found, lunch and tea, helpers to assist the infirm. A nice touch on several occasions was the use of a lovely old vintage coach from Wells driven by Charlie Talbot a regular driver on Bristol Tramways Bus Co.

Charlie had been the driver of the first service bus in Burtle, always arriving early each morning, he parked his bus up Robins Lane by the church. He had not been there long when a young girl from the nearby council houses asked whether he would like a cup of tea. That is how he met Arthur Baker and family and the start of a lasting friendship and a long time love affair with the village.

Nothing was shirked on the outings, the all day fixture was soon supplemented by a half day venture and an evening mystery tour. Car drivers would follow the coach with any pensioners who could not get seats on the coach and the helpers. No wonder that our local doctor once told me that Burtle did not need the welfare state, they had had their own for years! Age was no barrier to mischief, I once took a photo of Jim Hooper and Viv Moxey in their mid seventies, climbing a fence into an orchard by the tea room at Horner, near Porlock, to fill their pockets with "scrumped" apples whilst on one of these outings.

Sadly, the people who were running the lunch club were quickly becoming the beneficiaries, some passed away and the youngsters were getting married and having to move away to find work. The biggest single blow to the club was the tragic, premature death of Bill Reece, he had taken early retirement and was greatly looking forward to continued involvement. The club continued on a reduced basis but when Bill Vowles passed away the fund was used up and the club itself just faded away.

With the loss of Bill Reece, Bill Vowles, Harold Hill and Arthur Baker, the heart of the club was extinguished after some twenty wonderful years. However much we mourn its demise, it is, sadly, unlikely that it will ever be resurrected. A part of the Burtle "welfare state" just went!

I am very proud to have been involved with the Saturday lunch club, even if my part in it was rather peripheral. My business entailed a great of travel but I always made sure that I did not miss the main events. I took photos of almost every senior citizen and filmed the activities to justify my existence! It was an honour and a privilege, to enjoy the action along with so many worthy characters.

The village hall, like so many pre-war, were ex- army huts often made by Harry Hebditch of Martock and opened in 1939. Back row; 1) Mrs. Elsie Parsons, 2) Mrs. Frank Lockyer, 3) Mrs. Lucie Moxey, 4) Winsome Lee, 5) Mrs. Arthur Cox, 6) Mrs. Gilbert Grant, 7) Renee Moxey, 8) Mrs. Ivor Coombes, 9) Mrs. Tucker, 10) Mrs. Arthur Tratt, 11) Mrs. Ken Rice, 12) Mrs. Wesley Stone, Mrs. Frank Cox. Front row; 1) Mrs. Arthur Beakes, 2) Mrs. George Lee, 3) Miss Taylor, 4) Mrs Eva Vowles, 5) Mrs. Buchan, 6) Mrs. Bessie Butt, 7) Mrs. Rowland Norris and Mrs. Frank (Nacky) Lee. In front; Mary Stone. (Mrs. E. Bell)

The June 27th, 1911 Coronation festivities were celebrated in style in Burtle. Decorating the Marquee ready for the big day. (J. Heal)

Waiting for the procession to start outside Coombes's Burtle Inn. (J. Heal)

A celebratory arch is erected over the road. (P. Parsons)

The procession underway With Gatcome Farm (then White Rose Farm) in the background. (P. Parsons)

The Horses were followed by the foot soldiers in the shape of the four year old Burtle Silver Band. (P. Parsons).

Back in the marquee the children pose in their incredibly decorative best clothes. (J. Heal)

The 1937 Coronation was also great celebration. Standing at back; 1) Mrs. Queenie Lee, 2) Mrs. George Lee, 3) Mrs Fisher, 4) George Giblett, 5) Frank Cox. Seated on left; 1) May Groves, 2) Minnie Groves, 3) Ern Packer, 4) Bessie Packer, 5) Mrs. Winnie Lee, 6) Mrs. W. Groves, 7) Walter Groves, 8) Metford Whitcombe, 9) John Beakes, 10) Thurza Lee, 11) Lorna Norris, 12) Minnie Lee (holding Harold). Seated right; 1) George Shepherd, 2) Mrs. Edith Shepherd, 3) Eileen Fisher, 4) Mrs. Met Watts, 5) Met Watts, 6) Mary Jane Watts, 7) Harry Moxey, 8) Mrs. Tidball, 9) Mrs. Ted Tratt. (Mrs. I. Storey)

Standing; 1) Alf Highnam, 2) Mrs. Fisher, 3) Mrs. Joyce Coombes, 4) Arthur Tratt, 5) Jack Leigh, 6) Mrs. Arthur Cox, 7) Arthur Cox. Seated on left; 1) Gilbert Grant, 2) (at rear) Harry Cox, 3) Tom Mogg, 4) Hubert Rice, 5) Frank Lee (junior), 6) Bob Moxey, 7) Mrs. (Nipper) Cox, 8) 'Nipper' Cox, 9) ? , 10) Charlie Norris, 11) end of table?. Seated on right; 1) Jim Packer, 2) Charlie Sandford, 3) Mrs. Gladys Sandford, 4) Vince Norris, 5) Bill Vowles, 6) ? , 7) ? , 8) ?? , 9) child? , !0) mother of child, 11) ? , 12) Peering over 10), Far right Frank (Nacky) Lee. (I. Storey)

Standing and in background; 1) Walt Tratt, 2) Mrs. W. Groves, 3) Met Watts, 4) W. Groves, 5) Mrs. George (Emmie) Lee, 6) Mrs. Queenie Lee, 7) John Beakes, 8) George Giblett, 9) Mrs. Vowles, 10) Mrs Queenie Tratt, 11) ?? , 12) Ivor Coombes, 13 l) Mrs. Ivor (Joyce) Coombes, 14) Miss Hembury. Seated on left; 1) Alec Cox, 2) Percy Cox, 3) Rowland Moxey, 4) Mrs. Rowland Moxey, 5) Mrs Betty Fewings, 6) Mrs. Eileen Bell (nee Grant), 7) Mrs. Mary Bell (nee Fewings), 8) Miss May Cox, 9) Bessie Tippetts (nee Cox), 10) Mrs. Len Hayes, 11 Len Hayes, Seated On right; 1) Ern (Shocky) Grant, 2) Geoff Moxey, 3) Ken Rice, 4) Harry Cox, 5) Percy Ducket, 6) Allan Moxey, 7) Ray Court, 8) Winsome Lee, 9) Mrs. Syd Gardener (nee Lee), 10) Mrs. Reg Grant. (I. Storey)

Before and during the war Lysander aircraft from Weston Zoyland airfield used to tow targets for gunnery practice, this one came adrift and landed in Burtle. As always in Burtle someone turned up with a camera! Left to right; 1) Ralph Cox, 2) Rene Moxey 3) Kath Hooper, 4) Steve Pocock, 5)   6) Bert Whitcombe, 7) Mrs. Gilbert (Agnes) Grant, 8)   ??? , 9)   ???   , 10) Willie Pocock, 11) Mrs Allan (Lucie) Moxey, 12) Vince Norris, 13) Nelson Moxey, 14) Tom ????, 15) Frank Lee, 16) Allan Moxey, 17) Frank Cox, 18) Ray (Col.) Cox, 19) Vic Tidball, 20) Alec (Bunny) Cox, 21) Ern (Jumper) Lee.

Burtle Football team about 1930; Back row 1) Frank (Nacky) Lee, 2) George Giblett, 3) Alec (Bunny) Cox, Frank Lee, 4) Seward Rice, 5) Alf Highnam. Middle row 1) Wilf (Pickles) Parsons, 2) Ivor Meader, 3) Viv Moxey, 4) Ken Rice, 5) Art Watts. Front row 1) Ted Fisher, 2)   ? , 3) Ray (Col.) Cox, 4) Frank Cox, Charlie Norris. (Mrs. E. Bell)

125)Burtle Football Team about 1938. Back row; 1) Wilf Parsons, 2) Seward Rice, 3) Frank Lee , 4) Art Watts, 5) Ern Lee , 6) Viv Moxey, 7) Ken Rice, 8) Kneeling Alec Cox, 9) George Giblett, 10) Frank (Nacky) Lee. Front row; 1) Ted Fisher, 2) Bill Fisher, 3) Ray Cox, 4) Frank Cox, 5) ??????. (F. Parsons)

The 'A' team. In the past at least one skittle team was necessary to make a country pub a viable concern, two teams was a bonus, two winning teams gave a pub an enviable status. The Burtle Inn was in the happy position in the 1954/5 season their three teams 'cleaning up' in the Puriton league and in the Highbridge League. Back row; 1) Walt Clarke, 2) Henry Seery, 3) Percy Parsons, 4) Vic Leigh. Front row; 1) Met Watts, 2) Den Thorne, 3) Wilf Parsons, 4) Sid Gardener (landlord), 5) George Wilkins, 6) Lenny Baker, 7) Harry Moxey, 8) John Rice. (J. Rice)

The 'B' Team. Back row; 1) Bill Wilton, 2) A Baker, 3) Harold Lee, Front row; 1)Jim Hooper, 2) Frank Lee, 3) Dennis Walker, 4) Arnold Tucker, 5) Len Hayes, 6) Reg Norris, 7) Viv Moxey, 8) Wyndham Puddy. (J. Rice)

The Burtle Inn skittlers capped the foregoing successes by also winning the Highbridge league! Back row; 1) Wyndham Puddy, 2) H. Seery, 3) Percy Parsons, 4) H. Cox. Front row; 1) Ern Millet 2) Sid Gardener (landlord), 3) Met Watts, 4) George Wilkins, 5) Lennie Baker, 6) Len Hayes, 7) Dennis Walker, 8) John Rice. (J. Rice)

The Railway Hotel also had their successes. The traditional skittle supper about 1951/2, usually supplied by the landlord (Norman Moxey) and the silverware proudly displayed on the table all laid out in the old skittle alley.

More success in 1962, winning the Puriton League knockout cup. Standing; 1) Arnold Tucker, 2) Vic Leigh, 3) Frank Lee, 4) George Wilkins, 5) John Rice, 6) Ted Bishop, 7) Ray Bates (landlord), 8) Harry Cox. Kneeling Viv Moxey and George Baker. (J. Rice)

Very successful pram races were staged for several years. The participants and spectators assemble outside The Railway Hotel before the extensive alterations.

The costumes were taken very seriously and a lot of detail and effort went into making them. It was not just for children, most able (and some not so able!) bodied adults took part.

Frank Lee cuddling up to daughter in law, Margaret.

The school is always a focal point in any village. This 1893 photo shows a section of the pupils with Henry James Kidd, Headmaster.

The whole School about 1918 with the Rev. Leigh Phillips and Mr. Kidd, headmaster.

A class of about 1926 with Head teacher Alfie Wilcox and assistant teacher, Miss Short. Standing; 1) Geoffrey Moxey, 2) Frank Vowles, 3) Nelson Moxey, 4) Eric Cox, 5) Eileen Grant, 6) Minnie Lee, 7) Bessie Cox, 8) Evelyn Fisher, 9) Thurza Lee, 10) Dorothy Tratt, 11) Celia Denning, 12) Grace Denning, 13) Reginald Biffen, 14) Maxwell Young. Sitting; 1) Raymond Fisher, 2) Robert Moxey, 3) Margaret Lee, 4) Beatrice Fisher, 5) Lorna Ducket, 6) Lorna Norris, 7) Hilda Moxey, 8) Vera Rice, 9) Agnes Tidball, 10) Kathleen Hooper, 11) Elsie Packer, 12) Dorothy Cox, 13) Walter Cox.

Burtle School 1947, the numbers were falling by this time. Back row: 1) George Baker, 2) Ron Cox, 3) Jean Carp, 4) Fred Cox, 5) John Cox, 6) Alan Vowles, 7) Trevor Gillard, 8) Ruth Lee, 9) Margaret Sandford, 10) Eileen Lee. Standing; 1) Mrs. Williams (Head), 2) Esme James, 3) Kathleen Parsons, 4) Pat Moxey, 5) Geoff Parsons, 6) John Gooding, 7) Michael Thyer, 8) Delphine Tratt, 9) 3ean Cox, 10) Miss King (Teacher). Sitting: Valerie Cook, 3) Doreen Court, 4l Marlene Harris, 5) Esme Gillard, 6) Ivy Cox, 7) Sheila Vowles, 8) Sheila Moxey, 9) Mary Court, 10) Betty Court, 11) Ron Vowles, 12) Ray Boyer. Front row: 1) Tony Moxey, 2) Michael Harris, 3) Rex Moxey, 4) Ken Thyer, 5) Rod Gooding, 6) John Moxey, 7) Clive Moxey, 8) Graham Thyer, 9) Ray Baker, 10) Ken Bell.

A press cutting from the closure of the school, three of the pupils played Auld Lang Syne.

There were many novel ways of raising funds for village activities. Doreen Baker really getting down to it in the egg rolling race in 1970.

Derek Cox working up a fair head of steam! The shop ran out of Elastoplast for sore noses!

Chapter 4

BURTLE FOLK AND FAMILIES

Lucy Moxey: Centenarian

This is an interview carried out on August 9th 1975 by Pat Moxey with his Grandmother who was a month short of her 98th birthday at that time. She was the widow of Allan Moxey, founder of the Burtle Band, and lived to be almost 102. Two of her sons, Vivian and Norman became bandmasters as did her grandson, Jim. Her maiden name was Norris.

I remember my first day at school because me sister Frances took me and she went to the top of the school and I went down the bottom with the infants. My heart were in me mouth and after a bit I shouted out, "Frances", and the school-master

said "Frances is alright" and I never made another sound. I was just five at the time, they wouldn't take 'em before. I was born down Collin's Field. Your granfer was born in Catcott Burtle and when Catcott Burtle school were done away wi' and turned into the milk factory, your granfer came up to the new school at Edington Burtle. We were in the same class, the boys did sit behind and the girls in front.

There was ten of us in family, there was Bill, Sam, Bob, Oliver, and Rufus, five boys. Then there was Elizabeth, she died, Emily, Frances, Lucy (herself) and another Elizabeth. Frances were took bad down Burnham, opposite the

Mrs. Lucy Ann Moxey. Lived to be 101.

153

Manor gardens and I got the Doctor to send her out home so I could look after her. I couldn't stay with her 'cos I were cheesemaking. She died next morning, Bill died exactly a year later almost to the minute, I think 'twas the fifth of March. Bill was sixty something and Frances were fifty one. I was the youngest all but one. Elizabeth were the youngest, she were ninety three when she died, Emily were eighty seven.

I can just remember my old grandmother, my mother's mother. She came in from her cottage when my mother was nursing me in the rocking chair and said "Wha's the matter with the little maid"? Mother said "She've got a headache, I shall lay her down on her back on the sofa," and that's what she done.

I remember Bertha Pollard, she and I did sit together in school and what I didn't know she did and what she didn't know I did so we did copy one another. Mr Kidd (the schoolmaster) come along and said "What be you doing, copying"? I said "Yes sir". He said "Well, don't do it again and hold up yer hand". I held up me hand and he give me a smack wi' the cane. I started crying and kept on and on, bye and bye he come and put his arm round me and said, "Never mind Luce, just go on and do your work".

I remember when we used to dance out in the orchard when the band were learning, our dad (Allan Moxey, her husband) did get me to show the rest how to dance, he wanted 'em to learn the square dancing. I conducted the dancing and he did do the band.

I was twenty three when I got married out Burtle church. The choir were there and Mr Kidd had all the school children out and lined the church path both sides and throwed primroses over me. I were nearly overcome and me uncle who were giving me away said "Buck up, Luce", 'cos he saw 'twas a bit too much for me.

Your granfer worked for his father for a while, then we went up to Pennard where he worked as a signalman for some time. When he returned to Burtle he worked for granfy Moxey for some time before farming on his own account at Glebe Farm. His brothers and sisters were Flo Grant, Reggie Grant's mother; Lucinda (Coombes), Agnes, Annie and Kate. (The latter also lived to over 100) His brothers were Clifford and Hebdon.

When we started farming on our own account we bought an army horse, ol' Bob, father (husband) fetched 'un from Taunton. I used to go down Burnham and Highbridge delivering stuff, One day we went down Worston Lane and there were a great big tree cut down and the cut part were showing out towards the road. That blooming horse, he shied at that tree and our Viv pulled his head right round but he kept on going towards the ditch and tipped all the stuff out into the ditch. I bruised me ribs and couldn't stand upright, broke and cracked I don't know how many eggs. A lot of people come running and helped us get out and they went on at Tom Hale, a cattle dealer, for leaving a tree like that. We drove on into the auction and I told the auctioneer what had happened. He gave it out that we'd had an accident and do you know what, we made more of they cracked eggs than some of 'em did of their whole ones!

Granfy Norris said a little ditty at the carol singers' supper down the school one year:

It's a clever world that's as round as a wheel
The sting of death we all must feel.
If life was a thing that money could buy,
The rich would live but the poor would die.
But god in his mercy has ordered it so.
That the rich and the poor together must go.

I was living over Weston when I first saw a lady riding a bicycle. We used to walk everwhere before we had bicycles. When we were working at the peat, mother an' all of us, we used to walk from Collin's Field up past Shapwick Station, work all day and then walk back at night. I was quite young then.

The harvest homes were free for all parishioners but they;d have a collection and you could give what you like. They were always a good do.

Your father, Norman, was always very quiet. When he was going to school he'd walk along under the hedge not looking left or right. He were always a good child. I bought him a new straw hat for Summer 'cos he were always out in hot sun. One day I heard such peals of laughter I runned out to see what had happened. He'd gi'ed his hat to the pigs and they were shaking o'un like billy-o and he were laughing his head off. I told 'un that's the last straw hat you'll have bought for 'ee. Soon afterwards, Mrs Alfred Norris that lived down the bottom of the garden said "Have you lost your little boy"? I said "Where is 'er"? "Come on down yer", she said, "an' I'll show 'ee". He and the pigs was up top o' the dung heap, all fast asleep.

P. Parsons, Railwayman

Percy Parsons worked on the Somerset and Dorset Joint Railway and often found himself in charge at one or other of the small stations on the moors. Here are some of his experiences, mainly those at Shapwick Station which was actually much nearer Westhay.

'The main turf dealers were the Eclipse Peat Company, Godwins and Garvins, then there were others likes Phelps's with others like Paynes and Charlie Sandford. Whereas Eclipse would load 10 or 12 a day Charlie and the smaller dealers would load 3 or 4. Each morning or the day before they'd come in and say what they wanted. Eclipse and Godwins would want 10 or 12 each and the smaller people like Paynes might want 3 or 4. There were a lot of small dealers and producers and there weren't enough wagons available for all of 'em to have what they wanted, anyway the yards weren't big enough to take all the waggons that were wanted. We had to split the number of waggons between morning and afternoon so as to clear the loaded waggons and the train could bring down another batch of empties with the goods train from Evercreech in the afternoon to make up their daily total requirement. Although the peat trade was the biggest user there was other business as well. A lot of the empty box waggons used to come down from the old Southern line. We often had to push the empties in by hand because the train was facing the other way. You could fly shunt 'em in but t'wadde'n advisable because the engine would be on the main line and the waggons had to go into the siding.

I've knowed 'em come to fighting over waggons, some of the crafty buggers would throw a hundred or two hundred turves into several waggons and claim they were their waggons. Then somebody that didn't have a waggon would come along and chuck 'em out and claim the waggon for theirselves and the situation would dissolve into fisticuffs. That was just after the war when the

Right, Mr. and Mrs. Percy Parsons; Left, Betty Moxey.

156

peat job started to boom.

When they started cutting the branch lines 'twas like pruning a tree, if you cut 'un too hard you kill the whole bloody thing.

Between the wars I saw railcars running up and down the Castle Cary to Bruton line but I can't remember any on the Glastonbury to Highbridge line. They used to run the push and pull from Wells to Bridgwater one time and then it was Wells to Burnham. You know, the driver did drive the train to the destination and then, on the return, he got into the special push and pull coach and he could regulate the speed of the train and the stops from the front by a sort of remote control. On normal days we had 2 coaches on going to Bridgwater and on market days we put a third one on and also on a Saturday for people going shopping or to the pictures.

They did have containers which were used for farm and furniture removals and things like that. When I was relieving at Shapwick I had a farm removal over to South Wales, that was when Walt Cook was in the signal box there. I was relieving up there for some time and there was this gentleman from Shapwick, he brought down all sorts of stuff, hens, runs, coops, machinery like hay tedders and swath turners. I loaded 'em on and roped 'em down, he had 2 or 3 trucks of hay and the only time I had any help was on the Friday night when he moved out when he brought his cattle down, he had 4 or 5 trucks of cattle and some relief porters came in to help load the cattle and form the train up. I can't remember who it was now.

Going back to those containers, the Bridgwater Brick Company used to load them with bricks and tiles and things like that. If people were moving house they could have a container and fill it with their furniture and the container would be delivered the other end. They were demountable.

This was a book of regulations and charges etc, I handed mine in but this is one another one that was sitting around so I acquired it! All the types of waggons available are listed for almost every possible job. There were demountable containers and the like but the system was never really developed to meet modern needs. There were refrigerated meat waggons, one for bicycles so there were trucks for all occasions but nobody brought it up to date. We used to have a lot of containers at Glastonbury for Clark's Shoes. The railways were the common carriers for every thing.

I remember Bert Bartlett and Fred Wilton, they wanted to start up a general carriers business with a small lorry they used for peat etc. The approached the railways asking permission and the answer came back that the ministry would grant them a licence provided the railway could have first claim on them when their own lorries could not cope.

Pickfords used to load their traffic at Nine Elms, London and we used to have to sort out the deliveries at Edington to local warehouses etc.

All the crossing cottages like Sharpham, Stonend and the Huntspill were busy when the trains handled all the freight and passengers. There used to be enough traffic to warrant a person to be there all the time. You take the Catcott crossing, old man Cox (Arthur) would be up there a dozen times a day and there would be others as well. The Highnams, Frank and Glad, went on the Huntspill crossing after Nipper Cox went. Nipper were Henry Cox's father.

Huntspill crossing gates were a design of their own, the signals there worked off a pulley on the gates. Which ever gate you put across the line last, you had give the last yard an extra shove so that the pulley system worked the signal. That was the only one I knew like that. The other gates had separate levers but that one was sort of automatic.

When the buses came around they picked up at the station, the church and the Burtle Inn then on to Catcott. When they started there were 4 or 5 a day then the buses dropped off and it forced people to get their own cars, there weren't any choice. The railways were at a disadvantage in that they had to provide and maintain their own track. There were big lorries hauling from the Peatworks on roads that were never made for it. They've got to keep building up the roads to accommodate the lorries going up and down. It was always a wonder to me how the railway track stood up to it on the peat, of course it was built on faggots.

We used to have the stockfeed potatoes come into Shapwick after the war, some of 'em had purple stain on the outside of the bags, if they were loose they were sprayed over the top. People did eat 'em though and there were bags and bags of 'em perched on the engine going up and down the line. We used to keep a list of who wanted them, they were cheap food! I think we used to make about a shilling a bag on 'em, we'd pay five shillings and sell 'em for six.

There used to be a goods shed at Edington where farmers could pick up cattle cake etc and we kept the records in a big book. This was mainly Bibby's and Silcox. There was one at Glastonbury but I'm not sure what there was at Shapwick. Most of the stations had cattle pens but I don't think Ashcott did or Bason Bridge because it was near Highbridge. We used to load quite a few horses at Edington for old man Cowley at Holywell House, he'd average about two a week. He used to buy horses that were a bit run down and feed 'em up and flog 'em on again. I remember one time he said well I've had enough and he were going to sell out, Walt Cook were on one turn and I were on the other and we loaded ten horse boxes one day and some of 'em had two horses in stalls. They partitions were heavy to lug about though, they were big sturdy things and if you were on your own, well they wouldn't do it today, in fact the health and safety wouldn't allow 'e to do it.

When I was a junior we had a truck for delivery to various places around and the stationmaster would say you'd better go with the driver, and if you went down Greinton or somewhere like that you'd have to carry up fifteen or twenty stone steps. We used to manage but today they'd have to have a pulley or summat. Again if you were sheeting hay, if you had a truck that was loaded neatly you could probably get away with two sheets on 'un, one each end. When the trusses were cut out with a bloody old hayknife they could be all shapes and you had to be wary pounding about on 'em 'cos you could soon push the side right out and that would be it. They sheets used to weigh heavy and very often you were on your own to do it. you'd throw the ropes over and then you'd go and ask the stationmaster to come and help 'e strain 'em 'cos you couldn't do it on you own.

I remember down at Shapwick one time, we used to have the sheets come in truckloads, twenty, thirty or even forty in a truck. They used to come down from the sheet shop at Worcester, where they did go in for repair. I remember one day we had two trucks come in there and the weather was very hot and I suppose these sheets had been re-worked and tarred up and put in the waggons, the tar had melted and during the night the tar had cooled and the sheets were one solid block and we had to send 'em back. Now I know why they'm called tarpaulins! I suppose they had to warm 'em up and spread 'em out and sand 'em down or something.

There was a strict formula for positioning waggons in a train, there was a hell of a lot to it. The old hands could walk along the box vans and tell whether they were empty by tapping on the side. We used to get a lot of trucks come off the Southern line and we did open the doors and have a quick shufty and I remember one these waggons had something back in the corner and I got up and had a look and that was three Post Office letter bags, this was in February. I took these bags out and I thought what the hell be they doing in there so I took 'em up to the Postmaster up Glastonbury. Some time later when the local postman was empying the postbox down by Shapwick station I asked whether he knew what happened about the three bags, "Oh that was Christmas Mail, cards and that". I expect that somewhere where they handled a lot of traffic somebody said put 'em in here and I'll tell 'em where they are and didn't tell anybody. Another time a truck turned up down Highbridge loaded up with bacon, ham and all sorts for the Yeovil area, this was on a Saturday and we had to get the waggon back to Templecombe. This was probably caused by something simple like losing the truck labels through a faulty label clip.

Chistopher Denning's Move

In the early 1930's, Farmer Christopher Denning moved from Catcott Burtle Farm to Priddy Road Farm, about 5 miles north of Wells. The cattle were taken on foot by Ern Watts and George Giblet. The most direct route was along the road to Westhay, the road past the Turnpike Cottage, east through Westhay and Godney Moors, Fenney Castle and on through Wells. This would take many hours, dairy cows have to be milked, possibly en route, all in all it would be a very long day.

The farm equipment travelled by horse and cart and motor lorry. Cart horses were discouraged from using a pace faster than walking as it was reckoned to damage their legs. On those terms it would take quite a long day to make the journey in one direction, quite a marathon to complete the round trip.

It was and still is the custom for farms to change hands on Lady day, March 25th. or Michaelmass day, September 29th. It is a formidable exercise to move farms, there is much to do besides the physical movement of goods and chattels. For things to go smoothly there has to be full co-operation between ingoing and outgoing farmers and there could be any number of moves involved. It is not as if it is a straight swop between just two farmers but a frenetic mosaic of inter-farm activity extending throughout the whole country and everything has to be moved in the course of a few days.

The requirements of any two farms are rarely identical, farms of similar size in different locations can vary greatly in what is produced on them and consequently what equipment is required to farm them. Farmer Denning was moving from the low-lying peat moors with their lacework of ditches to the high, limestone soils and drystone walls of the Mendips, an area a 'good overcoat colder' than Burtle. Each farm must have a valuation by an auctioneer trusted by both parties, purchase and sale of equipment to and from the incoming and outgoing parties, in some cases an auction sale of surplus goods.

In a dry Summer, the lowlying moorland would

Farmer Christopher Denning enjoying his Christmas dinner in the hall at the age of 93!

produce very heavy shears of hay whereas the higher ground would tend to dry out, leading to a lighter crop. A wet Summer could spell disaster to the farmers on the peat lands, the soft nature of wet peat making it impossible to get onto the land. Many farmers in the Poldens region considered it necessary to have a mixture of both types of land to be viable.

When Farmer Denning left Burtle, he kept some fields in Burtle Moor, close to the River Brue and he had built two ricks of hay on the higher land along the river bank. He now needed this hay to feed his stock at Priddy, but a problem had arisen in the form of higher than usual floods, effectively cutting off any normal access to the ricks. There was well over half a mile of deep floodwater between the hay the nearest hard and accessible dry ground. Burtle folks are nothing if not resourceful, so the following is how the job was tackled.

The only safe way to reach the ricks was by boat and there was no shortage of turf boats in Burtle. Arriving at the ricks, the first job was to cut and tie the hay into trusses. The hay was cut into 'flops' about three feet square using a hay knife, layers about one foot deep formed the trusses which were then tied with binder cord and stacked alongside the ricks. This work was done by Roly Norris and Freddie Coombes, two Burtle men. Geoff Moxey undertook to ferry the trusses on a turf boat to the point on Green Drove above the water level. A truss would weigh around a hundred weight and the turf boat would take twelve at a time. Four in the bottom of the boat and eight on the top, a load of about half a ton on each trip.

The trusses of hay were stacked on the side of Green Drove, just above the water line and sheeted down. In those days the drove was not stoned, preventing any motorised road transport reaching the stacked hay. Mr. George Lee and his son Frank loaded the trusses onto waggons, hauled them half a mile up the drove and rebuilt it into a stack on the side of the hard road opposite the church, and, once more sheeted it down.

A week or two later, Mr. Willmott, a carrier from Wells, brought his lorry, picked up the hay and transported it to Mr. Denning at Priddy Road.

The whole exercise had taken over a month's hard work to complete. The amount of labour involved would be unthinkable these days, in those days it would simply have been accepted as just one more job that had to be done. Roly and Freddie would have been glad of the extra work it provided. Incidentally, the hard work did neither of them any harm, they both lived well into their nineties as did farmer Denning!

Evelyn Moxey (& Geoff)

I was born at up at Westham where Ern (Lee) and Edna, me sister, went to live in 1931. I was five when I left there and we moved out to River House Farm. I went to school over Blackford for six months before we moved. I mind as well as anything, coming home from school and they had a lot of stuff loaded on the horse and putt and they sat me up on the top and that's how I travelled out there. We didn't have to come round by road, we went out the drove off the Blackford road.

There's a pumping station on the next drove up and Harry Court used to live up there. Ray Court, his son, went down Burtle Moor Farm, Harry Court's place is gone now, all pulled down. There used to be a pathway across the grounds from River House to Harry Court's place.

Father made the roadway in round the eighteen acres and down to River House from the Mark Road in Burtle. There weren't any roadway there when we went to the farm. Ern Mutter over Wedmore hauled most of the stone with a steam lorry, there was already a bridge over the river.

I remember once when Francis fell into the River Brue and an auntie from Bristol was staying with us. She said he amused her because he didn't cry when he were in the river but when he come out he started crying.

Geoffrey's two years younger than I so I would have been seven when he started school. The way he used to carry on at school, what made me marry that man, I shall never know. He sat up in class and said to Mr Wilcox one morning "I fetched thee milk for thee s'morning, but I bain't goin' to vetch it vor thee no more". Mr Wilcox lived down where George Grundy do live now at Upper White's Farm and he were walking home from school one day and Geoffrey nudged 'un over in the gutter. Alfie Wilcox came from Westhay where there was a lot more Wilcox's.

When Ivor Coombes lived in Hill Farm and 'twas Burtle revel night, brother Tom, he did collect the money over a certain area for the Harvest Home. Mother wanted some sugar, she was making some wine so Tom had to

Geoff and Evelyn Moxey.

go up Ivor Coombes's with this money and I had to go to the shop for some sugar. When I come out of the shop he wad'n about nowhere, he were still in there. So I went down on the corner where there was quite a gang of 'em. There were Frankie Lee, Doris Taylor and the Denning girls. All of a sudden they did start to disperse and there was still no signs of Tom coming out. I walked on back to go in Ivor Coombes's to see if Tom were still in there then Geoffrey came along. Mrs Coombes and Madeline England who lived with 'em like a companion help, came back from Burtle revel where they'd been to get some gingerbread. Mrs Coombes said "Be you waiting for your brother?" I said yes and she said well come on in then. When we got to the door and as she looked round to see me in, she seen Geoffrey. "Is that another of your brothers?" I said no and she said "Oh I'm sorry to have taken you away from him" I said thankyou very much, I were very pleased about it! Geoffrey wanted me to come on home with 'un, he didn't want me to wait for Tom. He wanted to walk home with me, but said I wouldn't, so there. That were the finish of that romance for the time being!

Father milked cows and mother made cheese for so long as I can remember, then she gave it up and Edna took on, when Edna got married then I took on making the cheese. I made cheese for two years, caerphilly that was, we used to send it to Highbridge market. Dad said that he was never going to sell raw milk but the prices got so bad that he had to sell the milk and finish cheese making because he were losing so much a day on cheese.

I remember the Highbridge cheese market, everybody had their cheese down along the floor in rows. The dealers did come there with their borers and bore out the cheese and taste it. They had their dinner going round! Sometimes 'twould only make threepence or fourpence a pound when 'twas auctioned. You couldn't make it pay.

Yet see, I don't like cheese, I would never eat cheese, though I used to make it. I loved the curd when 'twas ready to vat, I could eat that. I remember when we went haymaking and that, we did have our tea in the afternoon, then last thing we used to have supper cos we used to be out haymaking 'til late. When we came in from haymaking once, the mother had supper ready there cos I always used to go out in the haymaking ground although I hated it. They said 'there's a piece of bread and butter you can have Evelyn, 'twere left over from tea'. Well I said that's dry now, I'm going to put some jam on it. So I put some jam on it and I just had one bite and I had to go out and spit it out, they had spread this yer soft caerphilly cheese on it to see whether I would eat it. No, I couldn't eat it.

Tommy Powell used to pick up our milk. He took the afternoon milk down to the old milk factory where he used to cool it overnight. He did pick up the morning milk and take all down to Bason Bridge factory. The creamery business shut down about 1921 when I were seven years old. I couldn't mind much about it. The Burtle creamery couldn't compete with Bason Bridge.

Dad bought the place up Hurst Farm where Harry Cox lives now and they all went up there except brother Tom and me, we stayed on down there farming. Dad kept the big field where you go in round on the track. Thats how we came to lose all our cattle with foot and mouth when we first got married because dad had all his young things in there, beautiful friesian heifers just calving down and they all had to be killed because he had foot and mouth. All ours had to go, because we had to go through 'em to go in and out of our place. We hadn't been farming long. That were when the war were on.

We were married in 1941 and our Rex were born in 1942. Francis were farming up Hurst, they lived in part of the house, 'twer divided in two then, father and mother lived in t'other part. Tom and I did carry on farming down Riverhouse, that were our business. Then when Tom got married and we got married, we parted that out, see. Dad wanted Tom to have that farm so we were the ones that had to get out. Tom didn't have it in the finish, he didn't want it, see. He went off down Mark to live. That's how we come to buy Hill Farm.

Francis let Harry Cox have Hurst Farm and he went up Station Farm. Father sold Riverhouse to Gilbey Sweet, he had it cheap. There were fifty acres of good ground with the farm and I think he got £11,000 for it.

None of us went out to work 'cos dad wouldn't let us, see, he wanted us home. When I sat for the scholarship I just failed to pass. Lorna Duckett, Ernie Duckett's daughter, she and I were the same age, and we were very great friends when they lived out Liberty Farm. We sat together, see, but she were that much younger than me, my birthday were in January and hers was in April, eighth of April was her birthday. Anyway, the first year we sat, she passed and I just failed. She had a step mother and they would not let her go on to the grammar school. I didn't think that were fair.

The next year, Mr Wilcox, our teacher wanted me to sit again, he said I should definitely pass if I sat. Well, we sent in the papers and all like that and I went for this exam and they said I were three days too old, because me birthday were on the 28th of January, see, and if I'd been born on the first of February, I should have been alright. So anyway, then Mr Wilcox, he came down to see dad, he wanted me to go on to be a teacher, but he wouldn't let me go, see. The rest had to stay home and work so I had to.

When our boys were growing up, we remembered all this. I always said, let 'em do what they want to and then they can't turn round another day and say I would have done so and so if it werd'n for you. That were the thing with our Rex you see, he stayed home on the farm till he were eighteen. Of course he were friendly with Ken Thyer and all they, they did go off weekends and everything. He did have some time off and he stayed home till he were eighteen. Barry were never interested in the farming, he never milked a cow in his life, he were always keen on electricity. He used to go out in the fowls' house and fix up batteries and lights and things, see. He went out to Hinckley Point as an apprentice electrician in 1960 and he've been there ever since. There's only one man been there longer.

We had the first milking machine that came into Burtle and Rex and his father did milk the cows. He said to his father on a Wednesday he wanted to go to town to have a haircut, so he went off to town, see. He went with Freddie Fear, anyway, he went in so-called to have this haircut. He didn't say any more about it till the Friday morning when he said, if I go in Cellophane 'smorning, I can get a job. Geoffrey said "How do you know you can?" "Because I went in there Wednesday and they said if I come in 'smorning they'd give me a job". That was why he'd gone in there. Well, anyway, I said to 'un I ain't going to stop 'ee doing it, but do you think you'll like working in a factory after working out in the open air all the time? Oh yes, he would like it, so he went in there, see.

While he were in there somebody or other told 'un that if he did go to Bristol, he could learn a trade under the government training scheme. Geoffrey said, "He wanted to go in there, now make 'un stay there" I said I'm not going to, let 'un do what he wants to do then he can't turn round another day and say you wouldn't let me do that. Now he is in demand as a welder all over the country.

Well, I said to Geoffrey, if they boys idden interested in farming, I don't see any sense in we milking all these cows. "Well, if we sell the cows", he said, "I shall go to work. I shall get a job". So he heard of this job going on the railway, and put in for it an' got it. That were in 1960. We had a sale and sold all the milking cows except we kept two for the house and then I did wean calves with the milk we didn't use in the house. Then I had some sows I did keep and farrow they down, see. That's how we went on, wi' he working on the line and me on the farm.

Geoffrey's father, Freddie, used to live down Lower Whites Farm, milking cows and turf digging. Geoffrey stayed home with his father, farming, turf digging and some casual work. When he sold the farm to Mr Ponsillo, he come up and lived with we at Burtle Hill. He was a very keen church man and were in with the school. He was a church warden and he helped with the school for years. Anything wrong out school, they did come for he, well there, he done a lot of work for the school and the church. We got a certificate here now that he had given to him for I don't know many years he went Sunday school and never missed once. He were over eighty and he'd had a heart attack and the doctor said he had to give up all that work. He stayed wi' we until he died, he went to church one morning and dropped dead at the church door.

Geoffrey's brother, Gordon, weren't interested in farming. He passed his scholarship and went to Dr Morgans but when he left school, he couldn't get a job anywhere. Eventually he went down Bason Bridge milk factory as a packer boy at fifteen shillings a week. He worked there over forty seven years and finished up as the milk checker.

When Geoffrey's father gave up as church warden they wanted he to take it on but he wouldn't. Then they wanted I to go on the church council. I told Kath Hooper if she would go on it, I would, so we both went on it at the same time, then I gived it up and Kath were still on it. We'm still friends though.

John Rice's Story

John Rice is a man who is true to his roots and beliefs, which emanate from such humble beginnings that they are difficult to reconcile with our comparative affluence some sixty years later. His story is one of a general state of happiness and humour in the face of hardship and deprivation. The cottage at Stone End was some two hundred yards down a peat track off the Chilton moor road.

"I were born in the crossing cottage at Stone End at the bottom of the Cossington bank in Chilton moor on the branch line to Bridgwater. I were only a few months old when we moved up to Chilton drove crossing on the Highbridge line. Bob Elver and his family moved in behind we. Mr and Mrs Walt Clark was in the house before we were, he did walk the line and she did do the gates. I lived all me school days up Chilton Drove crossing. For lighting we had little oil lamps and candles, I still got they old oil lamps out in the garage now. Then we got an Alladin table lamp wi' a mantle, you did pump 'un up and he gi'ed out a good light an' a fair bit o' heat too. Thees try to tell a youngster today

John Rice.

how things were an' they 'ont believe 'ee. With respect, they 'ant got no idea what twer like. Used to have a candle stuck in a jam jar to go to bed with. We used to have an old copper for to heat the clothes washing water and a gurt water tank to catch the rainwater off the roof. That water were nice and soft an' mother liked that for clothes washing. Mother cooked on an old black range and I still got her old flat irons she had for ironing and which she used to heat up on the hot plate of the range.

They cottages were very small and pokey with no proper toilet, electricity or water. Father was a porter on the line at Edington station and mother looked after the crossing gates. She got four hours off a week and a pass on the train for going shopping in the town. The porter would come out to relieve on the gates and she would go of on the train and come back on the train dinner time.

Our toilet was an Elsan bucket in a little outside shed. The railway supplied the Elsan acid in five gallon drums to go in the bucket to make it hygenic, 'twouldn't half sting your ass if you got splashed. To empty the bucket we would dig a hole out in the drove or down the side of the line an' sloush it in 'un and then vill 'un in. Our water was brought by train every other day in four five gallon churns and emptied they into a metal tank wi' a tap in 'un that was supplied by the railway an' sot up on a wooden 'oss in the house. When the train did come out to Edington station he had an hour to spare so he used to bring out our water and then carry on up to Stone End with the Elver's water.

Chilton Drove were only the same size as Stone End but at least 'twer closer to the village and on the hard road. Thic house is still there but Stone End have been demolished. Old Albie Wilton bought nearly a mile of line with the crossing cottage for thirty five poun'. 'E made a lot of money flogging the ballast off the track.

I remember the night the late train come out of Bridgwater, he were a goods train and always fully loaded because it brought all the day's goods from Bridgwater station. He runned into Baker Coombes's herd of cows down by Stone End. Thur was guts and blood and bits everywhere, the meat got all tangled up in the engine. The bull had unhung the gate and let 'em out on the line. Twer dark see and the driver couldn't see 'em, killed a fair few of 'em. Walt Clark come along nex' morning 'cos he were the patrolman at the time and there were the heart out o' one o' 'em and 'e took un home and 'e ate un.

I went to Burtle school for all me schooldays, I used to traipse all out along the canal to the Edington Road then up to the school. There wern't no school meals then mind, until the last few months of my school days. Mrs Williams were the head mistress and Miss King were the assistant teacher. I used to sit next to Joan Boyer 'cos she were more intelligent than I were and I could look over see what she'd done.

In the war we had some evacuees at school. Sheila Brown was one, she lived up in the monkey tree, Fairview House, wi' Perce Cox. I don't know what happened to her. Then there were Gordon Withers, I've seen him since, he were Norman Moxey's cousin and he come down to Burtle in a Rolls Royce one time, summat went wrong afterwards. There was one girl who would entertain the village lads any time and anywhere, had trouble with her nicker 'lastic and that made she popular! There was another girl, the sort that used to wear big 'ats an' 'igh heel shoes, she was vull 'o piss an' importance, but she werd'n so popular as t'other one!.

Mother used to come out along the track to the waiting room up Edington station with me sandwiches for dinner because between about half past eleven and two o'clock there werd'n no trains. She weren't s'posed to leave the gates but they didn't say nothing, turned a blind eye to it.

When I were about five year old, me father had a stroke and he couldn't work no more. Me mother had to take in washing to make ends meet. The rent werd'n very much and we lived very simple lives. If you 'ad a gun thees could shoot a rabbit or a duck for the pot. Ol' Walty Clark always had rabbit wires down which he did see to when he were walking the line. He'd drop in a rabbit from time to time.

All we young 'uns in the village had little part time jobs on farms or somewhere. I did always help Len Hayes in Chapel Hill, sometimes he'd give me a few bob, sometimes a bag of teddies or summat else. They was happy days and there werd'n the mischief and vandalism back then. We respected other people and their property, anybody getting out o' line would have got a bloody good hiding from their father or somebody. Times was very tight but we didn't go round pinching like today, they don't do nothing to 'em even if they catch 'em.

In the Summer this farmer, Len Ings from up Chilton somewhere did used to keep his cows on the verges alongside the road. When he were milking twer a real pantomime, one 'ould kick and break the span see, hit the bloody bucket over, spilling the milk. He had they old fashioned buckets with a little short handle wi' a knob on 'em. He'd cuss an' go, he'd start milking up by Bert Gooding's an' finish up down Harry Cox's! He were mad's a hatter and he's language, well, you could yer 'un up in the village. Then there were ol' Dickie House from down Mark, he used to milk out Chilton Drove behind we. He and his boy, they didn't get on, and they were nearly as bad.

Mother didn't have a pension, not a penny. We only had what we could earn, mother with her washing an' me with me odd jobs.

I started work on Edington station on Christmas eve 1946 when I left school at fourteen. Mr Arthur Beakes were the stationmaster and he were a gent. I worked one day and then had a day off. My wages was £1.13s.4d (£1.66p) and that were real riches to me. Father died soon after I started work.

When they closed the line in 1966, John Walton, he were the stationmaster then and he had to write to mother saying that as the line was closing, her services would no longer be required. She didn't get anything, no pension, no nothing, not a penny and she had to pay rent for the house. Not like tis today. She earned some money from the washing and I had my wages, such as they was and that's how we managed.

Now the line was closed we had to fetch our drinking water in buckets from up the station house, nearly a mile away. I was working on the station on by the milk factory down Bason Bridge, the line from there to Highbridge had been retained. Parker was the stationmaster, a little short fat bloke, I used to get on alright wi' he. He took over from Albert Coombes, bad ol' bugger, he was. This Parker, he were mainly interested in what he could get out of the system, in between whiles he used to run a bloody ice cream cart. He were a star turn, he didn't care a fig about the railway, he were only interested in what he could get out o' it.

Meanwhile, John Walton had a job as a relief stationmaster up Bristol and he were eventually offered a railway house at Sandford and Banwell up thick way. That left the station house at Edington empty for weeks and weeks. One day ol' Parker saw I and hollered 'Hey I want to see you'. I were a bit worried and said to 'un what do 'ee want then? He said, 'you got to put in fer thick house up Edington station'. Well I said there's a lot putting in for 'un, I shan't have much chance. 'You got to put in for 'un, there's a proper shithouse and running water in 'un which thees asn't got where you'm to. Yers the form, thee vill 'un out an' I be going to put a letter in wi' 'un', he said. So I filled in the form and he wrote the letter and sent 'em off. He kept asking me if I'd heard anything and I hadn't, see.

One day I were home wi' mother and she shouted out, 'Parkers coming down the line'. She could see 'un coming through the window, 'I wonder what he do want", she said. She went in t'other room wi' 'un and in a minute she come out hollering an' shouting, 'We got the house, we got the house, yers the key and we got to move in'. You could have hit me down wi' a bloody feather, I was so pleased for her. 'I'm going up now, straight away to clean it out'. She got her mops and buckets and trappings out she were gone. Old Jimmy Richmond down the First and Last moved us with he's ol' tipper lorry. We loaded up all the ol' rubbish and sticks of furniture, twerd'n hardly worth taking but twas all we had. We had a big wardrobe that wouldn't go in anyhow. Jimmy took out a sash window and he heaved it in through there, and that's how I came by Station House.

I stayed in there after they closed the line and one day I had a letter from some estate agents at Poole saying that the British Railways Board, as they no longer had any use for the properties on the old Somerset and Dorset line, they were offering them for sale to the sitting tenants. The price would be seven hundred and fifty pounds, no negotiations, take it or leave it. By this time I was fireman to driver Ron Andrews, working out of Highbridge and earning reasonable money. Although I like me beer I was always careful and able to put a bit by and I had the bloody money in house. I signed the paper there and then and sent it all off. It were a sudden transformation from Chilton Drove, we thought we was in Buckingham Palace, you could turn a tap and clean water came out! Mother kept twiddling and turning the tap, 'Where do it come from, I don't understand it' she said.

They old times were hard days, if you were tough enough to stick it you could keep going. You lived off the moor wi' a rabbit or a duck or two. You had to have a gun then but I've gived it all up, sold me gun and gived up me gun licence. I've turned right against it now.

John was made redundant on the railway, went to work at the Bason Bridge milk factory and then made redundant from there. He then went British Cellophane for several years and was once more made redundant. His age and a back problem prevented him from getting another job. He eventually bought a house in Bridgwater and lives there still. Following a slight stroke, John was glad that he was within a short distance of all the services and for that reason feels that it would no longer practical to move back to Burtle.

Arthur Barker: The Perfect Countryman

It is difficult to do justice to a man in a few hundred words when he could justify a complete volume to himself. I had known Arthur for some years but it was whilst making a cine film about the traditional ways of digging peat for fuel in 1975 I really came to appreciate his many skills and qualities.

Born at Westhay in 1900 and one of a long family he worked around the district peat digging, ditching, cider making, and various other rural activities. A man of average height, broad shoulders and the large, powerful hands of a man who had spent many years working with them. He moved with an economical grace and an athleticism belying his age. Under his seemingly inseparable flat cap was a weather beaten countenance with the brightest blue eyes, shining out like a pair of friendly, slightly amused diamonds.

After the tradition of the moors, he was a very good shot and kept the family pot full. Moreover, he often provided a duck, hare or rabbit for any neighbours in particular need. Any surplus after that would contribute a few coppers to the family budget.

The well respected and popular Arthur Baker was a true countryman.

Arthur and his family moved to Burtle in 1950, Westhay's loss was certainly Burtle's gain. It was not a great distance and he was already well known in his new chosen village.

I have been rivetted by tales of how, with his friends, he would set off with his gun, cover a considerable distance on foot or bicycle, shoot the next days meal, and still start work by 6.30am.

Arthur was a slightly shy, quiet man and, unlike some, could only be persuaded to embark on his reminiscences if he was sure that his audience would not be bored. The conversation would turn to matters of a past era, the Meare and Westhay revels, life in the peat fields, eel trapping, wildfowling and other occupations and pastimes.

Although a law abiding man, he undertook the occasional nocturnal excursions to the Shapwick estate where it was rumoured there were pheasants! "T'was always reckoned, if you zeed a man wi' a bag on 'is bike, he did come from Westee", (Westhay) Arthur once declared. He grew up in hard times but he was never bitter about them.

In 1976, Arthur and his wife celebrated their golden wedding anniversary, an event which might well have surprised his mother who once said of his youthful, romantic adventures, "Arthur, you be likely to sample the whole orchard and finish up wi' the crab if thees dissen mind out!". As in all things, Arthur did not waste his experience and it led to a perfect match when he eventually got married.

Arthur and his family moved to Burtle in 1950, Westhay's loss was most certainly Burtle's gain. No-one needing a helping hand would ever be refused and no reward was expected outside of his recognised ways of earning a living.

He was expert in all the local country crafts, a perfectionist, but he did not seek to impose his standards on others. He might well tease by way of gentle criticism of those of lesser ability, but there was nothing arrogant or harsh in his being. In his engaging way, he derived great pleasure in explaining how and why things were done in certain ways, he was also quite prepared to take the trouble to help those interested to improve their own skills. When trimming ditch banks, of which Burtle has many miles, the angle had to be correct and the edge straight. Traditional peat digging was a craft in which he excelled, using all the correct tools and methods, proven over the centuries. Tools can be a reflection of their owners, some of Arthur's were in good condition after fifty years of use.

Burtle had many good gardeners and Arthur was certainly one of these, growing amazing crops in his council house garden, much of which he gave away to those less fortunate than himself. Not satisfied with that, and in his mid seventies, he "did' several other gardens for some of "th' ole vokes!"

I can only once remember seeing Arthur really "worked up" over anything. He came into the Saturday lunch club in the Railway and his fury was uncharacteristic of the man. "They blighters 'ave pinched my traps", he announced. The "blighters" turned out to be the water board bailiffs and they had taken eel traps laid in the canal. It took a while to calm him down, the customs of his and many other lifetimes were being destroyed by bureaucracy. His usually humorously twinkling eyes had replaced by fiery look and his countenance had developed an unusually ruddy hue.

Sadly, Arthur Baker died suddenly in a very cold spell, early in 1977. A possible television programme of his life will never now be made. I feel greatly privileged to have known him. To borrow a phrase from A.G. Street, **"He was the gentleman of the party"**.

Elias Ernest George Lee

Ern Lee, a member of an old well respected Burtle family, was born in Burtle on April 27th, 1906, in a house on the Catcott road. His father George Lee worked on the railway and peat cutting, and gradually started farming. When the Henniker estate was sold up in 1918, George and his brother Frank, (nicknamed Nacky) bought the Burtle Inn with 26 acres for £1,460, a tidy sum in those days.

Ern (nicknamed Jumper) Lee was a very talented athlete, and, with his contemporary from the village, Ray (Colonel) Cox, travelled great distances on an old Douglas motor cycle to compete between morning and afternoon milkings. Ern's best events were sprinting and, as his nickname suggests, the high jump. How good he was is amply proved by the great collection of cups and medals together with wads of newspaper cuttings. Quite often the poles for the high jump were not tall enough and at several events the organisers resorted to placing matchboxes on the top of the uprights to enable them to continue to raise the bar. He could clear a bar well over six feet high running straight at it, a truly phenomenal feat.

When he married Edna Fisher in 1931, "a very good night was had by one and

Ernest and Edna Lee.

all" at the Burtle Inn. He took a farm at Westham that had been in his wife's family for over a hundred years, where he milked a dairy and operated a threshing outfit.

In the early 1950's, the family, now including daughter Margaret, moved back to Burtle to take over his father's farm. George had sold the pub some years previously, but had continued to make cider on the farm and for which he had earned a high reputation. Ern continued to make traditional cider under the brand name "Moonraker", winning many awards at shows such as the Bath and West. He milked a dairy until the early sixties when he turned over to beef production, winning numerous prizes for his high quality cattle. He was also one of the many talented gardeners in the village and, again, won many honours over much of the county and beyond.

One of his main village involvements was the Burtle harvest home and he was largely responsible for its resurrection after a break of several years. He was chairman of the committee until it finally finished in 1970. He was also associated with many other village organisations.

Ern Lee was a tall and upright man both morally and physically, he passed away on September 27th 1989 and was laid to rest in Burtle churchyard on October 10th. The familiar brown milking coat and pork pie hat is greatly missed in the village.

Harry Whitcombe

Harry Whitcombe was one of those men described as likeable rogues. He spent most of his time doing various labouring jobs on farms and in the peat fields. He lived with his wife in a dilapidated cottage just on the Catcott side of the canal at the end of a long drove that started on the Edington road although he was only one small field from the Catcott road. He mixed in with the villagers and developed a considerable reputation for his spontaneous wit. One of the Groves girls who lived in what is now the only remaining cottage on the Catcott Road described him in answer to a stranger's enquiry as "Upright and back over a bit".

Like most, he enjoyed a drop of cider and on one occasion fell off his bike and finished up in a heap under the hedge outside the post office. Mrs Seery who happened to be there was concerned and asked "Harry, did you fall off your bike?" "Naw" said Harry, "I do always git off like this!"

On one occasion during a conversation in the pub Harry exclaimed, "Thurs only one bloke in Burtle tha's unemployed and I be looking"!

Harry never had much money and hadn't paid his rates on the cottage. Eventually, after many abortive attempts to serve him with a summons, the local policeman caught him in. "Whitcombe", said the bobby, "I've wore out a set of tyres trying to catch you in". "Thees 'ull wear out the bloody vrame 'vore thees 'ull git the money", replied Harry. He never paid his rates and was sent to prison in Bristol. One day the warder said, "Whitcombe, I hear you are leaving us tomorrow". "Tell 'ee what", said Harry, "If thees could get I some cider I would'n mind biding up yer with 'ee for a bit longer".

Harry and his wife were evicted from their cottage and as they had nowhere to go, a local farmer parked a hay waggon on the verge side of the Catcott Road. Harry tied a couple of poles on top of the hay ladders at each end of the waggon and put a rick sheet over the top. He and his wife put their few sticks of furniture up in the waggon and lived underneath it. A passer by stopped for a word and asked where Mrs. Whitcombe was. "Oh, she's upstairs doing a bit of dusting', responded Harry!

He eventually moved up to Catcott village where he took a delight in tormenting Reg Pople. Reg had some hens on an adjacent piece of land and Harry enticed the hens through the fence and encouraged them to lay in his garden. His next step was to get a basket and fill the bottom with screwed up newspaper, carefully placing a layer of eggs over the top. The basket, apparently full of eggs was placed in his window with an eggs for sale sign.

In spite of his indulgence in cider and somewhat unhealthy lifestyle he kept up the Burtle tradition and lived well into his eighties. No matter what the situation, he always came up with a witty comment.

I allus gits off like this, missus!

Harold Whitcombe

Me great grandfather, 'e came from Shapwick, twer old Bert Beal the blacksmith up Shapp'ick told me about it. What happened was I wanted a plugging chisel 'cos when I started work in 1946 you couldn't buy tools 'cos they werdn' about. Jack Clark in Clarks (Shoes) gave me a piece of tool steel which I took over to old Bert. After about three weeks I went back and 'e said, "I used your bit o' steel, me son, to repair a tractor, but there's a plugging chisel so take 'e on".

I told 'un me name were Whitcombe an' you know how they would say "whose boy be you then?" I said we'em no relation to any other Whitcombes in the area, but he could tell me near enough where me great grandfather's grave was. We lost a lot of contact because dad's parents was both dead by the time he were eight. Granfather Whitcombe were only 38 when he died. He were a signalman down here and he dropped dead coming down over the platform. He lived over across the road with me grandmother who were a Norris and her sister were John Heal's grandmother. Sam Heal and his wife used to live down where the kennels is now. My father, Bert, were born 1897, my mother was a Symes from Chilton Polden one of the coal merchant's family.

Father bought two of they three cottages up by the canal two years before he were married and I were born in the middle one. Mr and Mrs. Nooks lived in the far one and Tom Mogg in the one agin the road. Reg Gillard moved in 'e after Tom Mogg moved up to Cossington. Tom used to ride a motorbike to work and old Reg Thyer was always cussing 'cos he reckoned he didn't go fast enough to keep 'un running sensible an' 'e were always in there for repair. I never had no brothers and sisters.

I done twelve months up Burtle school then I had polio and I never went back to school until I were eleven year old. I spent two years lying on me back on boards at home. There were an epidemic of polio about that time, 1937. Bath orthapaedic hospital were full up, and I used to see Dr. Forrester - Brown, she were an ol' battleaxe of a doctor, but she were very good. She used to operate her clinic in Bridgwater where the registrar is now. She had four beds wi' screens and as soon as one were finished with another would come in and her secretary did take all the notes in shorthand, 'twas like a production line. She showed mother how to do me exercises at home. The only bit of tuition I had were Mrs. Beakes, the station master's wife, 'cos she were a schoolteacher. I only did a half day at school when I went back and Mrs Williams who were the head teacher at the time put me in for an exam for the Bridgwater Technical School of Building down Blake Street, I were in the A class, the very first one.

I started there September '44 and that were a two year's course. I don't know how I passed the exam but whether she said summat to 'em that made a difference I don't know. Although I hadn't had much schooling I were good at maths and could tell 'em the answers though I couldn't write 'em down. I finished me two years in the Tech and I were looking around for a job, Ernie Tidball, Albert's son up Borough Hill out behind the Pipers Inn, (No relation to the Albert Tidball in Burtle) 'e got a job as a carpenter up Clarks and at that time they were running the train for trainees for the Redgate factory (Bridgwater). I seen Wormall, the building bloke when he come to the school an' 'e said you better come on up an' I got a job up there.

I worked for Clarks for forty years and one month exactly. I went in as a carpenter apprentice and ended up as building manager. When I started there were fifty two on the building staff. During me apprenticeship, to do the continuation classes you had to go to Bristol. Well I couldn' get to Bristol. Then the trains stopped and the buses so I got a motor bike and started to go to Bristol to do the course. I had some very good exam results up there and I never applied for a job afterwards. I went from carpenter to time estimating, in charge of the actual building section and finished up in charge of the lot. You couldn't do it today wi'out a degree or summat similar. Some of the young'uns today wi' a degree need a blowlamp up their ass to wake 'em up!

My father were a farm labourer and when he were 13 and living across the road at West Heath, he went up to Joseph Nuttycombe where Fred Conduit went later, living in and working on the farm. Everything found and he did get paid a shilling a quarter. When his mother died his father got married again, because there was three small children, to George Lee's widow so she was father's stepmother. They didn't hit it off but when he went up to Joseph Nuttycombe's they took 'un in as one of their own like, everything were provided and there were plen'y of it. Me step grandmother suddenly landed up wi' three children that weren't hers when me grandfather died three years after they married. I never knew what brothers and sisters me grandfather had because we lost touch. Father's brother learned his trade as a baker wi' Perce Drake down Mark.

Father's sister went down to Burtle Farm as a scullery maid to Lewis Grant, he was a bachelor, his brother Lucas Grant went over to Wedmore an' 'e had a son called Sid Grant. When father got married he were working down The Farm for Lewis Grant, so was Freddie Conduit. I can remember Ern Millet living in the little house where Connie Vowles do live now before Harry Selway an' 'e's wife come up there to live. "E were a miserable ol' so and so thic Harry Selway. I always remember father on about 'un cos Gilb Grant who lived next door had a fence down through the garden and had the posts on the wrong side o' the fence and he made 'em alter it, and there was o' Gilb all crippled up and couldn't do nothing wi' arthritis. 'Is wife brought some greens up to ol' Mrs Nooks, nex' door to we, tipped up the basket wi' the greens and apparently had her pension book in the basket see and tipped 'e out wi' 'em. Mrs Selway accused Mrs Nooks of pinching 'er pension book. Mrs. Nooks were a lovely ol' lady and would anything for we. I can only just remember Mr. Nooks, when father bought the two cottages, he paid £200 for 'em, he rented out the bottom one to 'em for three shillings and six pence a week. If mother were out ol' Mrs Nooks, she'd cook the dinner and she were a wonderful cook, she'd do anthing else that needed doing too. She were a pastry cook and she reckoned she'd use a sack of flour a day making pastry when she worked in Ludlow Castle. She 'ad one o' they little tin ovens cocked up on an old oil stove, she'd chuck some flour and stuff into a bowl and put it in th'oven and t'would come out lovely. The Nooks always made a lot o' wine, not just a few bottles but barrels full, I think they had 10 and 12 gallon barrels. She were deaf's a post but when they were bottling up, if a cork blowed out of a wine bottle she'd know, I don't know whether she heard it or sensed it some other way.

Father worked down The Farm 'til they said they couldn' afford to keep 'un on and he bought this plot wi' a few buildings on the Edington Road and had a smallholding here. He rented Elsie Heal's ground down here what John Heal got now an' did that until his heart packed up an' 'e couldn' do it. He died about two years after in the November before he were 65. When his health gave up he were going to sell the cottages and have a Woolaway put up yer but the day the contract come through father dropped dead. We sold up our place where the kennels is now and changed the two bedroom Woolaway for a four bedroom one. We sold our cottage which is the kennels now, mother sold her cottages and we all come up yer together. Mother lived wi' us for thirty one years.

I remember when there was a house out the bottom of Dobbins Drove where old Mr. and Mrs. Gay used to live. There was some nice damson trees down there. 'Twas a job getting in and out in the winter see 'cos the droves did go under water but i've never seen the water over the main road although I seen the wind blow the waves over 'un when I were a boy. They used to have white posts down each side of the road so you could see where the road was in the floods. They 'ad 'em on Chilton Moor as well. When Bert Heal did live down Box Farm I can remember father saying they had to put sleepers on the floor to keep 'em up out o' the water in house. Tidballs did the same an' Albie always 'ad a boat. There were another cottage down between Box Farm and the canal and the Burts used to live in there. That were a bungalow. There were another house in the corner of the same field down there in the opposite corner. If you go down the drove be Box Farm to the crossway there were one down there and father used to say there were one on down

West Heath drove. Fred Richards, the butcher up Chilton, he used to own the bit o' ground 'twer on one time. There used to be a lot of cottages out along the Catcott Road too. Fairview house, 'e wi' the monkey puzzle tree, were built by Perce Cox's father and wi' the four little servants' quarters on each side o' 'un, 'e cost nine hundred pound.

Did 'e ever find out the truth about Miss Field's gift? I can remember envelopes being given out when I were a boy an' father always used to talk about it.

Old Frank Pollard, Ralph's father and old Mrs. Rice's brother, their father used to more or less make his living catching moles. I remember ol' Mark, 'e couldn' get work one time and 'e cycled to Weston on a job. Ol' Mark 'ad a wonderful garden, all spic an' span. Perhaps I do take after 'un, I bought two cabbages since I been married! I've growed the same runner beans for yers from seed I 'ad from father.

I remember where the the council houses are was just a field of corn and after milking father cut round the outside wi' a mowing scythe and it took him until nearly ten o'clock at night 'cos twas a fourteen acre field see. Thats a thing I could never get on wi', a mowing scythe, I still got 'is out there in shed now. He did 'ave a little whippy cane wi' a nail in the end of 'un an' a hole in the back of 'is scythe and there were two little straps an' 'e did strap 'un on to the handle to put a bow on 'un an' that did lay it down flat so as you could pick it up and sheave it. He did sort of rock from one foot to t'other and twere a cut every time. Back in the war when they 'ad to plough up grass ground to grow corn they sowed oats in Clover Ground down The Farm and it growed up eight foot tall. The binder didn' 'ave enough adjustment to tie the sheaves in the middle and they were like damn great fans. Sid Mayled used to come down with the steam thresher. There used to be three grades, the best corn, the middling stuff and the small corn wi' weed seeds an' that for the fowls. Sometimes the corn would be nearly black wi' vetch seeds. Of course wi' weedkillers an' that now there's very little weed in the corn, you don't see a poppy in a corn field now.

Out The Farm there were a nail in one o' the trees where they used to hang the geese up for Christmas. They used to do a lot of poultry, they had one on killing all the time and they did hang 'em up on the nail to drain. There was Gilb Grant and his wife Ag Grant, now she usualiy used to draw 'em after they was picked, then they was singed off wi' methylated spirits, then she dld powder 'em wi' cornflour and tie their legs wi' tape but you lroned the tape first mind. When she'd done 'em they really did looked the business, she used to tie 'em somehow to make the breasts all plump up. They'd lay 'em out on the kitchen down there and then take 'em all round and by next Christmas they'd probabiy cieared up the feathers! Perce Drake (the baker from Blackford) used to take the feathers home and put 'em in the oven overnight to bake 'em so they couid use 'em in pillows and mattresses and such like.

I remember we used to go down to Met Watts for a haircut In amongst all the spar shavings which he used to keep the vire warm wi'.

Ol' Lennie Buttle, the blacksmith, used to live In a little bungalow on the Catcott Road down below the Bow which is gone now. Up t'other side of the Bow was another little cottage which ol' Coulty Lee that worked on the rallway used to live in. The Groves's that lived in the tiny little bungalow on t'other side of the crossing were very shy and they'd hide rather than come out and speak to 'ee, 'twere difficult to talk to 'em. There were Daisy, Liz, Mabel, May, Ern and Frank. Ern were the most chatty, you don't see Frank a lot, you 'ad to corner 'un to talk to 'un, he were alright though if you did.

Ruth Pollard

Me husband, Ralph, was born down in that little house where Harry Whitcombe lived. You go down by the Catcott crossing and in across one ground and there's the heap of rubble. The honeysuckle Ralph's mother and father planted there is still growing up through the tree. When Dave Whitcombe was up yer one day he said to Ralph, 'twas lovely hot weather like 'tis now, thees want to take a couple deck chairs down there and sit beside thic rubble and you'd thlnk you were back home again. So 'pon me soul one day Ralph said let's have thic chairs an' we'll go in round from the river and if 'tis alright we'll sit down there for a while in under the trees 'cos 'twill be nice there, so we did. And poor old Arnold (Tucker) coming down from 'ees pheasant patch wi' the pens, he did sit on 'is bike wi' his hand on the rails o' the bridge, he did bide an' look out cross an' thinking what the hell do they think they'm doing out there.

Frank Vowles

The Vowles's originally came in from Wedmore way, Blakeway or somewhere like that. I was born down by the lock in Catcott Heath, Harry Selway was my grandfather on me mother's side. When I was a few months, father bought the house where Kath and Jim Hooper lived. Me grandson, Farron, lives there now. I used to go up there as I grew up 'cos grandfather didn't leave there until I were seventeen or eighteen years old. He and grandmother went up to Little Burtle in the cottage known as Jefferies where Connie's living now. I don't know where the name came from but the farm where Arthur Tratt used to live was called Jefferies. Grandmother died up Little Burtle and grandfather went to live wi' mother up yer in the council houses.

Mr. and Mrs Frank Vowles.

I went to Burtle school, Alfie Willcox were the schoolmaster then, Miss Short was also there, she were the tall one! Mr. Kidd were the master before he but I don't remember much about 'un. Then there were a Mr. Scholfield after Mr. Willcox. Funny thing, there was a short Miss Short used to teach Missus down East Huntspill. Towards the end of me schooling days 'twere all women teachers then.

I were the oldest one in the family, I left school when I were fourteen, father, he left when he were twelve and went on turfin'. There was me brother Bill, then there was Joyce, Annie and Ivy. I stayed on helping father when I left 'cos he werden very well, later I went on farm work for Farmer Frank Lockyer down Catcott Burtle Farm. He followed Farmer Denning in the early thirties. Frank went up to Kent farm, Shapp'ick after Farmer Dick Vearncombe about nineteen thirty six or seven. After Frank Lockyer I worked for George Lee up in the farm next to the post office, that's when I got married. Then I went to White's up on the hill and from there I went on for Buckie Hurford up Edington. Then I come back to Burtle for Farmer Hole, who followed Farmer Lockyer in Catcott Burtle Farm, worked for he for some time. Then I went on for Arthur Cox for a year or two. Then I had a chance to go on wi' Art Baker on the rhynes and that, which were a much more interesting job doing turf digging and anything else we could get hold of. He were a good chap to work with, everything had to be right mind for Arthur. In the Summer we dug a lot of peat for burning and in the Winter 'twas horticultural peat, Tommy Whitcome used to sell that to Alexanders. In nineteen sixty I went on for Bert Smith on the building and stayed there until I retired.

I were in the band for quite a few yers, in later years I was in the Harvest Home committee, after we got married. The Harvest Home and the revels were the high spots of the year. For the revels they used to have the skittle boards all along the Burtle Inn fence, Mrs. Betty from Bridgwater did have her cockle stall where she sold shellfish, all sorts of sweets and ginger bread. That was before they had the skittle alley. Cliff Wynn used to bring out his swing boats and cocnut shy and that and set they up across the road from the Burtle Inn. 'Twere an evening turnout. Pococks from Pawlett used to come out there too, I think they were connected to the

Wynns.

People in Burtle were very friendly, helping each other out, a lot of us wouldn't have got on at all wi'out 'em. Didn't matter whether 'twas farmers, labourers or anybody else, if anybody needed some help they always knowed where they could go an' get it. They'd always pitch in and help. "Twas a wonderful community spirit. Mind, we used to play practical jokes on people but they were never harmed by it. Down Back Drove by the corner of the Westhay Road there was a little shed used for a communal toilet for the three cottages. One day a gang of 'em put this yer toilet on a trolley wheeled 'un down to the cross and put a sign up - One penny for a pee and a poop!

I remember one Winter, Farmer Lockyer had some cattle down by the river, all the ground used to be flooded pretty deep between the river and the house, and we had some very hard frosts. Course, he didn't think 'twould happen, he thought they'd walk back up but one or two of 'em went down and all the farmers went down and helped pull the injured ones back on a sleigh and a r007. George Lee and Reg Grant and all the lot of 'em all pitched in to help. They used have a sleigh with iron runners and a couple of sleepers which they used to keep up the factory in case any farmer had a cow bad out in ground so as they could get 'un back. They'd hitch a hoss on one end and pull 'un back to the farm.

1941, a cow was rescued over the ice by rolling it into a ricksheet and towing it home. Those present; Bill Packer, Len Hayes, Ern Grant, Charlie Sandford, Arthur Tratt, George Lee, Freddie Moxey, Cliff Moxey, Desmond Lockyer, Frank Lee, Reg Grant, Ray Cox, Frank Cox, Arthur Cox, Frank Lockyer.

Father died in nineteen thirty six, I were eighteen when 'e died, just before we were married, he was called Frank too. People were very helpful, they'd see you didn't starve. Father were in the peat job, digging and selling on a round. I used to go round wi' 'un 'fore I left school on Saturdays. When I left school I did the round 'cos father were bad for some yers, I used to go up checker patch up beside Shapp'ick station and get thousand turf up there for ten bob. Then we used to haul 'em down round Mark and out to Rooksbridge to make another ten bob. 'Twas hard work for the money. When father died, mother sold the place and ol' Bill Coombes bought it and we stayed there for another twelve months 'till we could get somewhere to live.

Among the older generation I can remember George Clark, George Moxey, that were Roland Moxey's father - I can only jus' remember he mind, when I were about seven or eight I used to see 'un leaning on the gate where he lived in Chapel Row. Tom Clark lived in the cottages across the road from the Burtle Inn, he bought all three in the estate sale for £130. Mrs. Fred Tratt bought two of 'em off o'un, he probably made a bit o' profit out of 'em. Tom had one arm, had a crook on t'other, he were Walt's father what used to walk the line to Bridgwater. I used to do a bit of ditching wi' Ern Gillard who lived next door when I first got married to earn some extra money. I used to do a lot of shooting especially when I were working wi' Art Baker, also when I were working wi' Farmer Hole, he and I would take it in turns with the work so as t'other could go. Tom Clark lost his arm when a gun exploded and blowed his arm off. Arnold Tucker had an accident up in Edington Heath with Ern Millet. They went up 'cross in the boat, apparently the gun went off and hit Ern in the side, that's the two gun accidents I can remember. With the number of guns twere a wonder half of 'em didn't get shot, there were a gun in every house back then. Father had a nice gun and he sold 'un to Frank Lee when he got past it. How I come be mine, I were working in Farmer Hole's and ol' Roland Moxey were living on the corner there by Back Drove and he used to come and have a chat wi' Farmer and he said to I one day "Diss ever go down wi' a gun?" I said "No I an't got a gun". "Wull", a said, "If I lend you my gun will 'ee bring I in a bird or two occasionally?" I used to take 'un in rabbits, wood pigeons, ducks and anything else that come along. When The ol' man died I said to Edgar, the son, that I had the gun and he said "Wull you hang on to 'un".

Life used to be a lot slower in they days, there werden none of this keeping up wi' the Jones's like. People were happy with what they'd got, today they all want more and more. People were always so friendly and helpful, if anybody were ill they always come and help 'ee out, take 'em in a meal and suchlike. One year Arthur Cox were ill and they all pitched in and hauled his hay from up Catcott Heath, they didn't need to be asked. If anybody got behind they'd lend 'em a horse and waggon or anything else. All the farmers had two or three blokes on, there idden any farm workers now. There was always plenty of jobbing work like thatching (ricks), spar making, ditching, anything. Frank Groves, he'd never work on a farm but he'd always find work, ditching and that. Met Watts worked for Pococks in Chapel Hill for some years then he went on spar making, thatching, haircutting and one thing and t'other. Mother worked in Chapel Hill as a housemaid when she were young. When I were younger, ol' Joe Clark down ther had a few cows, Bill Martin, 'ee had a few, grandmother used to have some but she never sold any milk, she couldn't bring it down from up the lock, so she reared calves. Frank Pollard, he lived just up over the railway and he had some cows, Alf Highnam, he had some at one time, used to keep 'em up Catcott Road in an old tumbledown place down Shepherds Drove, only about three or four.

Missus's family came from Mark and they went over to Huntspill to live and that's where I did me courting. I used to cycle over there nearly every night. When I first started work I were getting about seventeen shillings week, when we got married I were only getting £1.3.6d a week. Things didn't cost so much then and yer clothes, boots and that did last so much longer and you did look after 'em better. When you had a hole in your sock you didn't throw 'un out, you did darn 'un, yer trouser knees, they were patched, we didn't take any notice of it back then.

The blacksmith's shop was going, the first I can remember were Reg Arther, then there were a lot after Reg. I can't remember 'em all, There were Lennie Buttle and a bloke be the name o' Jack Hallett who come out from Bridgwater. I think he were about the last to work there. That belonged to Fred Tratt's wife, see, and Farmer Denning rented it for some time and Jack Hallet come there to work for 'un.

Highnams had a little shop down on the corner on the Westhay Road, Reg Grant did go round delivering coal, Reg's father did some butchering. On the other end from Highnams there were a saddler's shop, Jack Adams, he was related to Eileen. There was Charlie Burnell down Collins Field, uncle Charlie, he retired off the railway and he'd do a few small carpentering jobs, nothing very big mind. He were a good carpenter, mind, he'd sharpen saws, anything like that. We did always call 'un uncle Charlie, nice old chap, he was. I can see the old chap cycling up through Collins Field now on his way to have a pint.

A lot of people in Burtle did say that Victor Cox had the first car in Burtle but I don't think that were right. Roland Norris always told me Mr. Young down Blagdon Farm, where Clive Sweet is now, were the the first one 'cos he reckoned he rode in the first car in Burtle. Victor Cox used to do a bit o' taxi work, me sister Joyce did go up to Chilton wi' un for cookery classes 'long wi' others.

There used to be a lot of big families back then, they'd sleep several in a bed, some at each end in the smaller cottages. I used to have some old photographs and I let 'em 'ave 'em down school and they kept the bloody lot! I forgot about it see for two or dree months and when I realised what I'd done 'twere too late, I never had sense enough to put me name and address on the back, I could kick meself now.

When I were young we used to have all the dances and that down the school, yes, whist drives, dances and concerts. The school children used to get up a concert every year, the school were the village hall.

Victor Cox were in the post office, he come out about nineteen thirty and Nacky Lee went in. Then there were Mr. Stone, he built the new post office and went there about 1939.

Everybody who had a chance would get on the railway 'cos twere a constant job, the money werdn't much better but 'twas regular. Most of 'em kept a cow or two and, of course, they had Saturday afternoons and Sundays off and some of 'em finished up farming. Twerden like working on a farm, that were seven days a week.

Missus and I got married in 1937 and went into one of the new council houses and we'em still here over sixty years later. We had four children, three sons and a daughter. I s'pose I've had a pretty good life, really.

Jim Moxey: Bandmaster

Well, let me tell 'e this, if I could model my life on my grandfather I'd be a wonderful fellow. He were a wonderful chap, a very charismatic man. He was a man who would never hear a bad word said about anybody. He worked on the old S & D railway, a signalman up West Pennard until he came back and started to farm down Glebe Farm.

Me grandmother was a couple of months away from a hundred and two when she died and I don't suppose anybody will see the changes to transport and that that she did. She saw the first push bike, the first motor bike, the first motor car, the first aeroplane, the first train to Bridgwater and the first man on the moon. That's a hell of a lifetime! Grandfather helped to build the Bridgwater line.

Grandmother, she were a hard ol' woman mind. When I was 15 or 16 I was one of the strongest kids around (Jim was about 6ft 2" and around 13/14 stone then!) When we was hay making, grandfather would be on the load of hay, I would stop between the cocks and I would pitch one side and grandmother would pitch t'other and she'd keep up wi' me. When she came out of Glebe Farm she lived down Chapel Row where she had a garden across the road where the chapel used to be.

Jim Moxey is still leader of the band after 44 years.

There's a house there now. She felt she couldn't do it on her own so I said "We'll grow some spuds and we'll go halves". So I got it all dug up and I said I'll be out one night in the week to put 'em in. When I turned up to put 'em in she she said "Huh, I've done that! The scouts come round for their bob a job week and so I made the holes and they put the spuds in". When I dug 'em, she picked 'em up, she were ninety then.

So far as the band was concerned, he bought an old cornet for £2 and taught himself to play when he were up West Pennard in the signal box. The band is still going after nearly a hundred years though 'tis hard work now. I had hoped to retire after 43 years as bandmaster but the chap that took on was ill and I'm now back in the hot seat. People outside the band might think there's nothing to it but there is a lot of work and a lot of worry.

Grandfather taught some of the locals to play, 'twas all local lads at one time, see. Mr Kidd, the schoolmaster, taught a lot of 'em music though I don't think he ever played in the band. If you were taught by my grandfather, he was a real old stickler for having it right, the dicipline that man had was unbelievable, he had so much respect. We'd go 'round Christmas carol playing nobody did know we were coming, you didn't make noise and if anybody coughed 'twould be a muffled "Oi, shut up"!

The band started in 1907. Grandfather were bandmaster for 35 years, uncle Viv for about eight years, father for six years and me'self 43 years. I started to play when I was 11 years old, that was back in the war. We used to play in all the carnivals, the last one we played in was at Wells and it rained so hard 'twas running out the ass of our trousers before we even started. Wells carnival used to have about eight or ten bands and we were the only silly sods that went round and when we come round by the cathedral it were like a river down there. At the next practice I said well you can go to so many carnivals as you like but that's the last one I be playing in. Rain, you never seen anything like it! Frank Lee split the big drum when 'e got wet and the hide shrunk, 'e didn't slacken 'un off see.

We used to do all the flower shows around here and all along Mendip, Westbury, Henton, Theale, etc. Ashcott and Middlezoy used to have bands in me grandfather's day but I can't remember 'em, 'twas before my time. Burtle used to and help 'em out sometimes if they were a bit short. Glastonbury tried to start up again but they didn't have much success, Wells try to keep going with some help from Bridgwater and that. One Burtle band member said one night,, "If there's any bickering or arguments, 'tis always sorted out there and then in front of the whole band and 'tis done with. There's no secrets, everybody knows what's happening. It's more like a club than anything else.

We've got the band hut down Mark Road but now Charlie Tratt and Tony Mayled have died I'm not sure what is going to happen. We had a smashing little generator pinched from there, cost us over £600 from down in Devon. It ran all our lighting and a couple of heaters. It would be nice to have our own bit of ground with a band hut with electricity etc so we could remain independant. They used to practice in the old milk factory one time and also in Burtle House when Arthur Cox had it.

There was a lot of characters in Burtle back in they days. Ol' Harry Whitcombe (nicknamed Drasher), grew a beard and when he turned up in the First and Last one night, he used to go there every night, and Perce Ducket said to 'un "tis about time thees 'ad a shave Harry". "I s'pose tis said Harry", and Perce took a razor blade out of 'ees pocket and cut it off there and then! Another time, in the fog, he missed the plank over the ditch out to the road from 'ees cottage down by the Catcott Crossing and he thought he'd fallen in the rhyne but 'e'd pushed his bike through the canal 'cos he said "I come up on the railway line". 'Twas feasible 'cos when they were pumping the canal werden all that deep. Then there was 'Captain' (Frank) Groves, we used to get 'un on the cider in the Burtle Inn, we'd go over Harry Moxey's and get a corrugated galvanised sheet, stick 'un out on The Cross and get 'un dancing on 'un wi' 'is hobnail boots. He'd hammer thic sheet out flat in no time. He always had a gurt plaster on 'is nose. Tha's one aspect of village life that's gone for ever, we shan't see times like it again. Then there was 'Doff' and Ern Watts who lived down Middle Whites Farm down Green Drove. They were both cripples and both used to go the Railway dinner time every day for their drink. They never used to walk together, one were always about 50 yards behind t'other, walking wi' sticks but one did limp one side and one on t'other. Doff also had a cleft pallet. One day Bert Bartlett from up the King William at Catcott, who also had the same problem, brought down a load of stone on 'ees lorry and when he spoke to Doff, he thought he was mimicking him and challenged him to a fight!

Down opposite the Burtle Inn, down where Lindsay Coles do live, there used to be Coles's, Clarkes then Jimmy Packer and Sammy Packer. I remember Charlie Norris when Sam died saying that if he had all the Star cigarette packets from what Sam smoked he wouldn't need no dirt to fill in the hole! Henry Tratt lived on the corner. We used to ride our bikes round and round. One day he grabbed Mike Thyer's bike and gie'd 'un a shove. The garden gate flew open and the front door, he went straight through the passage and out t'other side into factory lane. We used to get up to all sorts of mischief but there was nothing vicious and nothing broken. One of things we used to do was to swap peoples' gates 'round or moving Perce Cox's milk stand around 'cos 'ee were on wheels and that were an open invitation.

Roley Moxey used to live in a cottage on the corner on Westhay Road and Charlie Norris in behind.

A few years ago I sat down and went round the village mentally and at that time I could only calculate 12 new houses built since the war. There's never been any speculation building in Burtle only the odd house tucked in here and there.

Burtle were a wonderful place to live. I was six when war broke out and I must say that in spite of that we had a wonderful childhood. When father and mother got married they lived up the end of Robin's Drive, there was some cottages up where Den Thorne built his bungalow. Allan were born down Collin's Field, the house is now called Burnells, I was born in Chapel Row. We lived next to Fred Tratt, we used to call 'un uncle Fred, he had his old cider house down the garden. I was only about three years old and I went in house and kep' saying "Ditch mum, ditch mum". Apparently I'd turned on 'is cider tap and 'twas all running away in the ditch.

I can remember when the war broke out as if twere yesterday. Somebody come out and said "You boys better go home". We were all down by the shop. Our mother had four o' we and four evacuees back in the war, by then we were living in the council houses up Station Road. When the bombs blowed up the railway line down by the canal, 'twas a wonder that half a dozen of us werden killed thic day, we all used to go down there swimming by the Baulk (the wooden footbtbridge over the canal). The bombs started out by Catcott Crossing and the last one pitched out between the station and Chilton Drove. We'd actually been swimming there that day! One of the evacuees used to travel quite a bit and whenever he was in the West Country he'd always come and see mother and father, right up until father died.

When I was a kid I used to get so much a week for counting these sheep for a farmer out on the Quantocks who bought grass keep down Burtle. When I used to ring 'un up he'd say "If you do find one in ditch make sure she's right under before you phone me up". Drowned mutton were very handy when meat were on ration! That's how things were in the war if we'm honest.

We kids used to know every inch of they moors, we'd go ditch jumping and birdsnesting. If we wanted to go the fair or something we had to go blackberrying or mushrooming to earn the money, not many of us got pocket money so you had to go out and earn it one way or t'other. Most of us had part time jobs on the farms to earn a bit. I used to help me grandfather and Harry Moxey haymaking. Times have changed when you hear people saying they give their kids £10 a night to go up fair.

When I started work, I used to cycle from Burtle to Bridgwater to Ellison, Ellis and Jacksons. I used to start at 8 o'clock in the morning, finish at 6 o'clock at night, Saturdays was 8 to half past twelve, two nights a week I used to have to go to night school. I left home at seven o'clock in the morning and got home seven in the evening, when I had night school 'twere ten o'clock at night. When I was eighteen years old my money was £1.16.10d a week. When brother Pat started work up Clarks they used to pay their fare on the old S&D, the fare on the bus from Glastonbury to Street and at 15 he were bringing home up to £15 a week at the same time. It made me feel like chucking it all in but father told me to stick it out, I'm glad I did now. Then I had two years in REME for me national service, I often wish I'd stayed in. I spent 12 years down Bason Bridge milk factory, I left there and went into bonded fibre in Bridgwater. Within a year I was made up to chargehand, in two years I was foreman and finished up as manager. I travelled all over the world, India, Israel and so on, I had a marvellous time.

One day we had a hell of an air raid down yer, the whole of Huntspill Moor were afire. Some said they were turned back from Bristol and others that they were after the factory over Puriton. My uncle Bob that were killed, that were the last leave he were home on and I remember him coming over and saying to mother "Come on, we got to get 'em out', and we went over in the ditch across the road. There was a plane came down out there and father and a few more in the home guard went off on their motorbikes to see what was on. The band didn't operate during the war, there was so many of 'em away at the time.

To get 'round with the band we used to hire 'Gilbo's' coach from down Mark, Gilbert Wall that was. The payments would cover that and leave a bit for the band funds. For example, Wells carnival would pay us twelve pounds and the coach, we might have a drink out of it. Come Christmas, we never used to go anywhere else bar Burtle, it used to take us three weeks to get 'round Burtle. We used to walk everywhere and visit every house in the village, everybody had some Christmas carols. The music had a job to stand up to the hospitality, come the end of the night we had a job to find our way home! Some said if you weren't never carried home from carol playing, you werden a member of the band. The concoctions we used to drink was unbelievable, two or three o'clock in the morning when we used to finish

Charlie Tratt, a good old trooper and supporter of village functions.

sometimes. When you got to some houses there would be a basket of sandwiches and a bucket of cider outside the door 'cos they'd gone to bed. We'd eat the sandwiches, drink the cider, play a few carols and then off home. You can't imagine that happening today, cannee'?

Ol' Charlie Tratt were the best band supporter we ever 'ad, no matter what, he was always there. If I saw Charlie I always used to stop and speak to 'un and this particular day I said to Gwen, "There's ol' Charlie there, I better pull up and have a word". "Coo", said Charlie, "I'm glad to see you, you bugger". I said "What have I done wrong now Charle"? "Nothing", he said, "I've made me bloody will out and I've left the band a hundred pound". "What do 'ee think of that"? I said "That's very nice of 'ee Charlie, thank you very much". Then he said, "But now I've bloody altered it, what do 'ee think o' that"? I said "Well what you've never had, you never miss". Then Charlie said, "I thought to meself I shall never know what they buggers 'ull do wi' that so I'll give it to 'ee now". He put his hand in his pocket and pulled out a hundred pounds and give me. He was a good old trooper.

Mrs Williams was the head teacher down school and Miss King and Miss James were the other teachers there. Children used to stay until they were 14 unless they were one o' they bright swines that passed the 11 plus and went to the grammar school. Later they started that secondary modern business and the older ones went over to Weston Zoyland. We caught the old S&D train into Bridgwater, about where Sainsburys is now and we had a good 2 mile walk up to Dr. Morgans at Durleigh and there were only one morning you were allowed to be late and that were fair morning!

On the corner of West Street there was Bowerings the bakers, we used to go in there and get a little loaf of bread for tuppence farthing, 'twas all hot and lovely. West Street area was all little narrow streets, every other house seemed to be a pub. I drive a school bus now and I do 120 miles every school day all up 'round Street, Somerton, Charlton Mackrell and back to Ashcott. 'Tis crazy really, I can't see how that can be cheaper than the village schools used to be, and, the dicipline used to be much better.

Dr Beeching done a lot of damage to the villages, took away their transport. 'Tis like a river, if thees assen' got ditches and rhynes running into 'un, 'e don't amount to much and that's what's happened to your main line railways now.

Burtle Memories

Dr. Philip Williams grew up in Burtle where his mother was the headmistress of the village school for many years. There being no school house they lived in a part of Catcott Burtle farmhouse. He progressed to Dr. Morgans Grammar School in the same year as myself where he played rugby with a muscular enthusiasm as a ferocious fullback. He excelled academically and gained his degree at Aberystwyth and has spent six years in Australia and the last thirty four years working in agricultural plant breeding sciences in Canada. He is now a prominent member of the Canadian Grain Commission. The following are some of his memories of his youth in Burtle. His long time in North America comes through in his phraseology.

'My most vivid memories of Burtle start in about 1940. I was raised on a dairy farm operated by Mr. W.J. Hole. Mr Hole, everybody called him 'Varmer Awl' had a son Reg and a daughter Mary who married David Gwilliam.

Burtle used to flood every year prior to and during the war years. I believe that a lot of the land is below sea level. Burtle Moor, Mark Moor, Westhay Moor and Shapwick Moor would form a big lake. We used to build a raft every year and tour the waters. Reg and I would try and talk Mary into taking the first voyage in case the raft proved less seaworthy than we thought. We always wound up getting wet of course. Burtle would be cut off completely some times, except by train. In those days there was a pretty good train service to Bridgwater, Highbridge and Glastonbury. In some years the frost would be heavy enough to freeze it thick enough to skate on and people would drive down from Bristol to skate.

The Burtle of 1940 was quite a bit different from modern Burtle. There was a chapel on the right hand side of the Westhay Road about 200 metres from the "S" curve. Rowl Moxey lived on the corner of the curve. There was a great big stone laid into the ground right on the corner to protect his house from some shithead driving into it! At that time there were about two cars and two or three tractors in Burtle. Ivor Coombes had a car for sure, but I don't know who else did, it was all horses. We were haymaking from June through September every year and October some years.

All of that was done by hand, except the mowing was done by double-horse mower and there were horse drawn swathe turners, tedders and horse rakes. All the hay was pitched onto waggons and from them onto the ricks. Tough times - good to have lived through them but hard work at the time.

Reg and I, when we were about 13 and 12 respectively (1945) used to go ditching in the evenings. The farm had about 4 miles of ditches (rhynes pronounced rheens). They were essentially bottomless. It was peat country, even though the water may not have been very deep at times the mud was very thin and you could push a 10 foot pole down out of sight. Needless to say, if cattle fell in they couldn't get out and had to be pulled out by horse or later tractor. You had to dig away a bit of the bank so that you wouldn't strangle the cow.

In about 1941 we started digging peat at the bottom of the eastern-most 20 acre field. Frank Vowles was working for Mr. Hole at that time. Frank is still around and lives in the first council house by the church that he and Mrs. Vowles moved into when they married in 1937. He is a fine guy, used to whistle a lot. I thought so much of him when I was about 7 that I taught myself to whistle too! I've often thought about that - I am now a reasonably good whistler, or so I am told, and that is due to Frank's influence (and constant practice).

Reason for bringing up Frank's name is that he was a mine of information about many things, including peat-digging, or turfing as it was called. He figured out where the old diggers had left off years before. When we opened the first trench we found a whole pile of rubbish the old diggers had thrown into the last trench. This included old solid horse shoes and worn turfing tools, probably worth a fortune now. I've forgotten the term for the trench. I know that the actual cleared peat before removing it was a "bench", the main digging tools were very sharp, flat spades called turf scythes and we had special turf barrows to bear the cubes (mumps) of turf (peat) back to dry, and broken pieces of turf were called "brocks", the small piles 14 pieces of semi-dry turf were "hiles" and the big round 7-8ft high stacks were "ruckles", but there it ends - turf lore in retrospect!

Golden days. Reg and I used to go for miles jumping ditches across the moors looking for bird nests on the ground. Lapwings, curlews, several species of ducks, skylarks and many others. Those moors were a naturalist's paradise. I recall that you were pretty interested in wildlife when we were in school.

They built a big draining system during the war, ostensibly to improve the land more likely to ensure the ordnance factory at Puriton of a lasting water supply. Even by the time I left Burtle the character of the land had started to change. The engineering geniuses who came up with the drainage scheme has characteristically not thought it through, and hadn't taken into consideration the effect of the weight of thousands of tons of water compressing the soil for several weeks. The last time I was down on what was Farmer Hole's land it looked sort of spongy, the herbage composition had changed from predominately ryegrass and other good species like crested dogstail and cocksfoot to poorer species.

Burtle received about 26 bombs during the war, some of them are probably still at the bottom of Collin's Field. A plane crashed out on the moors between Burtle and Chilton Polden and several bombs fell out there too. We had a searchlight battery in Collin's Field for several years, it was powered by a Lister diesel engine/ generator on the corner near our farm. There was an old milk factory at the end of what used to be Factory Lane, it led due East directly off Burtle Cross. That closed down when the big milk factory went in at Bason Bridge.

There were three pubs in Burtle then. The Burtle Inn and the Railway Hotel (now the Tom Mogg) are still there but the First and Last closed several years ago and became a private house. It was the first house in Burtle coming in from Westhay. Rowland Norris was the landlord. It was a cider house but also sold beer, all virginia creeper, flagstone floors and quart cider cups - history in the embryonic stage! I knew old Rowl very well and used to go down to Burtle when I was in the UK just to see him. Just a few years ago I ran down from Edington to see him, then ran back via Catcott - I am a long distance runner ever since Morgan's and have run 6 marathons - lots of work - but a good way to stay in shape. Ron Vowles, Frank's youngest son, lived next door to Rowl during Rowl's golden years, he was well over 90 when he passed away.

In West Manitoba there are two towns, one called Birtle, the other Somerset. Both of them are bigger than Burtle was when I left. I believe that some pioneer from Burtle must have settled out there and founded Birtle first, then probably a member of that family founded Somerset, not far away. If the pioneer had come from anywhere else in Somerset it is unlikely that they would have named their town Birtle, most people don't know it exists even now, in those days communication was all by foot or horse.

A Moorland Journey

The following illustrates the interest in local activities held by almost everyone living in rural areas. An individual's problems were a source of genuine concern to their neighbours and friends. I have not discovered who wrote the following in 1930, he was probably from Ashcott, but it demonstrates the strong sense of community that used to exist.

'Having had my new car for three weeks (and now correctly insured) I decided to take my nephew for his first ride in a motor car. I will describe my journey through Shapwick and Burtle.

Driving down to Shapwick we were able to see the church of St. Mary where the vicar the Rev. Seamer was talking to Bill Marsh who is Farm Bailiff to Miss Strangeways of Down House and looks after Church Farm, he was leading two cart horses which he probably brought back from having them shod at Bert Beale the blacksmith. In H.D.Barnett's yard there was a new waggon for Leonard Jenkins of Beerway Farm. We passed Francis Cox delivering bread to John Burroughs of Manor Farm, we overtook Bill Durston the butcher passing the time of day with Henry Barnett who was painting the front of Mr. Anthony John Clark's home at The Lawns.

We stopped at Fred Wren's to buy sweets for my nephew and met Fred Hunt getting his tobacco, he is the head gardener for Miss Strangeways. Fred said he was on his way to Northbrook Farm for a putt load of manure, and he said that both Mr Lockyer of Moorgate and Charlie Jennings of Bowerings Farm had finished their haymaking. We passed the Griffins Head where the landlord Richard Chick was loading peat onto a cart for Joseph Loader of Brickyard Farm, we met Joseph walking to collect his cart and he told my nephew about the Holy Well and mineral springs which used to be sited on Northbrook Farm before it was built.

Driving across the moors to Burtle we can see Ivor Coombes of Burtle Hill Farm, Ralph Cox of Lilac Farm and Oliver Tratt still haymaking, do hope the weather stays nice for them, at least its better than last year, 1929.

In the distance we could see the smoke from a train going towards Evercreech from Highbridge, it will be dropping off empty milk churns at Edington, Shapwick and Ashcott stations. Alan Moxey of Chilton Burtle, Clifford Moxey together with Sam Heal are always prompt in collecting their churns. No doubt they often stop off at the Burtle Inn, landlord George Lee or the Railway Inn, landlord Bill Selway, to quench their thirst.

The Rev. William J. Leigh-Philips was just coming out of Frank Lee's shop and was talking to Charlie Norris, the sexton.

We collected as arranged Mrs. Lucinda Coombes to enable her to catch the train to Bridgwater from Edington station.

The gardens of Lt. Col. Begbie at Pines Farm and Mrs. Hughes at the Great House were a picture at this time of the year. Henry Arther's ladders and paint were outside Jan Swain's Cottage where Mrs. Trenchard lives and breeds dogs.

We passed the waggons of Tom Brain who lives at Burnthouse Farm and Robert and Bill Durston from Hill Farm with their loads of hay. Tom Granville was working on a house not far from the shop of Mrs. Ada Hull.

We arrived at the station in plenty of time, Mr. John Hibbard of The Spinney and Arthur Granville who is the parish clerk were on the station.

On the way home I will order some more turves from Jim Wilton of Cockhill. We were late home for tea as we were held up by Arthur Bastable and Charles Ackerman's cows.

A young lad from Burtle caught a large conger eel off Burnham beach and excitedly told everyone he met in Burtle about it. When he got to Viv Moxey, Viv told him that he often went fishing at Burnham. One day he hooked something that took him over two hours to land.

"What do you think it was?" he asks the boy.

After several guesses the lad gave up.

"It was one of those old ship's lanterns, all brass and bevelled glass," says Viv, "and what's more the candle were still alight. Tell 'e what," he said, "if you knock a couple of feet off your eel, I'll blow out me candle!"

Mr. and Mrs. Francis Fisher.

Mr. and Mrs. John Fewings.

Walter and Joyce Cook.

Mr. and Mrs. Tom Willis.

Jim and Kath Hooper.

Ivor and Eileen Bell.

Lionel and Margaret Burroughs.

Nelson and Dorothy Moxey.

Vivian and Betty Moxey.

Mr. and Mrs. Domenico Ponsillo.

Above left: Freddie Coombes with daughters Eileen and Sylvia.

Above right: Rowland Norris.

Right: Mr. and Mrs. Met Watts.

Reg Thyer and Reuben Fisher.

Left: Fred Haste, drove the lorry collecting milk churns for many years. Right: May Cox, a remarkable lady who was deaf and dumb but communicated well with the villagers.

Ray and Eileen Bates when they retired from the Railway Hotel after 21 years.

Frank and Dorothy Cox.

Mrs. Bert Whitcombe.

On the left, Mr. and Mrs. Ron Atkinson who set up the school for dislexic children and was a generous benefactor to the village with two of their guests at the Lunch Club's Christmas do.

Left: Met Whitcombe. Right: Mrs. Dennis Thorne.

A scene seldom seen these days, a Christmas game of cards in the Burtle Inn; Jim Hooper, Gilbey Sweet, Viv Moxey and Reg Thyer.

Tom Willis chatting to Cliff Fursland.

Frank and Queenie Lee.

Arnold Tucker.

Above left: Norman (Henry) Moxey.

Above right: Bill and Connie Vowles.

Right: Bill Vowles and Bill Reece.

Mr. and Mrs. Arthur Baker.

Mrs. Mary Bell, moved to Blagdon Farm when very young with her parents.

Above right: Old Bobby Tratt by the door of his little cottage by the entrance to Catcott Burtle Farm. He always walked with a bicycle but never rode it. Born in 1853 he lived with his father, Thomas, who was a butcher, and his mother, Susan. It was said that he would walk to Moorlinch and back to pluck and draw a fowl for 2d. When his parents died the villagers looked after and fed him.

Mr. and Mrs. Frank Vowles proudly holding their diamond wedding telegram in the garden of their home since 1937.

Left: Wilf Parsons in his turf boat outside his home on the Catcott Road with four of his children; Percy, Evelyn, Fred and Mary. (F. Parsons)

*Below: **Dad's Army!** A strong contingent from a village the size of Burtle was due in part to the large number of small farmers who were exempt from military service. 1) Walt Clarke, 2) Nelson Moxey, 3)　?　, 4) Frank Lee, 5) Hubert Rice, 6) Charlie Sandford, 7)　?　, 8) Met Watts 9) Ralph Pollard, 10) Alan Moxey, 11) Wilf Parsons, 12) Len Hayes, 13) Ivor Bell, 14) The 6ft 6 inch figure of Captain Pook, 15) Bill Smith, 16) Tom Willis, 17) John Fewings, 18) Norman Moxey, 19) Eddie Cox, 20) Charlie Tratt, 21) Arnold Tucker, 22) Vic Pollard, 23) Frank*

Right: Every body in Burtle had and could use a gun, very necessary for some families to fill the pot. This sportsman was photographed outside the front of The Farm about 80 years ago.

Below: Hubert Cox of Fairview House with sons Percy and Leonard.

Mrs. Arthur Tratt, (Dorothy Moxey's mother), with her mother in law, Mrs. Cox, in front of Petherams Farm, now demolished.

Mr. and Mrs. Watts outside their home at West Heath Farm, just off the Edington Road.

Mr. and Mrs. Fred Tratt outside their cottage in Chapel Row. (M. Moxey)

Watts Farm has changed very little over 90 years.

Mr. and Mrs. Hembrow from Burrow Bridge used to visit Burtle every Christmas Day to dispense oranges and other treats to the village children. (E. Bell)

Miss May Cox with her mother outside Elm Tree Farm.

Some of the Frost children when they lived at Hill Farm; Bill, Nora, Gladys, Edwin, Olive, Jessie (married Wilf Parsons) and Dorothy. (H Willcox)

Washday was hard work at Hill Farm; Nora, Olive and Jessie. (H Willcox)

In honour to those who did not return.

Rural Jottings

Footpaths are not such a straight forward part of country life as they may appear to be on the surface. Landowners can receive a lot of flack from the Ramblers Association and the public at large, much of it misplaced. Firstly, many footpaths are termed estate paths, created when almost all the local inhabitants worked on the land, they were internal, informal tracks which would not appear to connect any two points of any importance. Then there were the public paths providing the direct route between villages, used by almost everyone travelling on foot, or, as in the case of bridleways, on horseback.

The question of the upkeep of paths and bridleways has always been a source of contention. It would seem that in Chilton Polden the Parish Council accepted the cost of much of the repairs provided that the paths were used. As the importance of footpaths in everyday life receded their use has become almost entirely recreational. The people using them are no longer villagers visiting friends and relatives but more likely those that have temporarily migrated from the town to the rural idyll to exercise their dogs. The lack of country experience, leaving gates open etc. has led to considerable friction with farmers.

The landowners and farmers view point should be taken into account. They stand to gain very little and could lose a lot, so it is rather unfair to expect them to finance the upkeep of paths purely used for recreational purposes. Either the whole of the population should accept the financial responsibility, through local rates or from central government or those wishing to benefit such as the Ramblers Association should pay for their privilege, much as anglers have to purchase a rod licence, even to fish on their own water. Additionally, each footpath should be systematically designated as such with a clear undertaking of who is to take responsibility for upkeep. The argument has been going on for a hundred years and will probably continue for another hundred!

As people today have a resurgence of interest in footpaths and rights of way, it may be interesting to look into what has transpired over the years since they formed an important part of everyday life of the villagers of Chilton Polden, in particular, Chilton Burtle. The Ramblers Association occasionally hit the headlines, often through the irresponsible actions of some more militant members, cutting fences, cutting swathes through maize crops etc. There has been a radical change in emphasis now that most footpaths are used for recreational purposes, not as they originally served as the shortest route between two points by a population largely without other means of transport. Why should farmers and landowners be losers in our 'everything on a plate culture'?

Using to Chilton Polden as an example of the importance of footpaths in the community it is interesting to follow the course of events in the early 20th century.

In February 1901 the Parish Council agreed to provide a plank over the ditch in the public footpath leading to Edington over the boundary between the two parishes. In February 1902 a letter was written to Mr. Tom Boyer pointing out that he had ploughed up part of the public footpath leading to Edington in his field called "Pulpits" and requested him to abstain from doing so in the future.

A special Council meeting was called in December 1903 to consider an application from Major Kennedy to divert a footpath that ran through his shrubbery at the Priory. The Council agreed subject to the approval of the District Council. The proposal was confirmed in April 1904, presumably with the sanction of the District Council.

In April 1905 the Council decided that the stiles on the Edington footpath should be repaired. A bill for 17s.6d was received from Mr. Francis Rugg in December but was not paid as one of the stiles was in the wrong place. Mr. Rugg was eventually paid in March 1906, when one presumes that the job had been satisfactorily completed.

In December 1907, a number of parishioners living in Chilton Burtle complained by letter that they were being prevented from using a footpath between Robins Lane and Chilton Drove, over a field called "Five Acres", occupied by James Grant and owned by Thomas Moxey. This developed into a long running saga with a vigorous exchange of letters arguing the respective points. Following a further complaint by a group described as "ratepayers from the other end of the Parish" in January 1908 the Council instructed the Clerk to write the following letter to Mr. Moxey.

CHILTON POLDEN PARISH COUNCIL

January 22nd 1908

Dear Sir,

Right of way at Chilton Burtle

In consequence of a letter signed by many of the inhabitants of Burtle, stating that you <u>deny</u> that there is a public right of way from Robins Lane to Chilton Drove across your field called "Five Acres" in the occupation of Mr.James Grant, a committee of the Chilton Polden Parish Council visited the spot on January 10th to enquire into the matter.

It appeared quite clear, both from letters received from former owners and occupiers, and from the evidence of those who know the locality (evidence extending over the period of 60 years) that there is and always has been a public footpath across the field in question, and that no-one has ever been prevented from passing that way until you came into possession of the property quite recently.

The Parish Council are quite convinced that there is a right of way across your field, and I am directed to write and inform you that if you persist in preventing any member of the public from passing that way you will doubtless render yourself liable to an action for assault.

An early answer will oblige,

I am, yours faithfully,
T. Westlake,
Clerk of the Chilton Polden Parish Council
To Thomas Moxey,
Farmer
Chilton Burtle

Burtle,
January 30th 1908

Dear Sir,

I am in receipt of your letter of 27th in reference to right of footpath claimed by the Parish Council, across my field called "Five Acres" at Burtle in the Parish of Chilton Polden. I have made careful enquiries myself but cannot find evidence that there is such a right of footway over the land. I do not want to be unneighbourly and provided fair use is made of a footpath over the field in question, I have no objection to such a path being used but it must be clearly understood that this concession on my part must not be considered as consenting to any other right of way over that piece of land or any other lands I own in the Parish of Chilton Polden.

Yours Faithfully,
Thomas Moxey

To Mr Tom Westlake,
Clerk to the Parish Council,
Chilton Polden,
Bridgwater.

* * * * * * *

The Parish Council wrote to Mr Moxey, asking his consent to the erection of two wicket gates and the making of a foot bridge over the ditch in order that people may go through without opening his gates.

Mr Moxey replied refusing permission for the wicket gates and bridge, no doubt fearing that it would form some sort of precedent.

The saga then goes quiet for several years with apparently no resolution of the problem. Meanwhile, in April 1911, Mr F. Rugg was asked to repair a stile in the Church Path through Mr. Wilce's field leading to Cock Hill. His bill for 17/6d (87.5p) was paid in January 1912. Things did not move very quickly in those days.

In January 1912 the Council received a letter from Chilton Burtle stating that a Mr. Samuel Coombes has erected notices and prevented the public from using an old right of way leading from Robins Lane to Chilton Drove through a field and yard in the occupation of Mr. Walter Shepperd. The Council wrote to Mr.Coombes pointing out that the ancient right of way undoubtably existed through the field in question. In April 1912 yet another player enters the argument, Mr. Eastwood wrote to the Council denying that any public right of way existed across his field but that he would permit the public to cross by permission. By this point, the Parish Council, obviously feeling out numbered, decided to enlist the help of the District Council.

The reply from the D. Council was considered at a meeting in September 1912, also a letter from Mr. Eastwood's solicitor which suggested the Parish Council should acquire the right of way by purchase under sec.8.ss.1.(g) of the local government act 1894. The Parish Council decided to ask the District to supply details of Mr. Eastwood's proposals. In October 1912 the piece of land to create a roadway was on offer at £80. Not surprisingly the P.C. declined the offer as unreasonable to be expected to pay that much where they considered a right of way already existed. In order to avoid costly legislation, however, if he would give the strip of land the Council would consider making a fenced roadway on it.

The erstwhile footpath had developed into a proposal for a road, Mr. Eastwood then reduced his price to £40 presumably considering that half a loaf was better than no bread! In spite of this the P.C. decided not to entertain the purchase and wrote back to the D.C. in those terms. The matter then appears once more to have been allowed to lie without any resolution.

As the O.S. map surveyed in 1884 appears to clearly show the footpath it is surprising that this or the later maps were not referred to by the Council as evidence of the footpath's existence. So, is there is or is there ain't a footpath leading from Chilton Drove to Robins Lane?

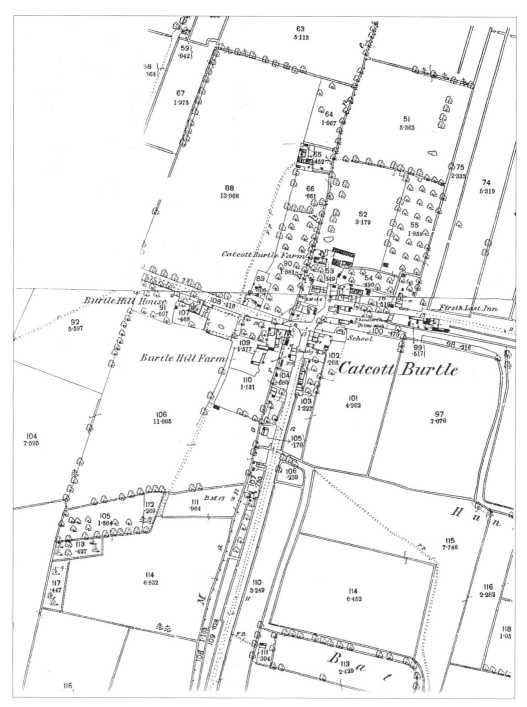

1884 O/S map, part of Catcott Burtle, many of the little cottages are gone.

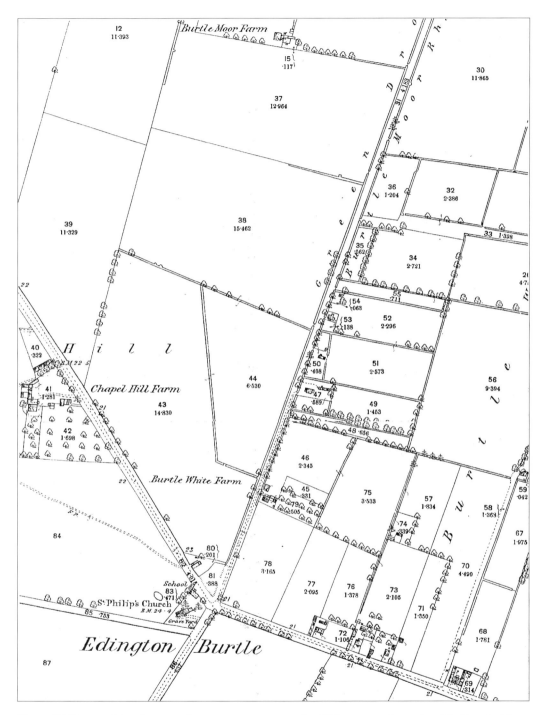

Part of Edington Burtle, note the remote cottage at the S/E corner of number 56. Burtle Moor farm would be completely cut off by the Winter floods.

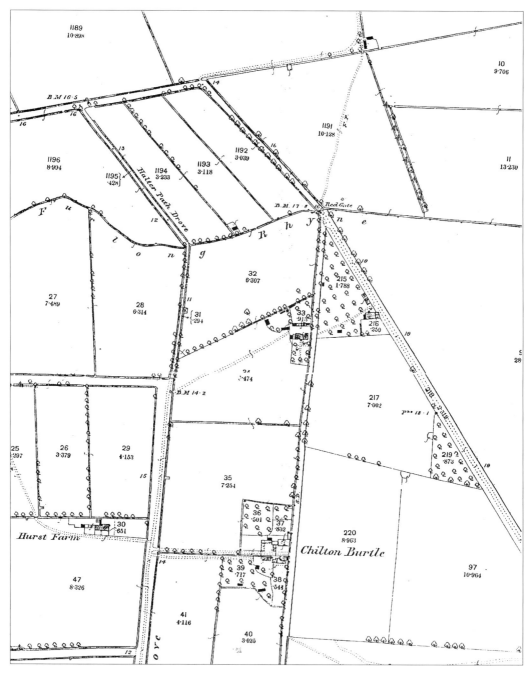

Part of Chilton Burtle, there is no shortage of footpaths

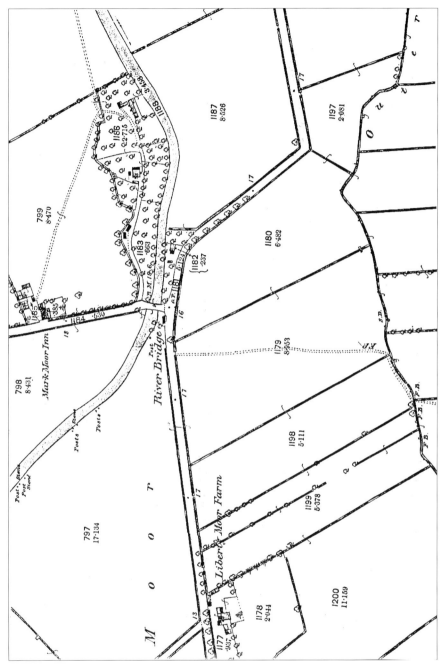

In 1884 there was a cluster of cottages around the river bridge on the Mark Road.

Past and Present People and Occupations

Researching village history is becoming a popular past-time, one aspect of which are the movements of population. As one grapples with tithe and census records, patterns begin to emerge. Burtle has experienced a larger upheaval in terms family movements than most other villages in this area. Some families were so numerous as to almost qualify to be called tribes! It was often quipped that if you removed two or three families from the "Burtles" there would be no-one left to carry on!

In simple terms, the records back to 1801 are fairly comprehensive although for some reason the ages given before 1851 are considered to be unreliable. Were there reasons for this or did people then not know their ages? It is difficult to form an opinion on these quirks.

The enclosures, in the early 1800's in the Burtle area, also provide further information on the settlement of the land into individual hands, although it must be said the major landowners on the hill scooped the majority of the land pool in most villages. Burtle land ownership was more fragmented than most, there being no one major estate encompassing the whole area.

The wide verges gave locals the opportunity to erect their "long acre" cottages alongside the roads on what was often reckoned to be common land. If they could conform to certain conditions such as erecting a chimney within a twenty four hour period it was usually accepted that they had acquired the right to remain. Many of these dwellings along the Catcott Road were no more than hovels and they have long since gone. "Squire" Henniker claimed ownership of the common land and numbered all the cottages in order to charge them rent. It would have been virtually impossible for the occupants to contest it in those days.

To illustrate the situation, in 1851 there were as many as seventy souls living in this type of accommodation on the Catcott side of the Glastonbury Canal, mainly on what used to be known as Catcott Broad Drove. There were some houses, small farms, way out in the "five hundred acres" the large block of peat land to the East of the Catcott Road, contact with the village was as much as a mile over peat tracks with such names as Skimmers, Batchkey, Stubbylawn, Shepherds, Upper and Lower Ropes, Lady's and Jane's Droves and by boat during the Winter floods. By 1891 this number had dropped to around twenty, half a dozen by 1918 and there were none from about ten years ago when the Groves family died out, until now when the sole remaining cottage has been renovated.

1891 Census: Burtle Families

Many villages have a preponderance of certain families and Burtle has always been recognised as one of these. An analysis of the family groups shows this quite clearly. The total population was as follows; Chilton Burtle, including Moorgate and Moor Farms was 60, Edington Burtle 141, Catcott Burtle 171, a total of 372. The breakdown was as follows.

Name	Chilton Burtle	Edington Burtle	Catcott Burtle	Totals
Coombes	–	2	4	6
Cox	12	8	12	32
Fear	14	–	–	14
Grant	2	7	11	20
Grove	–	–	11	11
Groves	1	–	10	11
Lee	4	6	7	17
Moxey	–	11	14	25
Norris	2	17	9	28
Pollard	–	13	–	13
Rice	–	–	12	12
Tratt	14	9	8	31
Watts	–	13	14	27

The population of Catcott Burtle in 1851 was 229, which dropped by 58 during the period up to the 1891 census largely due to the evacuation of cottages on or near the Catcott Road. The total population today has dropped to possibly less than 50.

The main families from 1851 until the present day are as follows. For some reason, best known to themselves, the Grove family always insisted that they were not connected to the Groves family! Could there be an interesting reason for this?

1891 Census: Burtle Families in Catcott Burtle

	1851	1891	1997
Coombs	8	4	--
Cox	30	12	--
Grant	4	11	1(Mrs. E.Bell)
Grove	--	11	--
Groves	10	10	--
Lee	24	7	--
Moxey	6	14	--
Norris	38	9	--
Rice	--	12	--
Tratt	4	8	--
Watts	34	14	--

The population shift is quite staggering and is largely repeated in Edington Burtle and Chilton Burtle. The population of the 'combined Burtles' in 1851 was around 500, probably twice what it is today. Families tended to remain in the village, filling the shoes of their predesessors. There were "romantic raids" on other villages, no doubt nature's way to widen the genetic pool by bringing in a wife from 'away'. They must have been a hardy crew, going courting in a leaky old turf boat on a cold winter's day. I put the large families down to **no television!**

Most farms and some private houses had generators to provide electricity up until the connection to the mains supply in 1963. Mains electricity was taken along the hill villages in the late 1920s.

The occupations listed are quite different to those we are familiar with. Many are listed as live in servants, even in what were somewhat modest households. I suspect that there were some for whom the term "servant" was a convenience to cover up nocturnal sins! In **1851** William Trafford of Chilton Burtle was a 'want catcher', how many people reading this know what that was? (you will have to ask a native!). Henry Bradford was a tallow chandler, several others were listed as cardwinders. The road between Churches Farm and the Burtle Inn was called Fore Street and the one from the First and Last to the present village hall, Burtle Street. The blacksmith at Catcott Burtle was Charles Colman, William Pearce was baker and grocer in Edington Burtle and the wheelright in Chilton Burtle was James Plece. John Guppy was a draper in Fore Street, Sophia Meaker a dressmaker and William Tratt was landlord of the Burtle Inn and a farmer.

There were a surprising number of fairly large farmers, Joseph Tratt farmed 200 acres at Moorgate and Moor Farms Chilton Burtle and raised a family of at least 11 children, his son Isaac who took over the farms also raised nearly as many! William Tucker also of Chilton Burtle had 132 acres, in Edington Burtle Theodore Murch (probable discoverer of the "Burtle Hoard" of which more elsewhere) farmed 130 acres, William Norris 200 acres, William Pocock of Chapel Hill 180 acres. Stephen Pocock his grandson died at Chapel Hill some 100 years later. Some described their occupation as 'occupier of land'.

Today the farms are much fewer and generally larger, some no longer milking cows, employing no-one outside of the family. Mechanisation has completely changed the agricultural scene in the last 40 years. In 1947 there were nearly 40 people milking cows in Burtle although, to be fair, some only had 2 or 3 cows. Today there are six farms milking about the same total number and producing about 3 times the quantity of milk. Incomes were low but life was lived at a more enjoyable pace, everyone seemed to get through and have the price of a pint or more in their pocket. It was not many years ago that a pint of milk, a pint of beer and a loaf of bread were all the same price. There was a structure of self sufficiency, well tended vegetable gardens, a few livestock and a the skilled use of a 12 bore shotgun.

A regular Sunday morning practice was to visit one or other of the farm cider houses in the village, you could get around to several if you had a bike and were still capable of riding it! A number of part-time barbers used to visit and set up 'shop' in one or other cottage. Tradesmen selling every conceivable product called regularly often allowing credit where needed and passing on the news in the best tradition of the 'bush telegraph'.

A close-knit community like that which existed in Burtle helped each other out in times of need. Meals on wheels, usually a bicycle, operated to the advantage of the sick or imfirm. The late Dr. Hayne once told me that Burtle had their own welfare state long before the country as a whole. Without the continuity of the old families it becomes increasingly difficult to retain such values.

One can often hear that we have endured one of the wettest periods in our recent history. Claims that we have had the worst floods for 50 or 100 years are well wide of the mark, however.

Up until the second world war, the water covered much of the levels most winters. There are many accounts of coffins being carried, couples getting married and children travelling to school, all by boat. The Winter months were a difficult time for levels' families, many of the outlying cottages were only accessible by boat. The opportunities for even casual employment were few, some may be lucky enough to get a job with the local threshing gang but more had to make do and mend. Wild-fowling, using the turf boats as punts, was an essential part of moor life and necessary to put food on the table, a good result could add a little to the family budget. Other winter employment could be "reening" (rhyning?) which would be a pig of a job in bad weather and very hard work at the best of times.

Two men, working as a team, usually undertook contracts to clean out the ditches during the Winter months. Some of these would be for the drainage board, the rest private arrangements with local farmers or landowners. Working one each side of the ditch one would shear the bank and the other recover the spoil and weeds onto the other. Concientious men such as Arthur Baker would use a line to ensure that the banks were as straight as a die. The angle of the bank was also very important, too steep would lead to the banks breaking away, too shallow would encourage cattle to tread down the banks. The drainage ditches are so straight that shoddy work would stand out like a sore thumb and be the subject of much chaffing in the pub!

From the accounts of the times by those who lived through them, winters appear to have been colder than today. The flood waters often froze over sufficiently for skaters from far and wide to come and enjoy their sport. Some of the locals were also pretty good on skates and some of the latter are probably hung up and forgotten in local outhouses.

Many had a few cows, reared some calves and a pig and did some casual work on nearby farms. The late Arthur Baker once recounted how, at one time, his day started around 4.30 am with a "pot hunt" with his gun, return to breakfast then cycle to Winscombe to plant trees for the forestry all day before cycling home to tea! The late Mark Pollard cycled to work at Axebridge for several years to work for the council until it was discovered that he lived outside the area of that council's jurisdiction and lost his job as a result. He, incidentally, got married on boxing day, 1912, by boat!

During the second world war everything changed, the Gold Corner pumping station, the largest in Europe, was built. Four 240 hp Crossley diesel engines each with 6 ft diameter pipes to lift the water the 10 - 12 ft into the New Cut, capable of pumping a quarter of a million gallons a minute! Regardless of the real purpose of the pumping station, the beneficial impact on the area upstream, and therefore, the inhabitants was the greatest happening since the Romans built the sea wall some two thousand years ago.

Now, even if the order to start the pumps has to come from a clerk in an air conditioned office a "million miles away", today's floods still ain't what they used to be!

Up until the 1960's it was possible to buy almost every household need without leaving the home. Milk, bread, meat, hardware, paraffin, textiles and sundries, all delivered to the door on a regular basis. Some of these services were provided by local shopkeepers, some by town based businesses. Most villages had a variety of tradesmen to take care of other needs, carpenters, plumbers, stonemasons, cobblers, blacksmith/engineers, builders and the like.

The changes in village life over the last fifty years have been enormous, some good, some not so good. The younger generation were leached out of the system soon after the war by the shortsighted policies dreampt up government and rigorously enforced by Rural District Councils. All forms of industry, large and small must be concentrated in the towns, difficulties were placed in the way of anyone daring to apply for planning permission to build a new or convert an old building for business purposes in the villages. In spite of a recent directive from government (at least thirty years too late!) to look favorably on applications to convert redundant farm buildings into small business units there is still a reluctance to comply. Old habits die hard!

In the far off days of regular (and affordable) 'bus and train services to and from Bridgwater, Glastonbury and Highbridge young people leaving school had little alternative but to get jobs and training in the town. As the public travel network deteriorated the travelling became more expensive, the costs of running a car made a large dent in their income.. They duly married, bought affordable houses in the developing suburbs. Their children were born 'town children' with virtually no connections with the original home village other than occasional visits to granny at weekends. The villages became denuded of the younger generations with young families, keeping the village school open became more and more difficult. Those children that remained were being 'bussed' to larger schools being built in the towns further increasing the pressures on the traditional village communities.

The vacuum created in the villages became filled by the "white settlers", often folk with a very different view of village life. Some, with time on their hands, decided that the rural communities needed re-organising more to their taste and articulated their way on to various village committees and councils. Lists of the members became unrecognisable by the indigenous populations, councillors needed to answer queries were often found to have moved on. The balance of power had shifted away from the original village families, many of whom had been there for generations. In fairness it is only right to point out that some of the incomers have done a very good job and worked hard for the communities, becoming thoroughly integrated into them.

Most of the competant locals were too busy struggling to make a living. Anyway, it was nice to be seen to be doing one's bit, even getting a mention in the local press from time to time. Mind you, there were examples of locals staying on the RDC for ever. One retired farmer, a long time representative of a Polden village was so deaf that he had to read the account of each meeting in the Mercury to find out what had happened! It was difficult to know what he would have done on Mondays had there been no meetings!

Some of the younger generation who remained tried in vain to start businesses in their villages, some attempted to return with equally negative results. Embrionic businesses of great potential were ruthlessly closed down by the planners, a great loss to the rural community. Disallusioned entre preneurs moved away and some even emigrated taking their talents with them. Many of these proved to be highly successful, highlighting the folly of the planners.

The radio programme "Have Your Say" based on the problems of the Wiltshire village of Minety got closer to the facts than most, highlighting the problems but without identifying the root causes.

Jack showed up in the village the other day with the obvious benefit of a recent haircut. "Wurs thee git un done?" asked old George. "Up Glassunbury" replied Jack. "Vunny thing, while I wur waiting me turn, the barber wur cutting the hair o' one o' they 'ippies. 'Ad a mop 'o hair like a bale 'o hay wi' the cords broke, 'e did. 'E zaid to the barber 'ow 'e wos going back into normal life to work in a job vor which 'e wur qualified. I can zee 'ow as you 'ad a good eddication zaid the barber, I just vound yer school cap!"

Burtle Family Groups based on 1891 Census

The reference numbers refer to each house number and the census sheet number in each village. i.e. Ref7/2 in Catcott Burtle = Henry Pope.

SECTION 1, CHILTON BURTLE

Surname	Forenames	Year born	Where born	Comments
Biffen	William J.	1864	Mark	Ref.82/14, Dairyman, farming Dairy House Farm.
Biffen	Mary A.	1860	Sutton	Wife.
Biffen	Harold C.	1886	Chilton Polden	Son.
Cox	Samuel	1836	Edington	Ref85/15, Ag. labourer, Heath Cottage, Chilton Moor.
Cox	Ann	1838	Catcott	Wife of Samuel.
Cox	James	1866	Catcott	Son, Ag. labourer, single.
Cox	Walter	1872	Catcott	Son, "
Cox	William	1874	Chilton Polden	Son, "
Cox	Minnie	1878		" Daughter.
Cox	Lewis	1859	Edington	Ref.86/15, Railway plate layer, Stone-end crossing.
Cox	Esther	1863	"	Wife.
Cox	Arthur	1885	Chilton Polden	Son.
Cox	Maria	1887	"	Daughter.
Cox	Alfred	1889	"	Son.
Cox	Herbert	1891	"	Son.
Fear	Frederick	1864	Catcott	Ref.79/14, Railway labourer, Chilton Drove cr.cot.
Fear	Maria	1866	Chilton Polden	Wife.
Fear	Edward	1821	Sutton Mallet	Ref.81/14, Farmer.
Fear	Ann	1825	Chilton Polden	Wife.
Fear	William	1857	Chilton Polden	Ref.77/13, Agricultural labourer.
Fear	Maria	1862	"	Wife.
Fear	Edward J.	1882	"	Son.
Fear	Arthur J.	1884	"	"
Fear	Bertha H.	1887	"	Daughter.
Fear	Charles T.	1890	"	Son.
Grant	Jane	1831	Catcott	Ref84/14, Widow, living on own means.
Grant	Gilbert	1871	Edington	Son, agricultural labourer.
Groves	Alice	1877	Catcott	Ref.82/14, Live in servant to W.J.Biffen.
Haggett	William	1875	Mark	Ref.83/14, Live in farm servant to Thomas Lee.
House	John R.	1852	Banwell	Ref.80/14, Farmer, "Burtle Farm", Could it be Hurst?
House	Sarah	1853	Pennard	Wife of John.
House	Annie	1875	Mark	Daughter.
House	Raymond	1876	Mark	Son.
House	Frank	1879	Mark	Son.
House	Minnie	1886	Mark	Daughter.
House	infant	1891	Chilton Polden	Presumably not yet Christened!
Lee	Thomas	1829	Chilton Polden	Ref.83/14, Farmer at Parsonage Farm.
Lee	Sarah	1829	Theale	Wife.
Lee	Edward	1861	Edington	Son, farmer's assistant.
Lee	Sarah	1863	Edington	Daughter.
Norris	Wallace	1868	Edington	Ref.84/14,Cousin,ag.labourer,living with Jane Grant.
Norris	Eliza	1866	Shapwick	Cousin, living with Jane Grant. Poss wife of Wallace
Oram	Elisha E.	1875	Ham	Ref.82/14, Live in servant to W.J.Biffen.
Parsons	Edward	1830	Catcott	Ref.78/13, Railway labourer.
Parsons	Sarah	1854	Chilton Polden	Wife.
Tidball	Albert	1883	Huntspill	Ref.78/13, Grandson of Edward Parsons
Tratt	Isaac	1844	Chilton Polden	Ref.75/13, Farmer, Moorgate House and Moor Farm.
Tratt	Hester(?)	1845	"	Wife.
Tratt	Harry	1872	"	Son, farm assistant.
Tratt	Adam	1874	"	"
Tratt	Florence	1877	"	Daughter.

Surname	Forenames	Year born	Where born	Comments
Tratt	Ernest	1879	"	Son.
Tratt	Alice	1881	"	Daughter.
Tratt	Sarah	1883	"	Daughter.
Tratt	Florrie	1885	"	"
Tratt	Albert	1859	"	Ref.76/13, Ag labourer.
Tratt	Eliza	1862	Catcott	Wife.
Tratt	Albert	1885	Chilton Polde	Son.
Tratt	Florence M.	1886		Daughter.
Tratt	Ethel	1889		"

1891 SECTION 2, EDINGTON BURTLE

Surname	Forenames	Year born	Where born	Comments
Bending	Edward	1861	Bath	Ref.77/11, Railway signalman.
Bending	Emma	1861	Castle Cary	Wife of Edward.
Bending	Mildred A.	1887	Wincanton	Daughter of E. & E.
Bending	Hubert A.	1891	"	Son of E. & E.
Bending	Edward U.	1891	"	"
Biffen	Mary Ann	1867	Edington	Ref.76/11, Live in servant, Oliver Tratt, W.R.Fm.
Brice	George	1805	West Horrington	Ref81/12,Nav. Pens, uncle J&E Moxey, widr, lodger.
	Mary A.	1845	Wedmore	Wife of Joseph.
Moxey	Eva	1869	Catcott Burtle	Daughter of J. & E.
Moxey	Anna	1876	"	"
Moxey	George	1878	Edington Burtle	Son of J & E
Moxey	Louise	1882	"	D. of J. & E.
Moxey	Sarah	1884	"	"
Moxey	Lavenia	1816	Edington	Ref.91/14, "The Drove", widow, Farmer.
Moxey	Lewis	1856	Edington	Son of Lavenia, single.
Moxey	John	1854	"	" "
Moxey	Agatha	1876	"	Grand-daughter of Lavenia, lodging with her.
Norris	Albert	1844	Burtle	Ref.85/13,Robins Lane, Foreman on Highway.
Norris	Sarah	1843	Huntspill	Wife of Albert.
Norris	James	1870	Burtle	Single,Son of J. & S., Railway Porter.
Norris	Ambrose	1873	"	" Telegraph Clerk.
Norris	Lily	1875	"	Daughter of A. & S.
Norris	Miranda	1877	"	"
Norris	Earnest Albert	1879	"	Son of A. & S.
Norris	Burtha	1890	"	D. of A. & S.
Norris	Rufus	1867	Edington	Ref.92/14, Platelayer on Railway.
Norris	Elizabeth	1869	"	Wife of Rufus.
Norris	Oliver	1863	Edington Burtle	Ref.82/12, Robins Lane, gen labourer.
Norris	Emily	1868	Ludlow, Shropshire.	Wife of Oliver
Norris	Margaret	1884	Edington Burtle.	Daughter of O. & E.
Norris	John	1885	Edington Burtle.	Son of O. & E.
Norris	Joseph	1887	" "	
Norris	David	1889	"	
Norris	Mildred	1891	"	Daughter of O. & E.
Nuttycombe	Herbert	1875	Edington	Ref.76/11,Living with his uncle, Oliver Tratt.
Nuttycombem	Caroline	1876	Edington	Ref74/11,Grand- daughter of Hannah Tratt.
Phippen	Maria	1822	Edington Burtle	Ref.67/10, Widow.
Phippen	Alma E.	1884	Edington Burtle	Grand-daughter of Maria.
Pocock	Elizabeth	1829	Burtle	Ref.88/13,Chapple Hill Farm.
Pocock	William	1865	"	Son of Elizabeth.
Pocock	George Steven	1867	"	"
Pollard	John	1836	Edington	Ref.65/10, Farmer
Pollard	Betsy	1840	Woolavington	Wife of John
Pollard	Bessie	1870	Edington	Daughter of John and Betsy
Pollard	George	1876	Edington	Son of J & B.
Pollard	Bertha	1879	Edington	Daughter of J. & B.
Pollard	Rose	1880	Edington	Ditto.

Surname	Forenames	Year born	Where born	Comments
Pollard	William	1860	Edington	Ref.66/10, Ag. labourer, Edington Heath.
Pollard	Anna H.	1860	Catcott	Wife of William
Pollard	Rhoda E.	1880	Edington	Daughter of W. & A.
Pollard	Frederick G.	1884	Edington	Son of W. & A.
Pollard	Mark G.	1887	Edington	Son of W. & A.
Pollard	Joseph	1889	Edington	Ditto
Pollard	Bertha R.	1891	Edington	Daughter (Mrs. Rice)
Richards	Winifred Mary	1879	Berrow	Ref.77/11, Living with uncle, Edward Bending.
Salway	William	1883	Moorlinch	Living with grandfather, James Grant.
Salway	Henry Charles	1868	Othery	Ref.94/14, Packer on S. & D. Railway.
Salway	Eliza A.	1868	Chilton Polden	Wife of H.C.
Salway	William J.	1890	Catcott Burtle	Son of H.C. & E.
Searle	Thomas	1854	Bishops Hull	Ref73/11,Stationmaster on Railway, Edington Rd.
Searle	Sarah	1853	Ashcott	Wife of Thomas
Searle	Ernest	1879	Shapwick	Son of T. & S.
Smith	Elizabeth	1811	Meare	Ref.90/14, Independant Means, widow.
Symmons	George	1849	Meare	Ref84/12,Ag labourer, Robins Lane,
Symmons	Amelia	1851	Burtle	Wife of George.
Symmons	John	1874	"	Son of G.& E., ag labourer.
Symmons	Anna	1880	"	D. of G. & E.
Symmons	Ellen	1883	"	" "
Symmons	Hugh	1886	"	S. of "
Symmons	Walter	1888	Meare	" "
Symmons	Lucas	1890	Burtle	"
Tratt	Hannah	1811	Chilton Polden	Ref74/11, Railway Hotel, Farmer.(in Cottage?)
Tratt	Samuel	1832	Chilton Polden	" ", Married
Tratt	Charles	1836	" "	" ", Single
Tratt	Joseph	1839	" "	" ", Widower
Tratt	Oliver	1865	Chilton Polden	Ref76/11, Gatcombe / White Rose Farm.
Tratt	Hubert	1879	Catcott	Nephew of Oliver
Tratt	Fanny	1845	Chilton Polden	Ref80/12, Robins Lane, described as married.
Tratt	Hubert	1868	Edington Burtle	Son of Fanny. Ag. labourer
Tratt	Frank	1870	"	S of F. Gen labourer.
Tucker	George Brice	1866	Wrantage	Ref.75/11, Publican, Railway Hotel.
Tucker	Harriet M.S.	1867	Stoke st. Mary	Wife of G.B.T.
Tucker	Francis G.	1891	Edington Burtle	Son of G.B.T & H.M.S.Tucker.
Watts	George	1840	Wedmore	Ref.68/10, Ag labourer
Watts	Ellen	1843	Plympton, Devon	Wife of George
Watts	Charles	1875	Edington	Son of G. & E.
Watts	Joseph	1883	Edington	Son of G. & E.
Watts	Alfred	1890	Edington	Son of G. & E.
Watts	Robert	1844	Burtle	Ref.93/14, Turf dealer.
Watts	Mary A.	1849	Mark	Wife of Robert.
Watts	Robert F. C.	1877	Burtle	Son of R.& M.
Watts	Sidney J.	1881	"	"
Watts	Felix H.	1893	"	"
Watts	Marcus G.	1886	"	"
Watts	Oscar E.	1888	"	"
Watts	Herbert	1874	Burtle	Ref88/13,Live in servant to Eliz. Pocock, Ch.Hill.
Wheeler	John	1846	N/Known	Ref.83/12, Single, boarder M. Coombes, gen labourer.
Woolmington	Maria	1819	Burtle	Ref86/13,S.in l. Jas Grant,lodging with,ind. means.

1891: SECTION 3, CATCOTT BURTLE

Surname	Forenames	Year born	Where born	Comments
Ash	Thomas	1850	Wedmore	Ref.15/4, Farmer and Innkeeper, Burtle Inn.
Ash	Flora	1851	Cossington	Wife.
Clarke	Thomas	1855	Wedmore	Ref.17/4, Agric labourer, (by Blacksmith's shop?)
Clarke	Eliza Jane	1859	Mark	Wife.
Coombs	Henry	1856	Catcott Burtle	Ref3/1,Agric. labourer. Catcott Rd.
Coombs	Mary Ann	1856	Catcott	Wife.
Coombs	William	1867	Catcott Burtle	Ref13/3,Agric labourer, single, grandson Jane
Coombs	Samuel	1824	Catcott Burtle	Ref39/9, Agric labourer, Sam Curtis' F-I-Law.
Cox	Robert	1822	Catcott Burtle	Ref8/2, Agric labourer, Catcott Rd.
Cox	Margaret	1822	Meare	Wife.
Cox	John	1867	Catcott Burtle	Son, agric labourer.
Cox	Edmund	1837	Catcott	Ref.11/3, Farmer, 1st farm from Catcott crossing?
Cox	Jane	1838	Catcott	Wife.
Cox	Ada	1868	Edington	Daughter, cheese maker.
Cox	Arthur E.	1870	"	Son, ploughman.
Cox	Minnie	1872	"	Daughter, buttermaker.
Cox	Alexander	1876	"	Son, pupil teacher.
Cox	Ralph C.	1878	"	Son.
Cox	Ernest G.	1883	Catcott Burtle	Son.
Cox	Mary Ann	1858	Catcott Burtle	Ref.27/6, Farmer, single.
Curtis	Samuel E.	1862	Weston Super Mare	Ref.39/9, Carpenter.
Curtis	Marie	1864	Catcott Burtle	Wife.
Curtis	Samuel	1886	Weston Super Mare	Son.
Curtis	Ethel	1889	ditto	Daughter.
Dickie (Dicker?)	Rose	1879	Glastonbury	Ref7/2, Stepdaughter of Henry Ash Pope.
Dickie	Elinor	1884	" "	
Dickie	Adolphus	1881	Glastonbury	Ref8/2, Grandson of Robert Cox.Dickie
Giblett	Agnes F.	1883	Westhay	Ref.1/1, Live in Stepdaughter of E & E. Groves.
Giblett	George	1886	"	" " " Stepson of E. & E. Groves.
Gran	George	1854	Edington Burtle	Ref.14/3, Grocer and butcher, (opposite Burtle Inn)
Grant	Florence	1860	"	Wife.
Grant	Reginald G.	1884	Catcott Burtle	Son, (father of Eileen Bell?)
Grant	Hugh	1886	"	Son, (Shocky?)
Grant	Emily	1886	Sutton Mallet	Ref.27/6, Neice to Mary Ann Cox.
Grant	Robert	1851	Edington Burtle	Ref.34/8, Assurance agent.
Grant	Elizabeth	1847	Catcott Burtle	Wife.
Grant	Victoria	1877	Edington Burtle	Daughter.
Grant	Christopher	1880	"	Son.
Grant	Edith	1882	Catcott Burtle	Daughter.
Grant	Bertha	1887	"	
Griffiths	Eliza	1866	Catcott Burtle	Ref.18/4, Daughter of Chas Reading.
Griffiths	William	1887	Woolwich	Son of Eliza.
Griffiths	Edward	1888	Tunbridge Wells	"
Griffiths	Steven	1890	Londonderry	"
Grove	Henry	1850	Catcott Burtle	Ref10/2, Agric labourer, Catcott Rd.
Grove	Betsy	1851	"	Wife.
Grove	Elizabeth	1871	"	Daughter.
Grove	Frank	1876	"	Son.
Grove	Edmund	1876	"	Ref.14/3, Apprentice butcher with Geo Grant.
Grove	Gabriel	1831	"	Ref.19/5, Agric labourer.
Grove	Eliza	1839	"	Wife.
Grove	Matilda	1879	"	Daughter.
Grove	Victoria	1881	"	"
Grove	Bertha	1883	"	"

Surname	Forenames	Year born	Where born	Comments
Grove	Gabriel	1863	Catcott Burtle	Ref.38/9, Agric labourer, lodging with Geo Moxey.
Groves	Edwin	1845	Catcott Burtle	Ref.1/1, Agri. labourer. Catcott Heath.
Groves	Elizabeth	1862	Westhay	Wife.
Groves	Harriet	1879	Catcott Burtle	Daughter.
Groves	Bertha	1882	" "	
Groves	Edwin	1891	"	Son.
Groves	Mary	1831	Moorlinch	Ref2/1, Widow, peat saleswoman. Catcott Heath.
Groves	Mary Ann	1854	Catcott Burtle	Daughter, peat saleswoman.
Groves	Rose Ellen	1881	"	"
Groves	Octavius	1854	"	Ref.25/6, Agric labourer.
Groves	Joanna	1852	Chilton Polden	Wife.
Holly	Mary Ann	1823	Catcott Burtle	Ref.37/9, M-i-law to John Vowels, independant means.
James	William	1861	Bawdrip	Ref35/8, Railway porter.
James	Emily	1862	Mark	Wife.
James	John Albert	1885	Huntspill	Son.
James	Mabel Eliza	1887	"	Daughter.
James	Rhoda E.	1889	"	".
Jefferies	Rose	1881	Abington, Berks.	Ref.17/4, Step daughter of Thomas Clarke.
Jefferies	John G.	1883	"	Step son of T.C.
Hurlett	William	1886	Edington Burtle	Ref9/2, Grandson of Charles Parsons.
Lee	Elias	1845	Catcott Burtle	Ref.12/3, Agric labourer, Catcott Rd.
Lee	Mary Ann	1842	Mark	Wife.
Lee	?????	1839	Catcott Burtle	Brother, "
Lee	George	1880	"	Son, (Father of Ern and Frank?)
Lee	Frank	1882	"	Son, (Nacky?)
Lee	Betsy	1887	"	Daughter. (Nurse Lee)
Lee	George	1844	Chilton Burtle	Ref.38/9, Ind means, lodging with George Moxey.
Maidment	Louisa	1849	Edington Burtle	Ref.21/5, Widow, domestic servant.
Moxey	Robert	1840	Burtle	Ref.20/5, Farmer.
Moxey	Mary Ann	1840	Edington Burtle	Wife.
Moxey	Hebdon	1860		Farmer's Son
Moxey	Agnes L.	1870	Catcott Burtle	Farmer's daughter.
Moxey	Robert C.	1872	" "	Son.
Moxey	Allan	1876	" "	"
Moxey	Annie	1879	" " "	
Moxey	Ellen Kate	1882	"	Daughter. (Mrs. Stradling)
Moxey	Joseph	1851	"	Ref.31/7, Peat salesman.
Moxey	Eliza Jane	1850	"	Wife.
Moxey	Fred	1882	Edington Burtle	Son, father of Geoff.
Moxey	George	1848	"	Ref.38/9, Innkeeper.
Moxey	Anna Mary	1847	"	Wife.
Moxey	Roland	1870	"	Son, peat salesman.
Norris	Charles	1824	Catcott Burtle	Ref5/1, Peat salesman. Catcott Rd.
Norris	Harriet	1826	"	Wife.
Norris	George	1825	"	Ref6/2, Peat salesman, Catcott Rd.
Norris	Mary Ann	1841	Taunton	Wife.
Norris	Henry	1869	Catcott Burtle	Son.
Norris	Jane	1819	"	Ref.13/3, Widow, liv. on her own means, Catcott Rd.
Norris	Alfred	1858	"	Ref.33/8, Peat salesman.
Norris	Emily	1862	"	Wife.
Norris	Mathew	1846	Edington Burtle	Ref.38/9, Agric labourer, lodging with Geo Moxey.
Packer	William	1853	Catcott	Ref.36/8, Agric labourer.
Packer	Caroline	1860	Catcott Burtle	Wife.
Packer	Able	1878	"	Son.
Packer	Eliza	1887	"	Daughter.
Packer	Harry	1889	"	Son.
Packer	Florence	1891	"	Daughter.

Surname	Forenames	Year born	Where born	Comments
Parsons	Charles	1837	Catcott	Ref9/2, Peat salesman, Catcott Rd.
Parsons	Harriet	1840	Catcott Burtle	Wife.
Parsons	Frank	1878	"	Son.
Parsons	Wallace	1870	Huntspill	Ref.16/4, Platelayer.
Parsons	Harriet	1871	Catcott Burtle	Wife.
Parsons	Ann	1827	Mark	Ref.23/5, Widow, outdoor relief worker.
Parsons	Clara E.	1878	Catcott Burtle.	
Pope	Henry Ash	1842	Sherborne	Ref7/2, Railway ganger, Catcott Crossing?.
Pope	Annie	1842	Catcott	Wife.
Pope	Albert	1878	Edington Burte	Son.
Pope	Thomas	1890	Catcott Burtle.	Son.
Pope	Henry	1865	Sherborne	Ref.25/6, Lodger with Octavius Groves,eng driver.
Reading	Charles	1840	Catcott Burtle	Ref.18/4, Agric labourer.
Reading	Jane	1841	"	Wife.
Reading	Frank	1876	"	Son, agric labourer.
Reading	Emma	1882	"	Daughter.
Reading	Edward	1886	"	"
Rice	Samuel	1848	Mark	Ref.28/6, Railway labourer.
Rice	Mira	1847	Catcott Burtle	Wife.
Rice	Edward	1879	"	Son.
Rice	Beatrice	1881	"	Daughter.
Rice	Seaward	1883	"	Son, (Later Manager of creamery).
Rice	Dorcas	1885	"	Daughter.
Rice	Milborne	1887	"	Son.
Rice	Richard	1820	Bridgwater	Ref.30/7, Pensioner.
Rice	Eliza	1839	Edington Burtle	Wife.
Rice	Walter Tom	1872	Catcott Burtle	Son, agric labourer.
Rice	Alice	1876	"	Daughter.
Rice	Fred	1879	"	Son.
Symmons	William	1876	Catcott Burtle	Ref2/1,Live in servant to Mary Groves.
Symmons	George	1818	Catcott Burtle	Ref. 33/8, Widower, ag labourer,lodging A.Norris.
Symmons	Oliver	1866	"	Single, agric labourer, lodging with Alfred Norris.
Tratt	Eliza E.	1849	Chilton Burtle	Ref.22/5, Widow, farmer. (Petherams?)
Tratt	Celia	1870	Catcott Burtle	Daughter, working on farm.
Tratt	Arthur E.	1880	"	Son.
Tratt	Thomas	1819	Edington	Ref.26/6, Butcher.
Tratt	Susan	1822	Long Sutton	Wife. Laundress.
Tratt	Robert	1853	Chilton Burtle	Son, (Old "Bobby" Tratt?) No occupation shown.
Tratt	William	1822	Chilton Burtle	Ref.32/7. Peat salesman.
Tratt	Charlotte	1811	Street	Wife.
Vowels	John	1853	Wedmore	Ref.37/9, Agric labourer.
Vowels	Sarah	1853	Catcott Burtle	Wife.
Vowels	Albert	1879	Wedmore	Son.
Vowels	Frederick	1881	"	Son.
Vowels	Mary Ann	1884	Catcott Burtle	Daughter.
Vowels	Frank	1886	"	Son.
Vowels	William	1889	"	Son.
Watts	Frederick	1879	Wincanton	Ref3/1,Nephew of Henry Coombs.
Watts	Sarah	1821	Catcott Burtle	Ref4/1,Widow, outdoor relief worker.
Watts	Joseph	1859	"	Son, agric labourer. Catcott Rd.
Watts	Lucy	1884	"	Grand-daughter of Lucy.
Watts	Charlotte	1814	Wedmore	Ref.24/6, Retired dressmaker.
Watts	George	1844	Wedmore	Ref.29/7, Agric labourer.
Watts	Jane	1857	Catcott	Wife.
Watts	John	1877	Catcott Burtle	Son.
Watts	Elizabeth	1879		Daughter.
Watts	Dora	1882	"	"
Watts	Doffice??	1884	"	"
Watts	Louisa	1885	"	
Watts	Fred	1888	"	Son.
Watts	Infant	1891	"	Son.

CHAPTER 5

al History and Conservation

n unusual area as the Somerset lowlands, a re-cap in the form of a
chronological course of events may assist the reader to a better
what we enjoy today.

ago Britain was firmly in the grip of the ice age. The climate became
as the ice melted, the sea level rose by as much as 300 hundred feet, the
whole of the central Somerset saucer developed into an inland sea. A layer of
alluvial silt accumulated in the depressions. The surface became brackish saltings,
encouraging the growth of rushes, reeds and other plant life that could tolerate
these conditions. The climate, temperatures and rainfalls, fluctuated greatly over a
period covering several thousand years.

By 6,000 BC the mildness of the climate led to rapidly growing vegetation which
died down into the brackish, acid water, starting the formation of the extensive peat
beds. The rivers draining into the basin from the surrounding hills eventually
displaced the salt waters, slowly creating freshwater lakes in their place. This
accelerated the peat growth and some of the peat beds, as much as thirty feet deep,
were raised above the mean water levels for much of the year. The huge tidal range
of the Bristol Channel would occasionally flood the levels up as far as Glastonbury,
causing temporary salinity which would take several years to leach out.

Many thousands of acres of shallow lakes and swamp with occasional, gently
raised island areas, the Polden Hills through the centre, the higher hills around the
perimeter and the close proximity of the sea combined to produce an incredibly
diverse habitat. The water levels fluctuated considerably between Summer and
Winter. Fish were abundant and birds such as pelicans, bitterns, swans and
wildfowl flourished. Wild boar, deer and other large game were plentiful.

It is not surprising that such conditions should attract some of the earliest
attentions of man. The tribes living on the peat moors some six thousand years ago
were growing crops and raising livestock on the surrounding hills. Their primary
mode of travel and transportation of goods over the moors was by dugout boats.
Intricate networks of raised wooden tracks, some beautifully crafted, crossed the

Where the peat has been extracted there are thousands of acres of water of varying depths, providing a great variety of habitats.

firmer, less watery parts, connecting the prehistoric settlements on the small islands. The presence of these primitive communities, living mainly off the land and the abundant wildlife, would have made little ecological impact on the area.

The proportion of open water gradually diminished as the peat level rose, the 1,000 acres of the Meare Pool became the largest remaining area of open water. The first human activity to affect the levels was probably when the Romans reputedly built some sea defences, reducing the ingress of sea water over the low lying land. When water movement slowed down it released the particles held in suspension, gradually building up the five miles wide coastal belt which is usually called 'The levels", the lower, interior peatland is known as "The Moors". The former is an alluvial clay laid over thin, alternative layers of peat and clay and is at approximately sea level. This was the first part of the lowland to be reclaimed for agricultural use, the peaty swamps were considered to be mainly waste land, being as much as fifteen feet below sea level in the lowest areas.

The monks of Glastonbury Abbey had spent much time and energy improving the river systems by straightening and re-routing, in the 13th, 14th and 15th centuries. Although this was mainly to improve the navigational potential of the area it also improved the drainage a little. Some additional drainage rhynes leading into the rivers Brue and Axe were dug, the first grazing of animals on limited areas of peatland for a few months in Summer became possible. The Meare Pool was eventually drained in the late 17th century. The rivers could only discharge into the sea at low tide, the fall of the river beds was around 1:5000 so, at one foot per mile, without mechanical pumps, drainage was a painfully slow operation. The high tides would also make the rivers tidal for a considerable distance inland until the advent of one way clyses, the first was believed to have been fitted at the mouth of the River Brue in the fifteenth century. A clyse is large, often wooden, door hung between stone piers so as to allow fresh water to escape into the sea at low water but is shut by the pressure of the rising tide, thereby preventing sea water from entering the river.

For some, as yet unexplained, reason, the peat growth started slowing down around 500 AD. It has been systematically dug for fuel for over a thousand years, gradually lowering the land over a large area. Each time the land was dug the level would reduce by two to three feet. The virgin sections would remain several feet above the surround and become quite dry, encouraging the growth of heather and bracken, eventually over taken by birch, bog myrtle, sallow and alder. The actual level of the peat itself could vary by several feet between Summer and Winter. Being like a gigantic sponge, it would absorb the water in wet times and rise accordingly.

The rate at which peat was extracted accelerated rapidly in the first half of the twentieth century with the increasing use for horticulture. Since the second world war the arrival of sophisticated excavation machines which can take out five or six feet at a pass have speeded up the extraction by at least twenty times. These dig straight down to the underlying clay, leaving large lakes of open water. Hundreds of engine driven pumps worked day and night pumping the water into the lacework of rhynes, keeping the water levels in the workings low enough for the machines to operate. There is a now a growing number of pumps, operated by conservation groups, reversing the process by pumping water back onto low lying meadows to recreate wet land habitats.

Although not often getting much credit for it, the farmers and peat diggers have been responsible for developing the familiar open grassland areas which attract so many waders and wildfowl. For centuries life on the levels has been harder than it was on the more amenable higher ground. It is not surprising that when the opportunity to increase their incomes presented itself, the locals grasped it with both hands. They should not be blamed either for peat extraction or for stepping up the tempo of their farming operations.

It is easy for today's affluent society to criticise these practices from the insulated comfort of an arm chair. They have not experienced the rigors and uncertainties of past life on the moors, and should therefore respect the actions of those that have.

Old maps show how many smallholder families lived in remotely situated hovels right out in the peat moors. These were often more than a mile across the soft ground and only accessible by boat for the Winter months. Bearing this in mind, the younger generations who had been told of these times by their forebears, were not to be denied when better times were on offer. Subsidies, introduced to encourage the production of cheap and plentiful food during and after the war encouraged the agricultural improvement and exploitation of the moors. The result was an incredibly improved farming efficiency, if the rest of British industry had matched this performance, the UK would be in a league of its own in world trade. The subsidies were a political arrangement that worked so well that farmers became victims of their own success. In spite of stories of the over use of sprays and artificial fertilisers they were not much used on the peat moors until very recently and even then in nowhere near the quantities on the arable land on the hill ground. Many of the extravagant claims the uninformed and extremists make about farmers causing the degradation of wildlife habitats that hit the headlines are quite unjustified on the levels.

A main drainage rhyne, these are the responsibility of the area drainage boards and landowners pay drainage rates to cover their upkeep. These are fed by smaller field division ditches which are the direct responsibility of the farmers, they need cleaning out about every five years.

The agricultural grant system became an embarrassment to successive governments who were too timid to make the sort of changes that were needed. The focus should have been shifted much earlier toward more environmental and conservation based objectives. Lack of foresight led to the confrontational experiences with local farmers, government departments tend to be clumsy, bureaucratic organisations, lacking sensitivity. Having so recently experienced the greatly improved incomes and lifestyles, it is unrealistic to expect farmers to return to the conditions they fought to leave behind years ago.

A peewit's (lapwing or green plover) nest with its customary four pointed eggs which keeps them tightly packed in the nest with the points inwards. The numbers breeding on the levels have dropped drastically over the last 20 years.

Until recent years, the open meadow land hosted a wide range of ground nesting birds, lapwings, curlews, snipe, skylarks, wildfowl in abundance. The draining of the levels by the peat diggers' pumps certainly lowered the water table by several feet and had a major affect on botanical species in particular. The drainage has allowed access on to the land for chain harrowing and rolling much earlier in the Spring. Increasing use of fertilisers has hastened Spring growth, early cutting for silage has become the normal practice. This tends to coincide with the nesting of ground birds, and doubtless, has had some bearing on the decreases being reported.

The families in the lowland villages were almost born with a gun in their hand. It was an essential piece of equipment, enabling the owners to shoot wildfowl for the pot. In spite of the high numbers of shooters, they did not have any significantly detrimental affect on the wild life. Wildfowling has almost died out, certainly no-one has to shoot to keep body and soul together any more.

Much more serious than many of the urban and academic experts will accept, is that with the decline in shooting, predator species have got out of control. Magpies, crows, foxes and, in particular, mink are a curse. How any one can argue for the protection of these vermin is beyond the comprehension of those who really understand the wildlife of the levels. The problem is that an articulate idiot's plausibility tends to outweigh the earthy reality of the true, indigenous, working naturalists born and bred in the area.

When the Nature Conservancy Council became interested, their approach was very heavy handed and adversarial which put the backs up of those highly independent farmers who felt that their rights over their own land were under threat. This clumsy lack of diplomacy probably delayed the conservation cause by several years. Why is it that city based, single minded organisations verging on fanaticism, who are often represented by the least appropriate people, take it upon themselves to negotiate directly with a section of the public where neither party either trusts or understands the other? Had they been prepared to make more use of local conservation minded naturalists who already had lines of communication, this counter productive situation may well have been avoided. Many farmers are seriously interested in natural history and would have no doubt been prepared to promote the aims and objectives of the conservation movement, negotiating agreements as a readily acceptable part of the rural community.

The various conservation organisations involved with the levels do not always appear to have been pulling together in the past, exposing petty jealousies. Conditions that suit some species are anathema to others, whether insects, birds or mammals etc and this shows up by each tending to pursue their own encapsuled interest. I have long felt that a field study and interpretation centre on the moors would be a great asset but that it would have to operate under independent management in order to reflect all aspects of life on the levels.

Most farmers are now co-operating, entering into management agreements with English Nature, NCC's successor, and taking an interest in the conservation movement. There are still problems which must be addressed. One, quite serious in farmers' minds, is that although they pay drainage rates on their land, the Environment Agency maintain unreasonably high water tables by agreement with English Nature who, on their part do not appear to pay drainage rates on that land. One hidden hazard is the lack of water storage capability by not lowering river levels quickly enough. Perhaps the experience of West Sedgemoor in the Summer of 1997 where a sudden flood decimated the land for both farmers and conservationists have brought the message home. Although the management agreements pay regular compensation to farmers, some of them take a drop in income to participate. Only with diplomacy and patience will the problems and irritations that still remain, be sorted out amicably.

With the creation of lakes from the peat digging and the shallow water scrapes on low lying land, I am delighted to see that hides for public use are being built at strategic points. There has always been a danger that the wildlife would become a

An ariel view of some worked out peat diggings, Glastonbury in the distant left. Narrow strips of raised peat are left after digging which are quickly colonised by shrubs and trees.

"honey pot", attracting far too many people for the good of the conservancy efforts. People management is very important and is not much removed from systematic cattle and sheep handling, a matter that occupied most of my working life! When I first mooted the idea of hides to educate and control the public, it was rather poo-pooed, its good to see them get there in the end. Too many people in all the wrong places could be the biggest problem yet to be solved.

A recent illustration of a scheme, ill thought out and ineptly presented and promoted was Avalon 2,000. Like the curate's egg, it was good in parts. Among the ideas was the formation of a cycle track following the old railway line for much of its length. This would have taken it through some of the best wildlife reserves on the moors. As many as 200,000 tourists a year were forecast, not a situation conducive to good, undisturbed wildlife conservation. English Nature, who I was surprised to find backing the project, had seemingly been seduced by suggestions of as much as a million pounds to pour into its other reserves on Westhay heath. The promoters declared that farmers owning sections of the old rail track had been consulted regarding the cycle track although the ones that had were as scarce as hens' teeth. It was proposed to create an eco centre on the site of the old Moorlands sheepskin factory between Glastonbury and Street, together with the reconstruction of an iron age lake village on a purpose built lake. The total finance package amounted to an enormous thirty five million pounds and was eventually turned down by the millennium fund. I, like many others, I suspect, find it difficult to accept such incredibly expensive projects. Somewhat cynically, I suspect there may have been hidden agendas with some planning retirement in the Bahamas at the end of it all! Hopefully, the undesirable elements will not now happen.

The countryside the visiting naturalists enjoy is a consequence of many generations of man's activities, a point that should not be forgotten. Most of the raised peat beds have been systematically dug over for fuel, lowering the level to a point where they once more become so boggy that their agricultural value is reduced but they do attract wildlife. Drainage ditches and rhynes, pumping stations and improved main waterways gradually convert it back to good grazing land. Along come the peat diggers and create large areas of open water, once more encouraging wildfowl, waders and water plants. I have often been puzzled by the violent opposition to this cycle of events. Surely, the variety of environment has never been better for the enormous range of species that could be attracted to or regenerated on the levels.

One farmer had a knock on his door and found an earnest young man, complete with binoculars and camera standing in the yard. "I'm looking for nightjars and I wondered if you can help me?" "Got a couple upstairs, hold 'bout a gallon apiece", replied the farmer.

My Road to Damascus

At the age of five, I found my first bird's nest, a chaffinch had built in a conifer at the bottom of the rick yard. Within a few days, I found a missel thrush feeding its young in an apple tree in my grandfather's orchard. My lifelong love affair with nature was finally consummated by watching a pair of kingfishers feeding their young with minnows caught in the rhyne at the bottom of our farmyard. My first book on birds arrived for my birthday that Summer and probably did more to encourage me to read than any other factor. The Wembdon marshes, west of Bridgwater, and Cannington brook running through them to the sluice into the River Parrett were my idea of paradise!

Father was the tenant of a small, isolated dairy farm before and during the early war years. In April 1944 we moved to a larger farm at Cossington on the Polden Hills. One of my first actions was to get on my bike in order to explore the area. From a vantage point on the hill, I looked out over a vast expanse of low, rushy moorland, interspersed with rhynes, small covers and some scrub land. I rode my bike at top speed, down the hill into this unknown territory without a thought as to how I would find my way home! I felt that I had left paradise and found heaven. Fifty-eight years later, I have discovered no reason to change my mind.

The nearest moorland village to Cossington was Burtle and when I could give my father the slip and avoid farm chores I spent many happy hours in the area bounded by the Poldens and the River Brue. As one develops an affinity with nature it is easy to resent anything that threatens the sanctity of it. This normally took the shape of my father with a list of jobs awaiting my attention!

In the Winter of 1949 / 50, the Mid Somerset Naturalist Society was formed by a group of expert, dedicated naturalists centred around Bridgwater. I was in Winford Orthopaedic Hospital near Bristol at the time so I was extremely envious of my cousin, Alan, of the same age who had joined right at the beginning. The MSNS was a wonderfully well run forerunner of today's conservation movements, producing an excellent annual magazine with very detailed records which are most interesting to read today.

As a growing lad, my heroes were naturalists such as Seton Gordon, Mortimer Batten, E.W.Hendy, James Fisher, Eric Hosking etc. The eventual opportunity to meet some of these worthies, hitherto regarded as remote deities, was little short of miraculous to one of my tender years.

The Mid Somerset Naturalist Society organised regular field trips which were led by members who were each experts in their field. Points and items of interest would be discussed and explained to the juniors and less well informed members. Mrs Marie L. Colthurst was the dynamo with able assistance from her genial husband, Bill. A little like a 'Maggie and Dennis' duo in a rural setting! Louis Kelting of the Somerset Rivers Board, Claude Palmer a local auctioneer, his daughter, Eileen, Douglas Perrett the proprietor of a chemist's shop, John Cowley of Edington who was a prominent emptomologist and Mr Hamblin, a very knowledgeable botanist were just some of the great pool of talent on which the society could draw. Don Slocombe was the secretary for many years.

These outings stimulated a great interest in natural history and conservation. Not only did some of the leading lights promote the cause of conservation, they actually went out, and from their own resources, bought particularly important and sensitive sites in order to further the cause. In spite of their deep interests they were not fanatical, realising that responsible shooting and vermin control were part of the country scene and with some exceptions, an aid to conservation.

I feel very privileged to have had my interests nurtured, developed and shaped by such people. Today there are all sorts of career opportunities in the field that simply did not exist in my young days. I did work at Slimbridge for a short while in the early days as I had a hip problem and there was some doubt as to whether my leg would stand up to farm work. The surgeon eventually decided that it would and I was commanded to present myself for work on the family farm.

The Wildlife

My main interest was ornithology and there was no shortage of birds to watch. I have travelled extensively throughout the British Isles and I am convinced that few other regions can compete with the number of species that are found on the moors. In May 1980 I made a recording of the dawn chorus in one spot between Burtle and Westhay, now a reserve, and over thirty species have been identified from it.

Some species appear to have declined from their previously common status. Lapwings, curlew and snipe are among these, skylarks also much less common on the hill than they were. Corncrakes are no longer heard, they are rarely seen in any event. Nightjars were present until a few years ago, they favoured the drier, raised peat with some heather and bramble growing on it. The re-appearance of suitable habitat in the reserves will hopefully see their return. Many species of duck, on the other hand, are taking advantage of the lakes and reed beds and breeding well. It is to be noticed that large broods of ducklings on the network of rhynes and ditches are quickly reduced in numbers and I suspect that mink are responsible. Small birds are in abundance, nightingales can be heard singing almost anywhere there is some woodland.

Bitterns have re-appeared but as yet are not known to have bred. Marsh harriers are breeding, the first recorded in the county. Merlin are known to have bred on the moors. Sparrow hawks, hobbies, kestrels, buzzards, tawny owls and little owls are common. The moors are the major remaining stronghold of that beautiful bird, the barn owl, their population represents a high percentage of the total left in the country. Whinchats and wheatears are common as are the warblers. Amongst the large flocks of winter immigrants are bewicks and whooper swans in such numbers as to present some farmers with a problem. An occasional Summer visitor is the red footed falcon.

Following several drier than average Summers, the vole population can approach pestilential proportions. I have often watched the herons stalking them very successfully in the grass tussocks. Eels are plentiful and there are several heronries on and close to the moors. It can be quite amusing to watch the antics of a heron trying to swallow a particularly large specimen. The eel continues to writhe and twist on its way down the gullet. I have heard it said that the front end is being

242

digested at the same time as the tail is still flailing around in full view.

The presence of mink has, without doubt, had a detrimental affect on ground nesting birds and water birds alike. What those idiotic, fanatical animal liberationists were thinking of when they released them into the wild is beyond me. I suppose the truth is that they have no real understanding of wildlife other than that they picked up in their childhood from Beatrix Potter. Mink have no natural predators in this country, are as agile as a squirrel in trees and swim readily. Foxes have increased phenomenally and are becoming very bold, rummaging in dustbins and chasing cats away from bird tables in village centres. Magpies are every where, taking more small birds' nests than almost anything else. The increase in the crow population presents just one more problem to the small birds' nests.

A once familiar mammal that has all but disappeared is the water vole. As kids fishing in the South Drain we used to tempt them with small pieces of bread saved from our sandwiches. They could get quite tame and eventually reach a point where they would sit and wait for their titbits. I am sure that mink are almost entirely responsible for their decline.

Fishing is a wonderfully peaceful occupation providing good opportunities to watch the wildlife. Nothing equals the electric blue flash of a kingfisher speeding over the water. The whistle of an otter at dusk evokes a feeling of being at one with nature. Should an otter swim past it is as well to forget the fishing for a while and enjoy its company by remaining absolutely still.

The otter is making a comeback on the moors, several reserves are dedicated to their well being. The large areas of water and the close proximity of waterways bulging with fish should greatly enhance their chances.

Over the last twenty or so years, roe deer have arrived in considerable numbers. Their appearance could be connected with the reduction in shooting, they would never have survived the attentions of the 'marsh cowboys'. Their presence enhances an evening walk on the droves.

Grass snakes enjoy the wet conditions and live well on the bounty of frogs etc. Adders inhabit the drier parts and grow to much greater lengths than the two feet suggested in the text books, I have filmed adders in excess of three feet long. In Spring sunshine but with a cold wind they will bask in a small sheltered spot among the dry bracken. You have to be very careful to get near without spooking them by the vibrations of your footsteps.

Whilst I can appreciate and enjoy the many the plants, insects and other wildlife, there are many publications by such competent authors as Bernard Storer and Desmond Hawkins', in which they are discussed in detail. There are a multitude of butterfly and dragonfly species over most of the area. Strange plants such as tussock grass, can be venerable growths many years old. Fields full of orchids are visited by flirtatious flights of marbled white butterflies. Whatever the individual interest, its all there, so long as the public act responsibly, shutting gates and observing the requirements of the signs displayed at all the reserves.

The sun playing on some large willows.

CHAPTER 6

Reflections and Round-Up

In recent years, there has been a growing debate over the degeneration of rural life and standards, supposed and real. Opinions have been aired in the press, over the airwaves and even in the House of Commons. Many of these commentators, unfortunately, lack real, first hand knowledge, and as a consequence, often offer superficial, quick fixes ranging from the sublime to the ridiculous. These well meaning people, far removed from the grass roots, simply do not understand either the complexities of the rural situation or the people in it.

It is necessary to look back into history to find the platform upon which rural community spirit was born. The poor laws had a large bearing on families staying in the same villages for many generations, it was difficult to move to another parish on a permanent basis. Similarly, farmers would be discouraged from moving too far, it would be difficult to get a tenancy in an area where one was not known. A couple of hundred years ago most of the land was in the hands of the aristocracy, not much was owned by the farmers. The open field system operated for those who 'belonged' to that particular village, it was not easy to just 'pick up sticks' and carry on in another parish. Your rights related to your own parish and that was that!

This, almost enforced, family stability, ensured that generation after generation were anchored in their own parish, thereby each village developed its own character. The continuity gave rise to a tight knit community, jealously protecting what they perceived to be their very own patch of England. The families in the "big houses" also had a tradition of the estates passing down through their heirs. The whole scene was one of an interwoven society, very interdependent on each other but largely independent of the outside world. Associations between the squires in the Manor Houses, as employers, and families from the village labour pool would also carry on down through the generations. Where there were beneficent and understanding land lords the system could work very well, all villagers would be sure of a roof over their heads in old age, quite often rent free.

One evergreen reason for an excursion out side the confines of a young man's own village was the pursuit of the fair sex. This was not without its hazards, the menfolk did not take kindly to this type of invasion by the young blades of nearby parishes and could get quite "physical". Many are the tales told of the hair raising adventures by the old hands in their youthful attempts to widen the bloodlines of their own and neighbouring parishes! In Winter, the family turf boat would be used, even if leaking, this did not seem to quench the flames. In farming terms, the breeding of close relatives is called line breeding if it works, inbreeding if it doesn't! At least the collection of brides from neighbouring parishes tended to widen the gene pool within one's own.

Each village had its own microcosm of welfare organisations which, whilst not providing much comfort, usually kept body and soul together. The village charities, mostly set up by wealthier inhabitants with either a genuine wish to help the less fortunate or to salve their conscience, played an important role.

Many generations of this bonding developed the original village community spirit. It was much, much more than a few people getting together to organise some event or other once a year and enjoying themselves meanwhile. Leaders in the village community were not always the farmers and businessmen, ordinary working folks could be fully involved and play an important part in events. Because a man was not born with the proverbial silver spoon it did not exclude him from positions of relative importance in the community. Talent often shone through and could elevate a man's status. Community spirit is not something that can be constructed quickly. It is not like a trifle where a mixture of components can be dropped into a dish and the finished article is ready for serving. Community spirit is more akin to aging good port or wine, it must be handled carefully and encouraged in its development over many years. Even with great care things can still go wrong.

When the enclosures were in full flow, land ownership by ordinary people started to become a fact but there were also severe cases of hardship. Smallholders without a tenancy agreement in writing had no way of claiming their common rights. The big landowners and people with influence could steer an enclosure bill through Parliament regardless of others of less material wealth. Arthur Young, a farmer and writer whose career spanned the eighteenth and nineteenth centuries, tried with others to introduce a bill where by those who wished to participate could and those that did not would have the right to continue as before. That bill would have enabled dissenting smallholders to continue as before. Unfortunately for them the interests of bigger landowners prevailed and as a result many of them became general labourers. The whole process was a slow metamorphosis from the old feudal system almost imperceptibly to one with a less even spread of wealth and benefits.

This was the picture in most villages, but not to the same degree in Burtle. For a start the land ownership was fragmented, what is now the village, being originally outposts of the three hill villages, Catcott, Edington and Chilton Polden. There is a complete absence of big, manorial type houses on the moors, there are a few large farm houses. The most important houses are all located in the villages on the hill, but even there, there are no stately homes.

If life in the villages on the hill was hard, life on the moors was even harder and the people in Burtle tended to be rather looked down upon socially by their hill dwelling neighbours. Even in my time there was still some evidence of this. At the same time there was a grudging admiration for their independent lifestyle and attitudes. "Thur be a lot o' characters down in Burtle!", was a commonly heard quote.

Burtle had, and still has, its silver band, had its own harvest home, the revels, the repository sales, a plentiful succession of pubs and a well earned reputation for pulling together. Above all they have always shared a capacity to enjoy themselves!

When planning regulations were introduced, many small rural cottages were "condemned" as not being fit to live in. Bureaucracy had arrived with a vengeance. About forty dwellings in Burtle were compulsorily pulled down. This was appropriate for the hovels down on the peat moors but at least half, those situated within the village, could have been economically improved. The authorities were adamant, quoting chapter and verse from the regulations to support their actions. Whatever the merits of the legislation, the result has been that many pretty little cottages, which could have provided affordable, comfortable and attractive accommodation have been lost. Burtle did not have an influential landowner to stand up to the planners as did the villages up off the moors. It is quite clear that some of the condemned cottages were no worse than many of those allowed to stay in other villages and now so greatly valued by those who appreciate the rural scene.

For many years the village was largely self sufficient with what was produced and the trades and services contained within the community. Any other requirements could be met by neighbouring villages. This was more or less true until the advent of the second world war. There were many regular roundsmen selling an extraordinary range of household, farm and trade requirements. These were known as "Johnny Fortnights", an inaccuracy as the visits could be anything from twice a week to several months apart. The goods on offer could be of good quality and highly satisfactory customer relationships often continued over many years. In those days of limited transport options it was possible for, particularly, the poorer families to satisfy most needs without expensive visits to the town. This is a role now partly taken over by the mail order club catalogues.

There has always been a trickle of incomers to the villages including, to a lesser extent, Burtle which was not considered fashionable. The hill villages became highly desirable places in which to live with their splendid views over the moors. Many new houses were built to accommodate a huge influx from the towns, the trickle became a flood. Some of the new arrivals, unfortunately, brought their city ways with them. It was not long before there were demands for street lights, speed limits, playing fields etc. in pursuit of the utopian and elusive tranquillity they had read about in twee books and glossy weekend supplemental columns.

Burtle has been luckier than most of the villages, those moving into Burtle did so because of the friendly reception and have usually become involved in village activities. One Burtle farmer, however, received a phone call, from a new arrival, asking him to milk his cows later in the mornings as the hum of the milking pump was waking them up. The afternoon milking was a problem too, they normally had a rest about then! Why is it that the escapees from suburbia immediately attempt to transplant the environment they have just left, into their chosen village?

Some new arrivals mount vehement opposition to any extension of existing village businesses and almost go berserk on hearing of any proposed new ones. Since the second world war, it has been planning policy to force all business into the town based trading estates. This has left many villages bereft of tradesmen, businesses and employment opportunities.

After the war when country youngsters left school there was little alternative but to seek work and apprenticeships in the towns. Most rural areas had a reasonable bus service making this possible. As time progressed and these young workers got married they had to economise by buying or renting houses in the towns. Their children were born and grew up in the towns and were lost to the villages. Meanwhile, only established professionals and the better off, elderly people, were able to afford the steeply escalating village house prices. The costs of living in the rural idyll were escalating sharply, preventing the young village exiles from returning to their roots. With the changing generation balance, bus services declined and were eventually completely withdrawn, increasing the isolation of the village.

Other, similar rural areas, have encouraged the setting up of independent, owner operated buses, giving a valuable service to their communities. De-regulation of passenger transport made this easier in the short term and it seemed a good idea at the time. It quickly became apparent that as the new bus companies grew, so did their greed and hate of any form of competition, real or imagined. They did not show any interest in servicing these country routes until they had "stitched up" the more lucrative city and town services. That done they turned their malevolent attentions on to the smaller operators, running parallel services a few minutes earlier and charging below economic rates. In a short while the independent operator is forced out of business and the big boys take over. This is closely followed by a reduction of the service by at least half in order to reduce their operating losses to a minimum, their overheads are such that they cannot possibly make it pay but their presence acts as a deterrent to any aspiring rivals. If rural regeneration is to happen, urgent action is needed to prevent this sort of scandalous behaviour in future.

With the children of the economic exiles, now growing up in the towns, there are less village children to educate leading to the closure of village schools. Many of the upmarket occupants of the new executive houses send their kids to private schools and not many pensioners have children of school age. Bussing village children to bigger schools, with all the nonsense that can throw up. How silly some of the regulations governing who qualifies for transport, and who doesn't, are. Siblings attending the same school can be prevented from travelling together on half empty buses because of a difference in age. In this area many parents have to drive the kids to school to avoid the children being exposed to the dangers of busy main roads. As a school manager of one of these small village schools for some years, I have a deep seated belief in the important part they can play in the community. Whatever the IQ of the children, there was rarely a reading problem until the arrival of one of those (the children call me tony) trendy headmasters. He didn't stay too long but it took a very experienced and capable head teacher some time to restore standards to the previous high levels.

In fairness to some of the incomers, (locally known as white settlers), they become good villagers, joining in the activities and were quickly accepted by the more permanent residents. Others think that they can take over in order to create their personal view of "the new rural Jerusalem", arrogantly treating all rural beings as being beyond the pale. A third category merely came to sleep, complaining about early morning farming activities, - and cockerels! Nothing gets a dormophile more worked up than a good, old fashioned rooster at the bottom of a neighbour's garden! Some do not cause too many problems, they are rarely seen outside their garden gates except when swishing off to town in their cars.

Many of the old families who had been in Burtle for many generations are no longer represented. Those younger generations remaining were eventually forced to seek their fortunes elsewhere. This has brought about changes, the old stability has been replaced by a more mobile population. This situation was beautifully illustrated when a group of mainly recent arrivals formed a committee to arrange the V.E. day celebrations in May 1995. This was very commendable, but even in small villages there is a level of protocol and diplomacy that should be respected. The chairman cast covetous eyes on the unused funds still sitting in the Harvest Home A/C. This money is not fulfilling any useful purpose but the villagers who with their parents and relations had originally collected it, closed ranks and resolutely refused to sanction its use as a result of the chairman's inexperienced approach. I had been tipped off that the meeting was likely to be lively and worthy of Henry Williamson's *Tales from a Devon Village*. I was not disappointed and it prompted me to scribble some irreverent doggerel as a light hearted memorial to it. To be fair, the event was most enjoyable and successful, permitting a donation of over £400 to be made to charity.

Went to a meeting t'other night
All about V.E. day
Had to sort out what was right
For the merry 8th of May

Hast thee got a ten bob coin
to feed into the meter?
For without it we ain't goin'
to benefit from the heater.

The chairman says we have no cash-
but a programme's all mapped out.
Does the village want a bash?
No cash is what it's all about.

Villagers say thee cassen' touch
A fund tucked safely away.
Tidden that we'd need that much,
Still can't have it, come what may.

"These stupid folk", (an "alien's" slur!)
If he looked about he'd see,
To meet a stupid bloke down yer,
You'd 'ave to bring 'un with 'ee!.

Ideas are offered from the floor
and fielded by the chair.

Two or dree scoot out the door,
risk of jobs has caused a scare.

Chairman says there's not much time.
Committee heads nod assent.
Don't need a treasurer, we ain't got a dime.
Oh, where did the last month went?

"Pass 'round the hat", said a quiet man,
"A quid apiece will do,
give 'em a fund with which to work".
Now a treasurer's needed too!

We must have another meeting,
straight down the pub we'll goo,
get away from all the bleating,
by midnight we'll know what to do.

Reflect as time gets shorter
and assuming how villagers think.
Thees can take hoss to water
but thees cassen' make 'un drink!

Luckily for Burtle, progress "made haste slow", to use a village phrase. There has never been any large scale housing development although some of the houses that have been erected are of the large, executive type, attracting those with no wish to mix with 'the yokels'. Getting planning permission can be a complete nonsense, there appears to be an ambition to keep the rural rabble under control and not let them have what they want. In one case, a Burtle farmer wished to retire and build a bungalow in the large roadside, walled garden of the farmhouse. "You can't have a bungalow there because there are houses either side of the plot", said the planners. Directly across the road an application for a house was refused, it must be a bungalow! Another instance was that of Charlie Sandford, out on the Westhay Road. He tried for permission to build a bungalow for his family on several occasions but was refused. When Charlie died the cottage was sold and the new owner got permission almost immediately! Some of the planning decisions certainly leave one wondering....! Then there are the 'holiday bungalows' recently erected behind the Tom Mogg Inn. I do wonder about the inconsistencies!

Land on which planning consent can be obtained usually has, more recently, had to fall within the areas set out on the structure plans, drawn up for each village some years ago. My mother always told me that the road to hell was paved with good intentions, inspection of some of these structure plans confirms this. In Burtle, the plan makes little sense. The area designated for future development is a small part of the village at the Eastern end, at least three quarters of the village is excluded. The post office, village hall, school, church, one of the pubs, the council houses, the one engineering company and most of the farms all fall outside the development area. How were these structure plans drawn up and by whom? The illogicality beggars belief. Parish councils had very little say and the villagers appear not to have been consulted.

The plans for the future of housing development for the South West have just been released. If these targets are accepted, the pressure on villages will be severe. There is no point in building more and more housing estates in the rural areas unless business and employment opportunities are incorporated into a fully integrated plan. Without such a strategy, the degeneration will accelerate. The type of housing in the villages should also come under scrutiny, is the tendency toward large executive dwellings really in the best interests of the rural community? More individualism in the design and layout coupled with more thought on what type of development would best serve the particular interests of each village is important.

The planners have done their bit to enforce policies that prevented business startups in Burtle, several attempts with potential employment capability have been squashed. Colin Moxey and Chris Tucker started a glass re-inforced plastics business in the old blacksmith's shop. They showed flair and ingenuity, attracting orders from well known companies and employing several local people. For a while, the business could be contained within the rather cramped buildings but when the need to erect a modest extension to accommodate the increase in business, planning applications were turned down. Disenchanted, Colin emigrated to join his brothers who had already gone to Canada where they have all been successful. Several others have suffered a similar fate. If all this talent had been retained within the village, Burtle, like many other villages, would not need the upheaval of a major exercise to breathe life back into them.

One small engineering business was bludgeoned through the planning defences by a belligerently determined proprietor and, as a consequence, employs several locals. The independent Edington school for dyslexic boys employs several more, other than these and casual jobs at the pubs, there is nothing. All the farms are family affairs and non of them employ regular labour outside of the family. The peat digging is winding down and no longer offers any long term jobs. Even the great conservation movement will do very little for the locals.

Villages, like Burtle, placed at some distance form the main centres of employment desperately need a shot in the arm. The white paper, introduced by the government in the Autumn of 1995, is aimed at rural regeneration and could be a step in the right direction. The question is, whether or not, it is thirty or forty years too late. There are so many organisations listed it is difficult to see how they can operate without duplication. It makes the whole thing very confusing and the word kwango comes to mind. There are millions of pounds available from a multitude of sources but this is not of much use unless the objectives are sifted into clearly understandable form.

The term 'rural area' needs definition. Does it encompass towns of twenty to thirty thousand inhabitants or should we understand it to refer to villages and sparsely populated areas? The white paper looks at the problems from the top down whereas it would be better considered from the bottom up. If only the people that sit on these committees and occupy positions of authority would get really involved at grass roots level. Instead they make, carefully orchestrated by the local bureaucracy, flying visits which leave them with a totally distorted and superficial impression. How are the people that sit on the various committees selected? The White Paper's 146 pages could be condensed into less than 50 without detracting from its purpose and be more understandable to the layman. Perhaps the authors are paid by the word!

The 'power' of the parish councils would be a joke if it were not such a serious issue. One of the recommendations in the White Paper is that parish councils should have a much greater influence and control over matters in their parish. This sounds encouraging but there is the risk of creating a whole new tier of bureaucracy if, or when, it happens. On the other hand, many busy and able people feel it is a waste of time as things are, but might well be interested if they felt they were devoting their time to something worthwhile.

Village shops are under pressure, mainly from the large supermarkets and promotional activities that almost amount to brainwashing. As long as the traditional shop cum post office combination survives, the income from the post office side can make the shop viable, just. Supermarket mania keeps them under a pressure that is difficult to resist, in spite of the friendly, personal service and the fact that their prices are often very competitive.

Crime has become a very real problem in many country areas. Year on year could pass in Burtle with no crimes worth reporting but this happy state is no longer with us with the mobility offered by the modern road systems and vehicles. Items stolen in Burtle can be in London or Birmingham in a couple of hours or so.

Analysis of the thefts is quite interesting, some are the usual house burglaries, thefts from cars etc. A great deal of farm equipment has also been 'lifted', some from isolated locations such as fields well off the beaten track. A theory formed over a number of years suggests that the criminals are better organised and equipped than the law enforcers, with 'commission agents' based in villages. The latter are in a position to locate targets such as engine driven pumps, generators etc and relay the information to the mobile gangs who then pick up the items. The local contact is nowhere near the scene of the crime when it is committed but are often up the pub buying beer a few days later. Some thefts are unbelievably audacious, occurring in daylight with people around. This would have been difficult a few years ago, strangers would have been spotted straight away. Village bobbies knew nearly every one on their 'patch' and that knowledge alone was a deterrent. Whatever the hierarchy say, the system worked and, in many cases, still could. At a recent meeting in Burtle village hall the police informed us that they can only afford a maximum of fifty miles a day on rural patrols! It sounds like a rogues charter to me.

Contained within the waffle of the white paper are many worthy objectives but it will take a lot of effort to slow the impetus of a downhill slide. It is essential that the problems of the countryside are attacked at the grass roots by individuals and organisations that truly understand them. It can only be hoped that government, of whatever colour, has the will to see it through and, prove that it is not just a palliative to salve a persistent sore.

A change of government might have been considered an advantage but since May 1997 things have deteriorated rapidly. It would seem that M.P.s from city areas simply do not understand how rural life works, largely seeing our countryside through car windows. However, from wherever it is viewed, the farming fraternity have developed the rural scene we all enjoy today and will continue to care for it if they can afford to do so! The White Paper is no doubt collecting dust on a shelf somewhere.

Perhaps a new form of land setaside should be designed to encourage tree planting in order to produce the paper for the multitude of forms that farmers have to fill in these days.

Every village, particularly those situated at some distance from the local towns, should, at least, have the opportunity to encourage some small businesses, sympathetic to the environment and capable of employing, say, ten per cent of the population. It is asking a lot to expect planners to change the habits of a lifetime but unless they grasp the nettle firmly and quickly, our villages, like Burtle, will continue to die. It is imperative that the will is there to carry through imaginative, new infrastructural policies, quickly! Without positive action, our villages are rapidly becoming sterile, extensive clusters of retirement homes, far removed from the living, vibrant communities which they should be.

Charabanc outing, about 1914.

John Sparkes with his deerstalker hat, shepherd's crook and Somerset burr immediately conjures up images of orchards and cider, cricket on the county ground at Taunton, a man appreciative of cheddar cheese or a good cover drive.

A retired company director, he was born in 1933, the offspring of a long line of farmers. Today he lives in Cossington.

His father was the tenant of a small dairy farm in the Wembdon Marsh a few miles out of Bridgwater, moving to Trivetts Farm, Cossington on 1 April, 1944. At an early age he became deeply interested in the wildlife all around him. His first book on birds at the age of six did more to encourage his reading than any other factor. He attended Wembdon School and Cossington Junior School before moving on to Dr. Morgan's Grammar School and the Somerset Farm Institute at Cannington.

A hip injury when a boy prevented him from entering farming as a career so he turned his attention to the design, development, manufacture and marketing a completely new range of a modular livestock handling, penning and feeding systems on which a worldwide industry is now based. He is proud of winning over 20 regional and national awards for innovation and new ideas. He sold the Poldenvale group in 1987 and gained a new lease of life by having hip joints fitted. Within the group he ran his own PR, advertising and product development divisions. A keen photographer with some commercial experience, he sees things rural through the eyes of a true countryman. He gives illustrated talks on country subjects to groups over a wide area. He writes indignant letters to the press and articles on rural topics under the *nom de plume* Sylvanus.

During his business career he has been an active member of the Somerset branch of the Institute of Directors, the Agricultural Engineers Association, the British Agricultural Export Council and the Bristol Chamber of Commerce.

In past years, he has appeared on radio and television programmes mainly to discuss farming and rural matters. John feels passionately that many of the commentators and writers on country life do not dig deeply enough to establish the roots of the current problems and that needs to change if the countryside is ever to receive the understanding, and through that, the help that will enable it to recover its true status as a great national asset.

Michael Williams, Writing and Publishing Consultant